"*Sit down and feed,*
and welcome to our table."

WILLIAM SHAKESPEARE, *As You Like It*

AROUND THE TABLE

RECIPES & STORIES FROM
THE LARK IN SANTA BARBARA

FOREWORD BY BETTY FUSSELL

MACDUFF EVERTON

JASON PALUSKA

SHERRY VILLANUEVA

EDITED BY TAMA TAKAHASHI

AVP EDITIONS

SANTA BARBARA

First Edition 2017

ISBN: 978-0-938531-69-2
1. Cooking, Santa Barbara 2. The Lark Santa Barbara (Restaurant)
3. Santa Barbara (U.S.) 4. Cookbooks

Photographs of The Lark dining car printed with permission of
Joe Shine, Publisher, Four Ways West Publications
Southern Pacific menu courtesy of Bruce Morden, South Coast Railroad Museum
Photograph of George Castagnola printed with permission of Virginia Castagnola-Hunter

Photography, Layout & Design
Macduff Everton

Design Consultants
John Balkwill & Mary Heebner

Editing & Proofreading
Jackson Friedman, Matt Kettmann, Tama Takahashi

Text by
Jeremy Bohrer, Betty Fussell, Hilary Dole-Klein, Macduff Everton, Nick Flores, Mary Heebner,
Matt Kettmann, Jason Paluska, Trish Reynales, Tama Takahashi, Annie Villanueva, Sherry Villanueva

Digital files from film scans by Jeff Cable

Typefaces used in this book are Baskerville, Futura and Memphis

Printed on acid-free paper

Printed in South Korea

TABLE OF CONTENTS

FOREWORD BY BETTY FUSSELL
8

SANTA BARBARA
10

FROM THE KITCHEN
NOTES FROM THE CHEF
16

SNACKS
26

FROM THE FARM
64

FROM THE OCEAN
122

FROM THE RANCH
174

THE BASICS
NOTES FROM THE EDITOR
246

IN THE BEGINNING
NOTES FROM THE PROPRIETOR
NOTES FROM THE PHOTOGRAPHER
276

BEVERAGES
326

VINEYARDS
336

DESSERTS
356

INDEX
388

East Beach, two blocks from The Lark.

Wheeeho &
Zippittydodah!
I'm outta here.
On the go...

At last. Watching waves break on my left, sun rise over mountains on my right. Zipping along in the Coast Daylight streamliner streaked with orange, red, black. California colors. My colors.

Breathe deep. Put out cig. Sip coffee. Stifle scream of joy. I'm at heaven's gate and harking, even if I'm not breakfasting in The Lark Club on the classiest train in the country, The Lark.

Wish I were, but this is 1948. I'm poor and the Lark is luxey.

I travel chair car with thermos and lunch pail. But I'm on my way. "I got the sun in the morning and the moon at night."

Santa Barbara is just a curve in the coastline where it juts west to east as mountains meet sea between L.A. and San Fran.

Though born near the cities of angels and saints and Hollywood stars, I'm outta here and keep on going.

San Francisco, New York City and then—the World.

Now, after circling the globe for 70 odd years, I'm back. Instead of waking to the sound of New York sirens, I wake to morning doves at Casa Dorinda.

I'm one lucky oldie to choose this for my Last Stop. Came by plane, not train.

Hurricane Sandy blew me home to California.

I breathe deep of green air, sea air, laden with pollen. I sneeze. A sure sign of Home.

On a spring Sunday in 2013, sunlight filters through California oaks as I sit with a hundred families at one long dining table.

It snakes over the grass serpent-like to reach the apple trees and an old-fashioned cider press.

Today Rancho San Julian, in the San Ynez mountains above Santa Barbara, celebrates with families and friends their ritual harvest feast of beef and cider, redemptive flesh and blood.

In this Edenic garden, I find Eve in the guise of Elizabeth Poett with her baby Jack, the newest leaf on the tree of De la Guerras, Dibblees and Poetts that grew the Rancho.

At the table I hear a man describe a Maya family in the Yucatán, one of my favorite stops, so I introduce myself.

His name is Macduff Everton. A Poett and a Macduff in the same Garden. I can't believe my luck.

Macduff says he must take me to this brand-new place in the Funk Zone downtown.

Goody. I'm for funk; let's go.

At first look it's Soho 30 years ago—recycled warehouses, art galleries, small tasting rooms, bars, boutiques, breweries.

Only in miniature and bathed in warmth. My kind of place.

"Home again, home again, jiggity-jig. What a lark it is."

I've been dazzled by the blending of seascapes, landscapes, cityscapes, foodscapes and here is the heart of this throbbing body. Named for a bird, a train—LARK—pretends to be a restaurant but is actually an electromagnet connecting polar opposites of inside and outside, industrial steel and ancient fir, firepits and highboys, kids and oldies. Charged by a constant current of people.

Cooks, servers, purveyors, eaters, we're all connected.

When chef Jason, JP, walks by, I ask where he gets his sea urchins.

That's how I later meet Stephanie at the wharf, just back from a dive off the coast for urchins and abalone.

That leads to Bernie, the Oyster & Mussel man, who farms the ocean off Hope Ranch.

And inevitably to Chris at the Downtown Farmers Market, who sells whatever Bernie harvested.

Back at The Lark, which is joined at the hip to Les Marchands, Jeremy eulogizes his floor-to-ceiling bottles that witness the miraculous transformation of water and earth into local wines.

And first and last Sherry, the visionary, who set the charge when she imagined and created The Lark as "a magical train" designed to be "f*cking amazing."

Orange squash blossoms, red chiles, black-skinned avocados—the tri-colors of the namesake Lark—leap off the plate in glorious Hollywood Technicolor.

The construction of desserts astonishes like Gehry's Disney Hall.

New is old, old is new, nostalgia is futurism, nature is art, art nature.

We happy mouths simply join the song of warm days and cool nights, of sun and fog, of change and constancy down to the last pomegranate seed and olive pit.

We are here, now, eating and drinking and laughing and loving in a moment of infinite possibilities, like extended play, singing the sun, dancing the sea, tasting the seeds of our shared beginnings in ocean and earth.

Home again, home again, jiggity-jig. What a lark it is.

Betty Fussell has been writing about food, travel and the arts for 50 years. She is a winner of the James Beard Foundation's Journalism Award and was inducted into their "Who's Who of American Food and Beverage." Her latest book is Eat, Live Love, Die. *She lives gloriously in Santa Barbara.*

SANTA BARBARA

Overlooking Santa Barbara from the courthouse.

Santa Barbara is known for its bougainvillea-shaded lanes and sun-splashed hills tumbling to the sweep of the sea. The benign weather and the topography of Santa Barbara County create a vast range of microclimates, from cool coastal ones ideal for strawberries and salad greens, to the warmer, sunny, inland areas ideal for almonds and avocados. Almost every kind of fruit or vegetable can be grown here, with over 50 different crops grown on local farms.

Our long history of ranching stretches back to 1782 when Don Felipe de Neve built the Royal Presidio of Santa Barbara, a military outpost under the Spanish flag. The Santa Barbara Channel is a marine transition zone where the cold waters north of Point Conception mix with the warm waters of Southern California to create nutrient-rich waters, offering a multitude of different types of seafood. Our fisheries yield 6-10 million pounds annually. Ours is a land of plenty, full of possibilities, for a chef or food lover.

The Lark was created in the center of this abundance in an area of Santa Barbara with a colorful history. The Funk Zone comprises roughly a dozen blocks east of State Street—Santa Barbara's main corridor—just steps from the ocean and Stearns Wharf, California's oldest working wharf, dating from 1872. The wharf's construction allowed rapid development. Neither

Next page: Santa Barbara train station, a block from The Lark, is on the National Register of Historic Places. Begun in 1902, the station was designed by local architect Francis Wilson in the Spanish Mission Revival Style.

Highway 1 nor Highway 101 had been built at the time; intrepid drivers had to snake their way from Ventura along the beach and unimproved tracks at the foot of the bluffs.

In the 1930s, the wharf was surrounded by rowdy gamblers in floating casinos said to be run by New York mobsters. Legitimate businesses included the fishing boats of the Castagnola brothers George, Mario and Lino. They started peddling fish door-to-door and then grew their company into a seafood empire that included the chain of Castagnola Lobster House restaurants throughout California. Their first building, a 10,000-square-foot fish-processing plant, included 131 Anacapa Street, which

went on to become the Santa Barbara Fish Market and, ultimately, The Lark restaurant.

In 1916 Allan and Malcolm Loughead started the Loughead Aircraft Manufacturing Company in a rented garage at 101 State Street in what is now the Funk Zone. They built the F-1 flying boat, launching it at West Beach. They flew their seaplane from Santa Barbara to San Diego on 12 April 1918, setting speed and distance records. The brothers legally changed their surname to Lockheed so people would pronounce it correctly. Lockheed Corporation became one of the world's leading aerospace companies, merging with Martin Marietta in 1995.

Since 1887, Santa Barbara has been connected to Los

Angeles by rail, but it wasn't until 1901 that the link to San Francisco was completed. The same day also marked the passage of a lingering remnant of the Old West as the last stagecoach was pulled over San Marcos Pass. Southern Pacific inaugurated the Lark in 1910 with overnight train service between Los Angeles and San Francisco. In 1941 the Lark became an all-Pullman streamliner and quickly became a favorite among film stars and commuters looking for deluxe travel between the two cities. The Lark Club—a posh 130-foot-long, triple-unit dining car-lounge-dormitory was so popular people reserved a year in advance. The Lark was hailed as "America's most luxurious form of travel." Just a few feet from the tracks, our restaurant was named in honor of the fine-dining tradition the Lark Club represented. In a nod to its storied namesake, the restaurant's three enclosed booths evoke a vintage luxury dining car with period sconces and detailing.

Soviet Premier Nikita Khrushchev took the train from Los Angeles to San Francisco during his tour of the United States during the height of the Cold War. "I thought I could come here as a free man," said a disgruntled Khrushchev when he couldn't visit Disneyland. The next day, to the chagrin of the 175-man security detail, Khrushchev practically leapt from the train during his 13-minute stop in Santa Barbara on September 21.

"My first opportunity to go for a walk and talk with the people!" he said gleefully as he disembarked to greet the 2,000 spectators gathered at the station. It was an especially serendipitous moment for Vernon and Anne Johnson and family. After shaking hands with the mayor, the Soviet leader walked up to Vernon and said through an interpreter, "You have a nice face." A B-17 pilot in World War II, Vernon told Khrushchev he'd like to visit the Soviet Union. Khrushchev extended an invitation, and the two men shook hands.

Two years later, on the Fourth of July, 1961, the Johnsons and their eight kids, traveling the world in the name of world peace in a converted 1947 Santa Barbara municipal bus, reconvened with Khrushchev for a more leisurely visit behind the Iron Curtain at the American Embassy in Moscow. Their 30,000+ mile journey is chronicled in Anne Johnson's book, *Home Is Where the Bus Is.*

Grant Holcomb, a CBS reporter covering the trip, telephoned his sister, Kate Dole, who was living at the ranch house, to let her know when they should be passing through Hollister Ranch. After they left Santa Barbara, the train traveled west along the coast. Kate, married to the prominent artist William Dole, dressed their flock of kids into costumes they brought down from a big trunk in the attic. Kate wore one of her colorful Fiesta dresses. Her daughter Hilary remembers wearing a frilly, yellow, silk, Victorian, full-length dress; her brother wore a North African robe; another sister wore black tights, a black leotard and a black cape; another sister wore a Renaissance blue velvet dress and a cousin wore a Mexican serape. Along with other ranch kids that joined in they made an exotic contingent that waved at the train. A Russian journalist wrote in his dispatch about the "colorful peasants along the route." The "colorful peasants" made all the Soviet Union papers.

Urban areas transmute through cycles of growth, degeneration and renovation. At the turn of the 21st century, the Funk Zone largely fell into disrepair with dilapidated warehouses, artists' lofts and a strip club jumbled in with an amalgam of shops, including, the aforementioned Santa Barbara Fish Market, a few restaurants and a hotel in hopeless decline. The old Santa Barbara Fish Market complex was in bad shape. But it had great bones in the weathered brick structures and an exceptional location close to the beach and State Street.

The Funk Zone had already begun to attract renovation and renewal when The Lark restaurant debuted in 2013. Along with its sister businesses the Lucky Penny, Les Marchands, Santa Barbara Wine Collective and Helena Avenue Bakery, it helped exert a gravitational force—like a giant nebula drawing astral bodies toward it—attracting tasting rooms, galleries and retail shops into the Funk Zone. The Lark is part of Santa Barbara County's nexus of land, sea, food, wine, locals and visitors. It sits at the heart of community, both supported by and supportive of the people who live here and our guests from around the world.

Southern Pacific *Menu*

COFFEE SHOP

Dinner

1. Baked Fillet of Fish, Mornay	3.00
2. Potted Select Young Beef, Jardiniere	3.25
3. Fried Select Young Chicken (Half)	3.25

ABOVE SELECTIONS INCLUDE:

Fresh Garden Vegetable   Cream Whipped Potatoes

Hot Dinner Rolls

Strawberry Sundae   or   Rice and Raisin Pudding

Coffee   Tea, Hot or Iced   Chocolate   Milk

A La Carte Suggestions

Soup: du Jour (Cup) 50

Lettuce and Tomato Salad, French Dressing 1.10

Ham Sandwich (single deck) 1.35

Bacon and Tomato Sandwich (single deck) 1.75

(Above Sandwiches include:
Potato Chips, Ripe Olives, Pickles and Tomato Slices)

Cheese or Jelly Omelet (3 Eggs) with Toast 1.95

Assorted Bread 30   Hot Rolls 35

Ice Cream with Wafers 50   Rice and Raisin Pudding 50

American Cheese with Toasted Crackers 55

Coffee (Pot) 45   Milk 30   Tea, Hot or Iced (Pot) 45

Sanka (Pot) 45   Chocolate (Pot) 45

Executive Chef Jason Paluska and Executive Pastry Chef Nick Flores taste a dish.

THE LARK HAPPENED FOR ME out of thin air. I was parking my car in the Mission District in San Francisco when the phone rang. The caller identified herself as Sherry Villanueva. She was so chipper and full of life and excited to be on the phone with me. She told me about a project she was working on in Santa Barbara. "You've got to get down here and see this place and what I'm putting together."

My intention in life was never to be an executive chef in a restaurant. I actually wanted my rock band to become world famous with multiplatinum records. But the following week I flew out of cold and foggy San Francisco. When I looked out the window as the plane hugged the Santa Barbara coastline, I repeated to myself, "You have to make this happen. You have to make this happen. Just look at this place!"

Sherry picked me up at the airport. Our first stop was for coffee. I looked around. It was the bluest of blue skies. I'd always imagined California should be like this. Everyone around me looked relaxed and comfortable. And here I was in all black, coming off of no sleep. I already felt overdressed. I looked Sherry dead in the eye. "Do people really live like this?" I asked.

Sherry seemed confused by my question. I couldn't get over what a beautiful place I'd come to. A friend of mine had moved to Santa Barbara, and I remembered what she'd told me. "The produce in the markets will blow your mind." I thought of this when I bought my ingredients for the four dishes I cooked for Sherry in a borrowed kitchen as part of my job interview. The next morning I met her for breakfast, and she offered me the job.

I was pretty overwhelmed by the opportunity. I knew this would be a life-changing event. The proposed space was intimidating. It wasn't built, and Sherry asked me if I could see it. Seriously, I couldn't, but she could see it all. Her enthusiasm convinced me it would come to life.

I brought the tone and work ethic of a big-city kitchen to the beach. It caught most new employees off-guard. They had no idea how much work it takes to make something look effortless. My work ethic is something I won't compromise. I expect everybody to work cleanly, quietly and efficiently. Histrionics have no place in my kitchen. With all the attention to detail and the level of focus, we can't be distracted by anything. The expeditor shouts out food orders. The cooks shout them back.

Bussers are slamming bus tubs full of dirty plates to be washed, the dishwasher is nosily stacking hot and clean glasses in racks to be carried out, cooks are slapping cast iron pans on the French top range, another oven door smacks shut as the pastry chef turns back to plate another dessert, cooks are clicking open and shutting reach-in refrigerators for ingredients, and then a server drops and breaks a tray full of wine glasses. To paint this picture more clearly, the chaos needs to be completely controlled.

You don't have to attend culinary school to figure this stuff out. However, I found it really helpful. Culinary school gave me a reason to leave Texas and immerse myself in San Francisco, the most incredible city at the time. But what I found was the most helpful was to literally go out to eat and pay close attention to what I was seeing, smelling, tasting and experiencing. I watched the cooks and asked them questions. Was it bland or boring? Or was it spicy? Was it rich? If it was perfect, I wanted to know why.

I'm always trying to figure out why people freak out for certain things. Like the way I love the cheese tamale at El Bajio on Milpas Street here in Santa Barbara, or the epic burger at Nopa in San Francisco.

Some things work so well I remember them for years after I've eaten them.

Starting when I was 16, I spent all of my hard-earned money on trips all through Texas, New Orleans, Chicago, New York and California and to Spain, England, Switzerland, Mexico, Costa Rica and Belize. I had one goal—to find the absolute best food. I was getting my version of "being taught" by being so passionate about the food I discovered in all of these places. I knew if I could understand what I was eating, one day I could cook it.

When I was 23, I drove cross-country and rented a room near San Francisco in Daly City. Unfortunately, the Grand Cafe near Union Square didn't hire me to work in the kitchen prior to attending culinary school. Maybe it was because I showed up for my kitchen interview wearing a suit and tie and not wearing kitchen shoes. I looked as if I were there for a different job altogether. With my dull Wüsthof knife in hand, I didn't have a clue. I thought I could wing it. I couldn't. It was a reality check. "Where are your non-slip shoes? Did you bring work pants? Do you own a chef coat? Your knife won't work."

Morning prep list. Opposite: a well-used colander from The Lark kitchen.

The first thing I attempted to cut was a red bell pepper. My knife bounced right off. Then they asked me to go to the walk-in and bring back some frisée. I asked them, "What's that?" They said, "Dude, it's a green. Hurry up!" I also failed at poaching quail eggs, crushing their brittle shells and smashing the yolk. The chef told me I was not ready for the kitchen.

My life philosophy is to never give up on anything I care about. He hired me to check-in produce at 6 a.m. Monday through Friday while I attended culinary school. The chef once even chewed me out for allowing yellow chervil to cross the threshold of his kitchen. Once I graduated from Tante Marie's cooking school in August 2006, Town Hall gave me my first real cooking job. It opened my eyes to the reality of kitchens. Only the strong survive. Slowly but surely I developed skills I

will never lose. I loved every second of it.

I constantly remind myself how little I used to know about a professional kitchen. I learned a lot because I wasn't embarrassed to ask questions. I think too many people are afraid that asking questions reveals weakness. I think it is just the opposite. I try to create an atmosphere in my kitchen where no one is too intimidated to ask.

Most of my dishes encompass five to ten recipes because I love to cook with layers so that the first taste convinces you that all the preparation was worthwhile. Everything from butchering a pig to picking an herb, honor your ingredients and don't squander them.

Each recipe is a guideline. Personalize it. Please feel free to make your own little changes in ingredients. Do you need a little more of this? Or that? Taste it. Smell it. This is the joy of cooking.

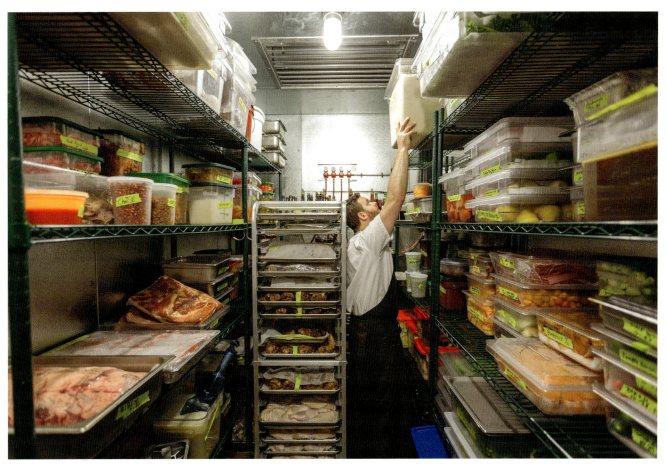

Working in the kitchen at The Lark.

Snacks

Crispy Brussels Sprouts
Medjool dates, garum, sesame, lime

Wine Pairing:

Scar of the Sea 'a | muse' Pétillant Naturel Chardonnay
Notary Public Chenin Blanc, Santa Barbara County
Kunin Chenin Blanc, Jurassic Park, Santa Ynez Valley
Spear Gnesa Vineyard Chardonnay, Sta. Rita Hills

Alternative Pairing:

M. Special Brewing Company Pablo Special Pale Ale
Pine Street Brewery Atom Splitter Pale Ale

Chef's Notes:

If you've never deep-fried Brussels sprouts, stand back. They have a tendency to explode as the oil tries to find its way into the tightly wound sprout. A splatter screen or lid will protect you. We love the balance between the sweetness of the date, the earthiness of the sesame seeds, the fish sauce adding umami, the spice from the serrano chile and the tartness from the fresh lime. The first time Nick Flores and I ate Brussels sprouts with a funky fermented fish sauce, we were barhopping through the Mission District and ended up in a small restaurant called Nombe (RIP). We owe the success of this dish to that rager of an evening.

Prep Time:

$\frac{1}{2}$ hour active preparation

Special Equipment Needed:

deep fryer (option: cast iron skillet with thermometer), splatter screen, slotted spoon

Servings:

2-4

Editor's Note:

Use rice bran oil, as indicated, for best results.

INGREDIENTS

Fish Sauce Vinaigrette:
1 large clove garlic (8 g), minced
2 serrano chiles, minced
½ cup garum fish sauce (140 ml)
5½ T water (77 ml)
8 tsp cider vinegar (40 ml)
8 tsp lime juice (40 ml)
5 T sugar (65 g)
1 T sesame oil (13 ml)

Toasted Sesame Seeds:
1½ T sesame seeds (12 g), toasted

Brussels Sprouts:
rice bran oil
½ lb. Brussels sprouts (226 g)
4 Medjool dates, halved, pits removed

Garnish:
½ lime, cut in wedges

DIRECTIONS

Fish Sauce Vinaigrette:
Whisk together all ingredients.

Toasted Sesame Seeds:
Toast sesame seeds on a sheet tray lined with parchment at 325°F for 8-10 minutes or until golden. Cool.

Brussels Sprouts:
Heat rice bran oil in deep fryer to 375°F. Halve or quarter the Brussels sprouts depending on their size and pat dry with paper towels. Fry 2 minutes or until golden brown and core is tender. Drain using a slotted spoon. In a bowl toss Brussels Sprouts with Fish Sauce Vinaigrette, dates and Toasted Sesame Seeds.

Plating:
Plate Brussels Sprouts, then garnish with lime wedges.

Morning prep team preparing Brussels sprouts, fava beans and English peas.

Fried Castelvetrano Olives
lemon and rosemary goat cheese, arugula, Spanish chorizo aioli

Wine Pairing:

Blair Fox Cellars Vermentino, Santa Barbara County
Lumen Pinot Gris, Santa Maria Valley
Margerum M5 White, Happy Canyon
Grimm's Bluff Estate Sauvignon Blanc, Happy Canyon

Alternative Pairing:

Ventura Spirits Wilder Gin Gimlet
Ballast Point Brewing & Spirits Fathom India Pale Lager

Chef's Notes:

I'm a huge fan of golden brown, crispy, warm and delicious fried food, but who isn't? With this dish we signed up for long hours of tedious prep, filling tiny Castelvetrano olives with goat cheese seasoned with citrus and rosemary. The end result is highly addictive.

Prep Time:

30 minutes active preparation, plus 30 minutes minimum chilling

Special Equipment Needed:

piping bag, deep fryer (option: cast iron skillet with thermometer)

Servings:

4

Editor's Note:

Chill the stuffed olives before cooking to prevent the filling from melting away during frying.

INGREDIENTS

Spanish Chorizo Aioli:
2 egg yolks (40 g)
5 tsp Dijon mustard (25 g)
1 large garlic clove (8 g), finely chopped
7 tsp champagne vinegar (35 ml)
1 tsp salt (3 g)
approx. 1¼ cup grapeseed oil (260 ml)
1 tsp ground cumin (3 g), toasted
2 tsp smoked paprika (6 g)
2 T pureed chipotle chiles (20 g),
  more to taste
2 oz diced Spanish chorizo (57 g),
  cooked, cooled
1 tsp lemon juice (4 ml)
¼ tsp cayenne
salt to taste

Lemon and Rosemary Goat Cheese
  Stuffed Olives:
8 oz goat cheese (227 g), room
  temperature
3 T fresh rosemary (15 g), very finely
  minced
4 T lemon zest (24 g), finely minced
½ tsp salt
heavy cream, if needed
40 Castelvetrano olives, pitted

Fried Castelvetrano Olives:
canola oil
1 cup panko (51 g)
½ cup all-purpose flour (62 g), sifted
1 egg, lightly beaten
salt to taste

Garnish:
wild arugula

DIRECTIONS

Spanish Chorizo Aioli:
Combine egg yolks, mustard, garlic, vinegar and salt in a blender, then add oil in a thin, steady stream until mixture thickens. Transfer aioli to a mixing bowl. Fold in spices, chipotle puree, chorizo and lemon juice. Season with salt and adjust spice with additional cayenne, if desired.

Lemon and Rosemary Goat Cheese Stuffed Olives:

In a mixer, paddle goat cheese thoroughly with rosemary, lemon zest and salt. Add cream so that the mixture is spreadable but stiff. Transfer goat cheese to a piping bag. Pipe into olives and chill until filling hardens.

Fried Castelvetrano Olives:
Preheat the canola oil in a deep fryer to 375°F. Pulse the panko bread crumbs in a food processor for an even texture. Divide flour, egg and panko in separate bowls. Dip olives in flour, then egg and then panko, using a slotted spoon for each bowl. Chill for one hour. Fry in batches until a golden brown. Drain on paper towels and season with salt to taste.

Plating:
Spoon Spanish Chorizo Aioli onto the plate. Arrange Fried Castelvetrano Olives in the aioli. Garnish with wild arugula.

Katy Villanueva carefully filling Castelvetrano olives with goat cheese.

Deviled Eggs
crispy pancetta, jalapeño, smoked paprika, chives

Wine Pairing:
Wenzlau Cuvée L'Inconnu Blanc de Blanc, Sta. Rita Hills
Palmina Malvasia Bianca, Larner Vineyard, Santa Ynez Valley
Rusack Chardonnay, Mount Carmel Vineyard, Sta. Rita Hills

Alternative Pairing:
Ice-cold Lone Star Beer

Chef's Notes:
An American classic. We loved the idea of incorporating the most familiar of all backyard snacks onto our dinner menu. The key is understanding how to make crème fraîche at home and using that to make your filling luxurious. Pancetta adds a subtle pepperiness and crunch. It's pretty simple but it packs a lot of flavor.

Prep Time:
30 minutes active preparation plus crème fraîche

Special Equipment Needed:
roasting rack, ice bath, tamis (option: fine-meshed sieve), piping bag

Servings:
4

Editor's Note:
Real buttermilk—created after milk is churned into butter—or cultured buttermilk with live culture is necessary to make the housemade crème fraîche thicken.

INGREDIENTS

Crème Fraîche:
1 cup heavy cream (240 ml)
⅓ cup live-culture buttermilk (80 ml)

Crispy Pancetta:
4 oz pancetta (113 g), sliced very thinly

Deviled Eggs:
12 eggs
⅓ cup Crème Fraîche (75 g)
1½ tsp Dijon mustard (8 g)
12 stalks fresh chives, finely minced
2 jalapeño chiles, finely minced

Garnish:
2 T smoked paprika (16 g)
3 T fresh chives (6 g), finely diced
1 jalapeño, finely diced

DIRECTIONS

Crème Fraîche:
Mix heavy cream and buttermilk together in a glass jar, then leave at room temperature for 48 hours until firmed up. Store in refrigerator.

Crispy Pancetta:
Preheat oven to 300°F. Place pancetta on baking rack with a pan underneath to catch drippings. Bake for approximately 15 minutes or until crispy. Drain on paper towels, then break into pieces.

Deviled Eggs:
In a large pot, cover eggs with water and bring to a boil. Turn off the heat and let sit for 10 minutes. Shock for 10 minutes in ice bath, then peel and cut in half, separating yolks. Place the tamis (or fine-meshed sieve) on a large mixing bowl inside a larger bowl full of ice. Scrape yolks through the tamis with a rubber spatula for a fluffy consistency. (Note: chilling yolks makes piping easier.) Fold in Crème Fraîche, Dijon mustard and chives, then diced jalapeño to taste. Place mixture into piping bag with a large tip, then pipe into whites.

Plating:
Place Deviled Eggs on plate, sprinkle with paprika, chives and diced jalapeño. Vertically embed pieces of Crispy Pancetta in the eggs.

The walk-in refrigerator. Opposite: Brunoise of jalapeño.

Southern Pimento Cheese
smoked Gouda, aged provolone, Shiner Bock, pickled serrano and bell pepper, grilled baguette

Wine Pairing:

Longoria Tempranillo, Santa Ynez Valley
Holus Bolus Syrah, Sta. Rita Hills
Qupé Syrah Bien Nacido Vineyard - X Block, Santa Maria Valley
Jaffurs Wine Cellars Upslope Syrah, Santa Barbara County

Alternative Pairing:

Ice-cold Shiner Bock

Chef's Notes:

White bread, mayo and store-bought pimento cheese got me through the 5th grade. At the Masters golf tournament in Georgia, it is the official food. I didn't realize pimento was even a "thing" until I left Texas. I guess kids in California eat avocado and alfalfa sprouts on seeded loaf? Either way, this is spicy as hell and delicious. Making this dish seems simple, but in fact it has a few key points that are important starting with texture. You have to understand it before you begin. Think creamy, crunchy, yet smooth. Make sure to spread the pimento cheese on the grilled bread while it is still hot.

Prep Time:

20 minutes, plus pickled vegetables.

Special Equipment Needed:

Servings:

2-4

Editor's Note:

Colman Andrews writes in *The Taste of America* of pimento cheese, "It's the pâté de foie gras, the hummus and the blue cheese dip of the American South..."
The recipe for aioli is scaled down as far as practical; you will have extra. Shiner Bock is a lightly hopped, American-style dark lager produced in Shiner, Texas.

INGREDIENTS

Pickled Serrano Chile and Bell Pepper:
¼ cup serrano chile (45 g), sliced, de-seeded
¼ cup bell pepper (45 g), sliced, de-seeded
½ cup champagne vinegar (104 ml)
¼ cup sugar (50 g)
1 T salt (9 g)
¼ cup water (56 ml)

Shiner Bock Aioli:
2 egg yolks
5 tsp Dijon mustard (25 g)
½ tsp salt
4 tsp Worcestershire sauce (18 ml)
approx. ⅔ cup grapeseed oil (140 ml)
approx. ¼ cup Shiner Bock (50 ml)
  (option: amber lager)

Pimento Cheese:
2 T Shiner Bock Aioli (30 g)
2 tsp smoked paprika (6 g)
½ tsp each cayenne and sumac
¼ lb each smoked Gouda and
  provolone (113 g), grated
1 T champagne vinegar (13 ml)
½ cup Pickled Serrano Chile and Bell
  Pepper (90 g)

Frisée Salad:
1 head frisée, separated
¼ cup olive oil (52 ml)
lemon juice and salt to taste

Grilled Baguette:
½ baguette
olive oil
salt

Garnishes:
fresh chives, sliced

DIRECTIONS

Pickled Serrano Chile and Bell Pepper:
Place serrano chile and bell pepper into a nonreactive bowl. Heat vinegar, sugar, salt and water to a simmer, then pour over the vegetables. Marinate in the refrigerator for a minimum of 72 hours. Drain before use.

Shiner Bock Aioli:
Combine the egg yolks, Dijon mustard, salt and Worcestershire sauce in a blender. With blender on low, slowly add oil in a thin, steady stream, just until the aioli is thick and emulsified. Adjust the consistency with Shiner Bock.

Pimento Cheese:
In a mixer fitted with the paddle attachment, combine Shiner Bock Aioli, smoked paprika, cayenne and sumac, then gently paddle in the Gouda and provolone. Fold in the Pickled Serrano Chile and Bell Pepper, using the pickling liquid to adjust consistency. Mixture should be thick but spreadable.

Frisée Salad:
Toss frisée with olive oil and lemon juice. Season to taste with salt.

Grilled Baguette:
Split baguette and season with olive oil and salt. Grill until nicely marked and warmed through.

Plating:
Scoop Pimento Cheese into a jar or serving bowl and top with chives. Serve with Frisée Salad and Pickled Serrano Chile and Bell Pepper. Serve with Grilled Baguette.

Sliced serrano peppers.

Jalapeño & Foie Gras Corn Bread

INGREDIENTS

Jalapeño and Foie Gras Corn Bread:
2 oz foie gras (57 g), diced
1 cup all-purpose flour (125 g)
1 cup cornmeal (150 g)
½ tsp baking soda
6 T sugar (78 g)
2 tsp salt (6 g)
2 eggs
1 cup crème fraîche (224 g)
1½ T honey (30 g)
2 jalapeño chiles, de-seeded, diced
2½ T tempered butter (35 g)
½ lb ripe peaches (226 g), pitted,
  pureed, passed through a chinois
pinch of Maldon Sea Salt
1 jalapeño chile, de-seeded, sliced for
  garnish

Grilled Scallion and Okra Corn Bread:
½ cup butter (112 g), melted
1 bunch scallions, grilled and chopped
½ cup raw okra (65 g), thin sliced, no stems
2 tsp onion powder (6 g)

Brown Butter and Rosemary Corn Bread:
½ cup brown butter (112 g)
1 T rosemary (5 g), finely chopped

How to make perfect brown butter:
Place cold butter in saucepot and cook on low heat. Don't rush the process or your butter will burn. Whisk constantly. The milk solids will slowly turn golden. Remove from the heat immediately and transfer to nonreactive bowl. Continue to whisk to cool. The milk solids should become the color of dark caramel.

DIRECTIONS

Jalapeño and Foie Gras Corn Bread:
Preheat oven to 325°F. Grease 8" x 8" baking pan with pan spray. Sear foie gras in hot, dry pan. Separate all solids and fat. Pass the fat through a chinois and reserve both solids and fat. Whisk together flour, cornmeal, baking soda, sugar and salt. In a separate mixing bowl, whisk together the eggs, crème fraîche and honey. Whisk the wet ingredients into the dry ingredients. Emulsify the foie gras fat into the mixture by whisking until incorporated. Fold in chopped foie gras pieces and diced jalapeño. Pour into baking pan and bake until the top is golden brown and a toothpick or knife inserted into the center comes out clean—approximately 30-35 minutes. Whip tempered butter with a paddle attachment in a mixer until aerated. Fold in 1 T (15 g) peach puree. Quenelle the butter onto the plate. Spoon remaining peach puree over the butter. Cut corn bread into squares and add to the dish. Finish with Maldon Sea Salt and a slice of jalapeño chile.

Grilled Scallion and Okra Corn Bread:
Substitute butter for the rendered foie gras fat and scallions and okra for the jalapeño chiles. Add onion powder to the dry ingredients.

Brown Butter and Rosemary Corn Bread:
Substitute brown butter for the rendered foie gras fat and rosemary for the diced jalapeños.

THERE IS NOTHING MORE AMERICAN than corn bread. For thousands of years, all breads in the Americas were corn breads. We might know them as tortillas, tamales, or griddle cakes, prepared over a fire or wrapped in leaves and steamed in a cooking pot, or baked in an earth oven or in the coals of a fire. Early European immigrants to the Americas learned recipes from Native Americans and revised them to include baking powder. They often added flour in addition to the cornmeal.

Corn is the grain that built America. Nearly every American culture in North and Central America cultivated corn (*Zea mays*) long before Columbus stumbled upon this continent. Nomadic groups first used it as a food, possibly in the Central Balsas River Valley in Mexico, when they began domesticating plants more than 9,000 years ago. Corn could store the sun's energy in kernels that would keep all year long. Early botanists developed the grain that would become the most productive food plant in the world. Corn was venerated by American cultures. It wasn't just a food—it was the symbol of fertility and the basis for religion. Combined with companion crops such as beans and squash, they provide all the essential amino acids and a complete protein.

Corn bread is the cornerstone of contemporary Southern and Southwestern cooking. I grew up eating it at my Nana's house. I learned to appreciate the South after I left. You can take corn bread in any direction you choose. You can add fresh blueberries, dried cranberries, cheese, okra or corn kernels; you can leave out sugar or flour; it is a perfect blank canvas to make your own mark. I don't think this cookbook would be complete without my favorite version.

Jalapeño & Foie Gras Corn Bread with whipped peach butter and a slice of jalapeño chile.

Spicy Root Vegetable Chips
goat cheese dip, pepitas, cilantro pesto, citrus zest

Wine Pairing:

Sillix Grenache Blanc, Santa Ynez Valley
Demetria Chardonnay, Santa Barbara County
Andrew Murray Grenache Blanc Estate Grown, Santa Ynez Valley

Alternative Pairing:

Captain Fatty's Craft Brewery Beach Bar Pilsner

Chef's Notes:

This is our take on chips and dip. When I was a kid, I hated root vegetable chips. All I wanted was Doritos. This dish comes full circle. You get a lot of variety of flavor between the carrots, parsnips and yam. The roasted shallots add a really savory element to the goat cheese dip. The spicy blend is tangy, and I love the addition of citric acid, the secret ingredient. This is a fun fall snack.

Prep Time:

30 minutes, plus 1½ hours chilling

Special Equipment Needed:

ice bath, piping bag with large tip, four half-pint glass jars, mandoline (option: slice by hand)

Servings:

4

Editor's Note:

Chilling the pesto makes it easier to pipe.

INGREDIENTS

Chip Spice Blend:
5 bay leaves
3 T fennel seed (18 g)
3 T coriander seed (18 g)
2 tsp black pepper (6 g)
1 T smoked paprika (9 g)
1 T salt (9 g)
¼ tsp citric acid

Cilantro Pesto:
½ cup pepitas (70 g), toasted
15 sprigs each fresh cilantro and
    parsley, stems removed
½ cup olive oil (105 ml)
1 T lemon zest (6 g)
salt to taste

Goat Cheese Dip:
5 oz goat cheese (142 g)
2 T crème fraîche (28 g)
3 T roasted shallots (36 g), finely chopped
1 T Cilantro Pesto (12 g)
1 tsp lemon zest (2 g)
salt and pepper to taste

Root Vegetable Chips:
rice bran oil
1 yam
1 parsnip
1 carrot

Garnish:
approx. 2½ T pepitas, toasted
zest of ½ lemon
zest of ½ lime

DIRECTIONS

Chip Spice Blend:
Remove stems of bay leaves, then combine in a blender with fennel, coriander and pepper until smooth. Fold in paprika, citric acid and salt.

Cilantro Pesto:
Toast the pepitas (for pesto and garnish) on a sheet tray lined with parchment at 300°F for 10-12 minutes. Let cool. Combine ½ cup of the toasted pepitas with cilantro, parsley, oil and zest in a food processor until smooth. Season to taste with salt. Chill in stainless steel bowl over ice bath.

Goat Cheese Dip:
Fold goat cheese, crème fraîche, roasted shallots and zest together. Season to taste with salt and pepper. Place in piping bag, then pipe mixture into glass jars to ¾ full. Smooth mixture so top is even. Pipe Cilantro Pesto on top of goat cheese layer.

Root Vegetable Chips:
Heat rice bran oil in deep fryer to 325°F. Shave yam, carrots and parsnips with mandoline or slice thinly by hand. Fry in batches until golden brown, then drain on paper towels. Coat evenly with Chip Spice Blend in a mixing bowl.

Plating:
Serve Root Vegetable Chips with Goat Cheese Dip. Garnish plate with toasted pepitas and fresh citrus zest.

SEA STEPHANIE FISH

Above: Catch of sea urchins. Opposite: Stephanie unloading her catch after a day of diving off Santa Cruz Island.

ONE MIGHT THINK, "SEEN ONE sea urchin, you've seen 'em all," until you meet urchin diver Stephanie Mutz. The owner and operator of Sea Stephanie Fish scans the waters off the Channel Islands at depths of 10 to 60 feet, hand-harvesting spiny red and purple urchins for uni, their prized golden roe. Watch her in action diving off Santa Cruz, San Miguel or Santa Rosa Island to learn what separates the average urchin from a chef's delicacy.

For starters, Stephanie looks for animals that proliferate near forests of *Macrocystis pyrifera*, the giant kelp emblematic of the Santa Barbara marine ecosystem. *Macrocystis* eaters, she says, yield sweeter uni than those feasting on other seaweeds. She also examines an urchin's location relative to ocean currents, food supply and the flow of available nutrients to assess quality. Then comes the final test: breaking one open and eyeballing the volume of its creamy roe. Known as "California Gold," Santa Barbara uni is considered among the world's best. Stephanie especially enjoys introducing its singular taste sensations to first-timers. "It's great with a Muscadet," she notes.

Stephanie studied marine biology at UC Santa Barbara and completed graduate studies in Australia, and then returned to California to teach. In 2007, she started urchin diving as a deckhand. "I found out I really enjoy it!" she says. The marine scientist in her liked the notion of sustainable fishing aimed at the healthy balance of local resources.

She launched her business in 2010. Of the 300 permitted urchin divers in California (and the three dozen or so in Santa Barbara), she's presently the only woman, though she's quick to point out she's not the first urchin diver. "I'm a newbie," she adds. "There are urchin divers here in Santa Barbara who've been at it for 30 years."

Three mornings a week, depending on the season and weather, she motors two hours to the fishing grounds in her 20-foot skiff, spends up to five hours in the water and bags 800 to 1,000 pounds of urchins. She sells some of her catch at the fishermen's market at the Santa Barbara Harbor. The rest she delivers fresh to local restaurants and specialty markets, updating her clients via cell phone, Instagram and Twitter: "Sea urchin tomorrow at the pier—6:30 a.m.!" She's usually sold out by midmorning.

—Trish Reynales

Sea Urchin on Brioche
oyster emulsion, Douglas fir, Meyer lemon, chervil

Wine Pairing:
Storm Sauvignon Blanc, Santa Ynez Valley
Brander Sauvignon Blanc, Mesa Verde, Santa Ynez Valley
Presqu'ile Brut Cuvée, Santa Maria Valley

Alternative Pairing:
Anchor Steam California Lager

Chef's Notes:
The sea urchin that thrive in the kelp beds off the Channel Islands along the Santa Barbara coast taste like candy. This is our caviar, our "California Gold." Almost year round you can see Stefanie Mutz at the harbor and take home as many you'd like. To me, urchin tastes like a combination of pine, citrus and the saltiness of the Pacific Ocean. All that comes out as soon as you crack the shell open.

Prep Time:
30 minutes

Special Equipment Needed:
sharp kitchen shears, rubber glove, towel, ice bath

Servings:
5

INGREDIENTS

Oyster Emulsion:
12 medium oysters, shucked
1 T salt (9 g)
1 egg yolk (20 g)
zest and juice of 2 limes
¾ cup grapeseed oil (150 ml)
1 tsp xanthan gum (6 g)

Douglas Fir Needles:
pinch of Douglas fir needles
one cup canola oil (200 ml)
salt

Uni:
1 live uni

Brioche:
1 thick slice of brioche
1 T butter (14 g), melted

Garnish:
picked chervil, Douglas Fir Needles, lemon zest and sliced radish

DIRECTIONS

Oyster Emulsion:
Blend oysters, salt, egg yolk, lime zest and juice on high speed for 30 seconds, being careful not to heat up the blender. If you do, add an ice cube to chill it quickly. Slowly emulsify the grapeseed oil into the blender. Lastly, sprinkle in xanthan gum. Pass through a chinois or fine-meshed sieve into a bowl over ice.

Douglas Fir Needles:
In frying pan bring canola oil up to 300°F. Fry needles until crispy, one minute. Drain from oil and season with salt.

Uni:
Wear a glove and use a towel to protect your hands from the spines. Turn the uni over and cut a 3" round circle through the shell. Carefully scoop out the five orange lobes with either an offset spatula or a teaspoon and put into a bowl over ice.

Brioche:
Brush brioche with melted butter. Griddle until evenly marked.

Plating:
Spread Oyster Emulsion on Brioche. Top with Uni and garnish with chervil, Douglas Fir Needles, lemon zest and radish.

Urchin diver Stephanie Mutz, at Santa Barbara Harbor.

Breakwater, Santa Barbara Harbor.

Fried Green Heirloom Tomatoes
buttermilk-thyme aioli, The Lark hot sauce, grilled lemon, arugula

Wine Pairing:
Liquid Farm White Hill Chardonnay, Sta. Rita Hills
Loubud Rosé of Pinot Noir, Santa Ynez Valley
Tyler Chardonnay, Zotovich Vineyard, Sta. Rita Hills

Alternative Pairing:
Sierra Nevada Nooner Pilsner
Trumer Pilsner

Chef's Notes:
This is the ultimate fried Southern dish. Going back to my roots in Tomball, Texas, ranch dressing and hot sauce was the foolproof addition to all fried food. I've elevated this dish with heirloom tomatoes and a grilled lemon to make it even better.

Prep Time:
1½ hours

Special Equipment Needed:
deep fryer (option: cast iron skillet with thermometer), grill

Servings:
4

Editor's Note:
Ask for green tomatoes at a farmers' market since they are usually not found in grocery stores.

INGREDIENTS

The Lark Hot Sauce:
½ lb ripe heirloom or Roma
  tomatoes (226 g)
5 T dried chile de arbol (22 g)
5 T dried ancho chiles
10 T dried chipotle chiles (44 g)
1 cup white vinegar (210 ml)
1 T salt (9 g)
4 cups water (944 ml)
xanthan gum (if needed)

Buttermilk Thyme Aioli:
1½ T coriander seed (9 g)
1 T fennel seed (6 g)
¼ tsp celery seed
1 egg yolk (20 g)
2½ tsp Dijon mustard (13 g)
1 T fresh thyme (5 g)
7 tsp lemon juice (35 ml)
½ tsp salt
approx. ⅔ cup grapeseed oil (140 ml)
⅓ cup buttermilk (75 ml)
Fried Green Heirloom Tomatoes:
canola oil (or rice bran oil)
1 cup panko (51 g)
¼ lb green heirloom tomatoes (113 g)
½ cup flour (62 g)
2 eggs, slightly beaten

Garnish:
2 lemons
wild arugula

DIRECTIONS

The Lark Hot Sauce:
Set oven to 500°F. Broil tomatoes on top rack until 50%
blackened. In the meantime, remove stems from chile de arbol,
ancho chile and chipotle. On a sheet tray lined with parchment,
toast chiles at 300°F for 10-12 minutes or until fragrant. Add
to a saucepot and cover with water. Bring the peppers to a boil
and cover with a lid. Turn off heat and let sit for 15 minutes.
Transfer contents to a Vitamix or high-powered blender. Blend
until velvety smooth incorporating roasted tomatoes in batches.
Use vinegar to adjust consistency and to maintain high acidity.
Strain through a fine-meshed sieve or chinois. Season with
salt to taste. If your end result is too runny, add just enough
xanthan gum to help thicken the hot sauce.

Buttermilk Thyme Aioli:
Blend the coriander, fennel and celery seeds in a blender into
a powder. Add egg yolk, mustard, thyme, lemon juice and salt
and blend until smooth. Slowly add oil in a thin, steady stream,
until emulsified. Fold in the buttermilk.

Fried Green Heirloom Tomatoes:
Heat oil in deep fryer to 375°F. (Option: use a cast iron skillet
with thermometer.) Pulse the panko in a blender for an even
texture. Quarter tomatoes, cut out stem ends and pat dry. Place
flour, egg and panko in separate bowls. Coat the tomatoes one
by one in that order. Fry until golden brown, then drain on
paper towels. Season evenly with salt.

Plating:
Halve lemons and grill cut-side down until evenly marked.
Spoon Buttermilk-Thyme Aioli on plate and add Fried Green
Heirloom Tomatoes. Arrange wild arugula across tomatoes.
Drizzle with The Lark Hot Sauce, and serve with grilled lemon.

From the Farm

Ras El Hanout Spiced Zucchini
saffron aioli, preserved lemon, crispy squash blossom, dill

Wine Pairing:

Margerum Riviera Rosé
Storm Santa Ynez Valley Demetria Vineyard Grenache Rosé
Martian Ranch & Vineyard Gamay Noir, Santa Barbara County

Alternative Pairing:

Smoke Mountain Brewery Citrus Medley White Ale

Chef's Notes:

This dish is a result of our friendship with Ellwood Canyon Farms. When Jack calls to tell us it is officially summertime, we listen. I write my menu based on the exceptional fruits and vegetables he brings. The Ras El Hanout spice blend is very floral and bold. I love the combination of saffron, dill and the crispy squash blossom. All these flavors and textures complement each other in perfect harmony.

Prep Time:

50 minutes active preparation plus preserving lemons

Special Equipment Needed:

deep fryer (option: cast iron skillet with thermometer)

Servings:

4

Editor's Note:

The recipe for aoili is scaled down as far as practical and you will have some left over to use later.

INGREDIENTS

Preserved Lemon:
6 lemons
6 T salt (54 g)
4 T sugar (52 g)

Ras El Hanout Spice:
2 T black peppercorn (15 g)
4 tsp cumin seed (13 g)
1 T fennel seeds (7 g)
4 tsps coriander seeds (8 g)
1 pod star anise
1½ tsp whole clove (3 g)
½ tsp allspice (2 g)
4 tsp cardamom pod (10 g)

Saffron Aioli:
8 threads saffron
¼ cup white wine (50 ml)
1 tsp lemon juice (5 ml)
1 large clove garlic (8 g), finely minced
2 egg yolks (40 g)
4 tsp Dijon mustard (20 g)
1 tsp turmeric (2 g)
¼ tsp salt
2 cups grapeseed oil (430 ml)

Squash Blossoms:
canola oil
1 small egg, cold, beaten
¼ cup flour (31 g)
⅓ cup neutral-flavored beer (66 ml)
2 tsp Ras El Hanout (4 g)
4 squash blossoms, patted dry
approx. 2 cups canola oil (400 ml)
1 tsp salt (3 g)

Spiced Zucchini:
1 each yellow and green zucchini,
  oblique cut
olive oil
2 tsp Preserved Lemon (8 g), diced
2 T Ras El Hanout Spice (12 g)
lemon juice to taste

Shaved Raw Zucchini:
½ zucchini, shaved thinly
olive oil
lemon juice
salt to taste

Garnish:
fresh dill

DIRECTIONS

Preserved Lemon:
Cut lemons into quarters and coat evenly with the salt and sugar. Pack into preserving jar or nonreactive bowl, then seal the jar with the lid or cover bowl with plastic wrap. Let sit at room temperature—they will be ready for use in 4 weeks. Once ready, remove 8 lemon quarters and separate rind. Wash the rind, pat dry and dice finely.

Ras El Hanout Spice:
Preheat the oven to 325°F. Toast all spices on parchment-lined sheet tray for 8-10 minutes, then cool. Put into a blender and blend until ground evenly.

Saffron Aioli:
Combine saffron and wine and bring to boil, remove from heat and let steep for 20 minutes, then cool. Blend the garlic, egg yolks, lemon juice, mustard, turmeric and salt in a blender. Add the wine/saffron mixture, scraping up the threads with a rubber spatula. Slowly add oil in a thin, steady stream, with the blender on low, just until the aioli is thick and emulsified.

Squash Blossoms:
Heat oil in a deep fryer or to ½" deep in a heavy skillet to 375°F. Mix together egg, flour, beer and Ras El Hanout, then use to batter squash blossoms. Fry them until crispy, rotating evenly. Drain on paper towels and season with salt.

Spiced Zucchini:
Sauté zucchini in a hot pan evenly coated with olive oil until caramelized. Fold in Preserved Lemon and Ras El Hanout Spice, then season with lemon juice and salt to taste.

Shaved Raw Zucchini:
Coat shaved zucchini evenly with olive oil, lemon juice and salt.

Plating:
Sauce the plate with Saffron Aioli, and add Spiced Zucchini Garnish with Shaved Raw Zucchini, crispy Squash Blossoms and dill.

ELLWOOD CANYON FARMS

Jack Motter picking peas at Ellwood Canyon Farms.

FOR FOUR GENERATIONS, JACK MOTTER'S family farmed land in the Imperial Valley, but he never planned to be a farmer. He knew he loved the ocean, though, and gravitated to Santa Barbara for college to be able to surf. He still looks as if he spends his mornings in the water, but now it is land that consumes his energies. He and Jeff Kramer, his longtime friend and Ellwood Canyon Farms business partner, are farming 50 acres between two properties.

After receiving his degree in economics, Jack worked for Smith Barney in Santa Barbara until he decided that wasn't for him. After quitting, he got a job writing a business plan for someone who wanted to switch from growing flowers to growing organic produce as community-supported agriculture. In the process Jack discovered an attraction for "local, organic and sustainable" and realized, "Hey, I do like farming—I do like working in the dirt."

In 2009 he heard about a few acres to rent and decided to take them on. "I was young and wide-open with few commitments," he says. "I called my dad.

He thought I was nuts, but he helped me out." Jack learned he likes following the weather and he likes to be challenged. "The easiest crop one month could be the hardest the next. You're at nature's whim, but there's always something new to learn. It's never boring."

A year after establishing Ellwood Canyon Farms, he partnered with Jeff. The two grew up together in Brawley—their grandparents had even been next-door neighbors. Like Jack, Jeff came to the Central Coast to go to school, fell in love with the area and never dreamed he'd end up in farming. "Life had a way of bringing me back to my roots," he says. Jack handles the business side and the production planning, while Jeff is the "machine and tractor-fixer extraordinaire" in charge of the mechanical operations.

For both farmers, life turned out to have better plans for them than they had for themselves. Although they both still love to surf, as Jack says, "Our passion is growing good, healthy food and treating the land well."
—Hilary Dole Klein

Ellwood Canyon Farms Ambrosia Melon
lardo, mezcal, pickled watermelon rind, Cotija, lemon basil

Wine Pairing:

Tyler Rosé of Pinot Noir, Sta. Rita Hills
Folded Hills Estate Lilly Rosé, Santa Ynez Valley
KITÁ Wines Grenache Rosé, Camp Four Vineyard, Santa Ynez Valley
Cebada Vineyard Rosé of Pinot Noir

Alternative Pairing:

Anderson Valley Briney Melon Gose

Chef's Notes:

Jack brought me an Ambrosia melon, and when I cut into it, I was overwhelmed by how good it smelled and tasted. I asked the kitchen, "Have you ever tasted anything this effing good?" In Texas canteloupe are pretty good, but they don't get anywhere near what Jack grows at his Ellwood Canyon Farm in Goleta.

Prep Time:

20 minutes

Special Equipment Needed:

juicer or chinois, Cryovac® (option: skim off foam with a large spoon)

Servings:

4 on individual plates

Editor's Note:

Mezcal is made from agave, like tequila, but cooked inside earthen pits with wood, rather than steam—giving it a distinctive smoky flavor. Del Maguey is made in a high mountain valley and is very aromatic—inexpensive tequila will not be a successful substitute.

INGREDIENTS

Mezcal Vinaigrette:
⅔ cup strained fresh Ambrosia melon
    juice (132 ml)
¼ cup lime juice (50 ml)
2 T Del Maguey Single Village
    Mezcal (26 ml)
1 tsp sugar (3 g)
1 tsp salt (3 g)
1 tsp xanthan gum (6 g)

Pickled Watermelon Rind:
¼ cup watermelon rind (25 g),
    peeled and finely julienned
¼ cup champagne vinegar (50 ml)
2 T sugar (26 g)
2 T water (28 ml)
½ tsp salt

Melons:
1 each Ambrosia melon, honeydew
    melon, yellow watermelon and sugar
    baby watermelon

Garnish:
2 oz lardo (56 g), very thinly sliced
½ bunch fresh lemon basil, de-stemmed
4 oz Cotija cheese (113 g), crumbled
2 sprigs flowering lime thyme
1 sprig lemon verbena
1 tsp Aleppo chile powder (2 g)
Pickled Watermelon Rind

DIRECTIONS

Mezcal Vinaigrette:
Juice approximately 1 lb (453 g) of Ambrosia melons to obtain strained juice. (Option: press through a chinois if no juicer is available.) Combine Ambrosia melon juice, lime juice, Del Maguey Single Village Mezcal, sugar and salt on high speed in a blender. Add the xanthan gum and blend for 45 seconds.

We use a Cryovac® to remove as much air as possible from each tray of vinaigrette so that the vinaigrette looks less foamy and frothy. (Option: skim off foam with a large spoon.) Adjust seasoning to taste.

Pickled Watermelon Rind:
Peel off all outer skin of the watermelon rind. Finely julienne similar to size of a toothpick. Heat pickling solution to a boil. Pour over rind and marinate in the refrigerator for minimum of 72 hours. Drain before use.

Melons:
Melon ball each melon, avoiding seeds, and toss in Mezcal Vinaigrette. Season to taste with salt.

Plating:
Plate four individual dishes with melons. Arrange lardo in ribbons across the melons. Spoon the Cotija cheese in pockets around the dish. Sprinkle Aleppo chile powder over the cheese. Place pieces of Pickled Watermelon Rind around the dish. Garnish with lemon basil, flowering lime thyme and lemon verbena. Pour a small pool of Mezcal Vinaigrette to the base of the bowl.

Lark staff visiting Ellwood Canyon Farms. Opposite: Ambrosia melons from Ellwood Canyon Farms.

Little Gems 'Wedge'
smoked blue cheese, chicory glazed bacon, radish, spicy pecans, fines herbes vinaigrette

Wine Pairing:
Ojai Vineyard KICK ON Riesling, Los Alamos Valley
Cold Heaven Viognier, Le Bon Climat Vineyard, Santa Maria Valley
Whitcraft Sta. Rita Hills Pence Ranch Mt. Eden Clone Pinot Noir
Clendenen Family Vineyards Pinot Noir, Le Bon Climat, Santa Maria Valley

Alternative Pairing:
Russian River Brewing Company Pliny the Elder

Chef's Notes:
The wedge has always been my favorite salad, but I'd never tasted my favorite wedge until now. This is it.

Prep Time:
45 minutes

Special Equipment Needed:
Cryovac® bag and sealer (option: sealable, food-safe plastic bag), PolyScience Smoking Gun Pro® with pinch of pecan wood chips

Servings:
4

Editor's Note:
Superfine pecan wood chips to work with the smoking gun can be purchased at www.cameronsproducts.com.

INGREDIENTS

Smoked Blue Cheese:
4 oz blue cheese (113 g)
pecan wood chips

Glazed Bacon:
4 oz slab bacon (113 g)
canola oil
1 cup packed brown sugar (200 g)
1 cup red wine vinegar (230 ml)
1 shallot, sliced
1 bunch fresh thyme, de-stemmed
1 T garlic (9 g), sliced
2 T ground chicory (25 g)

Croutons:
2 slices sourdough levain, large dice
olive oil
salt to taste

Spicy Pecans:
¼ cup pecans (30 g)
¼ cup reserved bacon fat (50 g), add
  canola, if needed, to make ¼ cup
1 tsp salt (3 g)
1 tsp cayenne pepper (2 g)

Fines Herbes Vinaigrette:
2 egg yolks (40 g)
5 tsp Dijon mustard (25 g)
2 tsp garlic (6 g), finely minced
2 T champagne vinegar (26 ml)
½ tsp salt
3 T each fresh tarragon, chives,
  chervil (10 g each), chopped
3 T parsley (15 g), chopped
1 tsp black pepper (3 g)
1¼ cup grapeseed oil (250 ml)
buttermilk, if needed

Little Gems:
2 heads Little Gems lettuce, washed,
  dried, quarterd lengthwise

Garnish:
2 T each fresh picked chervil,
  tarragon (6 g each)
2 T parsley (10 g)
1 bunch 1½" fresh chive batons, cut on
  bias
1 watermelon radish, peeled and sliced

DIRECTIONS

Smoked Blue Cheese:
Crumble the blue cheese and place in Cryovac® bag or sealable, food-safe plastic bag, then seal securely. Cut a hole just large enough for the tip of the smoking gun loaded with pecan wood chips. Insert gun and smoke for 3-4 minutes. Seal the opening of the bag securely by wrapping it tightly with tape. Let smoke soak for 6 hours.

Glazed Bacon:
Cut slab bacon into ¼" x ¼" x 1½" lardons. In a wide sauté pan, evenly coated with canola oil, brown lardons on all sides over medium heat. Reserve oil in the pan for the pecans. In a large pot, boil the chicory, brown sugar, vinegar, shallot, thyme and garlic. Reduce to syrup consistency, skimming as necessary. Strain through a chinois into a clean pot. Fold in cooked lardons. When ready to plate, remove lardons with a slotted spoon.

Croutons:
Preheat the oven to 300°F. Season sourdough evenly with oil and salt. Spread on a parchment-lined sheet pan, then bake until golden brown, turning occasionally to toast evenly.

Spicy Pecans:
Soak pecans in hot water for 1 minute to extract tannins, then drain and pat dry. In a sauté pan over low heat, cook pecans in reserved bacon fat until toasted, then drain on paper towels. Season evenly with salt and cayenne pepper.

Fines Herbes Vinaigrette:
Blend together egg yolks, Dijon mustard, garlic, champagne vinegar, salt and black pepper in a food processor. Pour oil in a thin, steady stream until emulsified. Fold in chopped tarragon, chives, chervil and parsley. Adjust the consistency with buttermilk if necessary; it should be thick and creamy.

Little Gems:
Wash Little Gems thoroughly to remove dirt from crevices close to the core. Dry completely. Quarter heads lengthwise keeping the core intact.

Plating:
Toss Little Gems evenly with Fines Herbes Vinaigrette. Place smoked blue cheese off center on the plate. Anchor the lettuce into the blue cheese to give elevation. Add watermelon radish, Croutons and Spicy Pecans. Evenly distribute warm Glazed Bacon. Finish with picked fines herbes.

Slices of watermelon radishes.

Butternut Squash and Candied Apples
fromage blanc, beets, black walnut, pomegranate, Calvados caramel

Wine Pairing:

Alma Rosa Pinot Blanc "La Encantada," Sta. Rita Hills
Tatomer Lafond Riesling, Sta. Rita Hills
Pali Wine Co. Huber Vineyard Chardonnay, Sta. Rita Hills
Amplify Carignane Camp 4 Vineyard, Santa Ynez Valley

Alternative Pairing:

Hollister Brewing Company Table 42 Red Ale
Anchor Steam Big Leaf Maple
Scar of the Sea Hopped Cider

Chef's Notes:

It is interesting tracking an idea to see where it goes. This dish began as an endive salad with apples and beets. I took the idea of carmelizing apples, glazing them in Calvados caramel and finishing them with candied black walnuts. I love the developed flavor of the pickled butternut squash in this dish. I like the play of textures—crunchy apple, pomegranate and endive, with creamy fromage blanc and velvety caramel.

Prep Time:

2 hours active preparation plus pickled vegetables

Special Equipment Needed:

blowtorch (option: hold over flame), cheesecloth, China cap (option: sieve double lined with cheesecloth), ice bath, Silpat, drying rack

Servings:

4-6

Editor's Note:

Be efficient by toasting the cinnamon and star anise for the Pickled Butternut Squash and for the Calvados Caramel at the same time.

INGREDIENTS

Pickled Butternut Squash:
½ lb butternut squash (226 g)
sachet:
   ½ stick cinnamon
   1 each star anise pod, bay leaf, whole clove
   2 tsp coriander seeds (3 g)
   ¼ tsp allspice
   1 T black peppercorn (6 g)
   5 tsp chile flake (10 g)
⅔ cup each apple cider and distilled white vinegar (132 ml each)
⅔ cup sugar (150 g)
⅔ cup water (153 ml)
1 tsp maple syrup (6 ml)
½ tsp ground turmeric
1 T salt (9 g)

Fromage Blanc:
2 cups whole milk (500 ml)
¼ cup each heavy cream and
  buttermilk (60 ml each)
1 T champagne vinegar (13 ml)
2 tsp fresh thyme (4 g), de-stemmed
½ tsp honey (3 g)
salt and pepper to taste

Roasted Beets:
3 each baby red and baby golden beets
2 sprigs fresh thyme
1 cup each red wine and champagne
  vinegar (200 ml each)
olive oil, lemon juice, salt to taste

Candied Black Walnuts:
1 cup raw black walnuts (125 g)
6 T sugar 78 g)
1 tsp salt (3 g)
1 T butter (14 g)

Cooked Butternut Squash:
½ lb butternut squash (226 g)
olive oil
4 T butter (56 g), melted
½ tsp salt
1 tsp sugar (4 g)
1 sprig fresh thyme, de-stemmed

Calvados Caramel:
½ stick cinnamon
1 star anise
½ cup heavy cream (115 ml)
⅔ cup sugar (132 g)
3 T butter (42 g), cubed, cold
3 T Calvados apple brandy (39 ml)
salt to taste

DIRECTIONS

Pickled Butternut Squash:
Peel and de-seed butternut squash, then cut in narrow ribbons. Steam for 3 minutes, then let cool. Burn the cinnamon and star anise with a blowtorch in a dry sauté pan or hold with tongs over a flame. Toast the bay leaf, clove, coriander seeds, allspice, black peppercorn and chile flake in a dry pan until aromatic. Tie up all the spices in cheesecloth to make a sachet. Bring cider vinegar, white vinegar, sugar, water, maple syrup, salt and turmeric to a simmer. Add sachet and pour over the squash in a nonreactive container. Marinate in the refrigerator for a minimum of 72 hours. Drain before use.

Fromage Blanc:
Over low heat, bring milk and cream to 170°F. Stir in buttermilk and vinegar, then remove from heat. Let rest for 10 minutes, allowing curds to form. Gently pour into China cap (option: sieve double lined with cheesecloth). When no whey is left dripping from the China cap or cloth, gently press mixture to remove all the whey. (Tip: save the whey and use in place of milk in baking.) Place fromage blanc in bowl and mix together with thyme, honey and salt and pepper to taste, then chill over an ice bath.

Roasted Beets:
Preheat oven to 300°F. Put red beets into a small baking dish, then add a sprig of thyme and equal parts red wine vinegar and water to a level halfway up the beet. Using champagne vinegar and water, do the same for the golden beets in a separate baking dish. Cover each with foil and bake until knife tender, approximately 1 to 1½ hours. Let cool to a warm temperature in cooking liquid, then peel. Season to taste with olive oil, lemon and salt.

Candied Black Walnuts:
Combine walnuts and sugar in a dry pan with a rubber spatula. Stir over medium heat until sugar melts and nuts are toasty and aromatic. Stir in butter, then spread on a Silpat to cool and season with salt. Pulse in food processor until roughly ground.

Cooked Butternut Squash:
Preheat oven to 300°F. Cut peeled squash into 1" planks. Coat evenly with melted butter, salt, sugar and thyme. Wrap in foil and bake 30 minutes or until knife tender. (The Lark uses a Cryovac® and steamer. Steam for 14-18 minutes at 200°F or until completely tender.) Drain, cool in a bowl over ice, then cube.

Calvados Caramel:
Have all your ingredients measured and on hand. Burn cinnamon and star anise with a blowtorch in a dry sauté pan or hold with tongs over a flame. Scald the cream over low heat; do not let boil. In a separate large pot, heat sugar over medium heat just until it reaches a golden brown color. Remove from heat and slowly add the warm cream in batches, constantly whisking to incorporate fully. Slowly whisk in the cold butter, then fold in the Calvados. Season with salt to taste, then add the burnt cinnamon and star anise and let steep 30 minutes. Remove cinnamon and star anise before serving.

INGREDIENTS

Caramelized Apples:
2 apples
canola oil
1 tsp sugar (5 g)
pinch salt
1 T butter (14 g)
sprig fresh thyme
1 T cider vinegar (13 ml)

Garnish:
¼ cup pomegranate seeds (45 g)
½ raw beet, shaved
several leaves of endive, radicchio, sorrel
½ apple, sliced thinly

DIRECTIONS

Caramelized Apples:
Quarter apples lengthwise, remove seeds, retain skins, then pat dry. Sauté in a hot pan coated with an even layer of canola oil until caramelized. Add sugar, salt, butter, thyme and cider vinegar and cook over low heat until a glaze forms. Cool apple quarters on a rack. Right before serving, rewarm and glaze with Calvados Caramel in a sauté pan.

Plating:
Plate Pickled Butternut Squash, Fromage Blanc, beets, Cooked Butternut Squash and Candied Apples. Top apples with Candied Black Walnuts, then garnish with pomegranate seeds, raw shaved beet, endive, radicchio, sorrel and apple slices.

Making Fromage Blanc

GOODLAND ORGANICS

Jay Ruskey with oak seedlings that he's inoculated with truffle fungus. Opposite: Jay pouring freshly harvested coffee cherries into a hand-cranked pulping machine to remove the seeds.

JAY RUSKEY HAS GOOD REASON to be proud of his impressive cherimoyas, the exotic fruit that Mark Twain called "deliciousness itself." Pollinated by hand, they take a lot of effort to nurture properly, but their aromatic ambrosia never fails to surprise and please his customers. "We grow organically and harvest at optimal maturity," he says. "We sacrifice shelf life for sweetness."

A pioneering farmer of the Central Coast, Jay majored in agribusiness at Cal Poly San Luis Obispo with the idea of growing cut flowers. But when his family found a farm in 1990 that was growing primarily avocados and cherimoyas, he switched to tree fruits.

Located on the Condor Ridge Ranch in the rolling foothills of Goleta, two miles from the ocean, Good Land Organics enjoys a distinctive ecosystem. Its elevation of 650 feet, warm southern orientation, frost-free winters and foggy-morning summers make it ideal for growing a diversity of subtropical delicacies, such as passion fruit, cherimoyas, avocados, pitaya, caviar finger limes and coffee. Jay takes full advantage of this, constantly experimenting with new ideas.

"I like the challenges of innovation, of pushing production and quality forward and finding organic solutions to produce the best crops," he says. "I'm still learning; every year is a new year." In addition to growing a hundred exotic fruit trees, he's the first farmer to grow coffee commercially in the continental U.S. He plants his shade-loving coffee beneath the canopy of his avocado trees. Sharing water and having the same soil requirements, they make fine companions. Good Land's coffee has been rated among the top 30 in the world.

Ever passionate about experimenting with crops, Jay has also partnered with Shanley Farms in Morro Bay to start Diversitree Nursery, which grows thousands of seedlings (including goji, passion fruit and coffee) and oak trees inoculated with the black winter truffle fungus to sell to farmers as commercial alternatives to diversify their farms. In 2010, Jay was named Outstanding Farmer by the University of California, citing his "willingness to share his knowledge with other growers and to open his farm to a variety of visitors."

In 2017, in a story about California coffee, the *New York Times* wrote that Jay is "widely regarded as the father of the state's nascent coffee business."

—Hilary Dole Klein

Red Kale and Pears
triple-crème brie, caramelized coffee bean, hazelnuts, wildflower honey

Wine Pairing:
Babcock Chardonnay "Top Cream", Sta. Rita Hills
Liquid Farm Golden Slope Chardonnay, Sta. Rita Hills
Brewer-Clifton Hapgood Chardonnay, Sta. Rita Hills

Alternative Pairing:
Dreamcôte "Original Dry" Hard Apple Cider

Chef's Notes:
I'd never heard of kale in Texas, let alone eaten it. Kale seems to be the equivalent of a religion in the great state of California. I like to remain secular. This became one of my favorite kale salads. I think the coffee bean is a surprising factor in the dish. It works well with the richness of the brie and the heartiness of the greens. Feel free to be generous with the wildflower honey.

Prep Time:
40 minutes

Special Equipment Needed:
Silpat, blender (option: coffee grinder)

Servings:
2

Editor's Note:
Extra Caramelized Expresso Bean Powder may be sprinkled on ice cream or stirred into hot chocolate.

INGREDIENTS

Caramelized Coffee Bean Powder:
3 T sugar (40 g)
¾ cup coffee beans (100 g)

Toasted Hazelnuts:
½ cup raw hazelnuts (60 g)

Caramelized Pear:
1 red Bosc or Seckel pear
canola oil
1 tsp sugar (4 g)
pinch salt
1 T butter (14 g)
sprig fresh thyme
1 T cider vinegar (13 ml)

Red Kale Salad:
½ bunch red kale, torn into pieces
olive oil
lemon juice
salt to taste

Garnish:
½ Bartlett pear, cored, shaved
3 oz triple-crème brie, cubed (85 g)
½ carrot, shaved
wildflower honey or honey comb
Caramelized Coffee Bean Powder

DIRECTIONS

Caramelized Coffee Bean Powder:
In a wide pot over medium low heat, fold sugar and coffee beans together with a spatula. Cook 7-10 minutes, until caramelized and aromatic. Watch carefully since sugar will start to burn soon after melting. Remove from heat and lower temperature, if necessary. Spread on a Silpat and let cool completely, then break into small pieces and pulse to a powder with a blender (Note: a coffee grinder is also an option.)

Toasted Hazelnuts:
Preheat oven to 300°F. Spread hazelnuts on a baking sheet, then toast for 10-12 minutes or until golden brown, stirring occasionally to toast evenly. Cool before serving.

Caramelized Pear:
Quarter pear lengthwise, remove core, pat dry. In a hot pan evenly coated with a layer of canola oil, sauté until caramelized. Remove pears, turn heat to low, stir in sugar, salt, butter, thyme and cider vinegar, then cook until a glaze forms. Add the pears and spoon the glaze over them. Keep warm until serving.

Red Kale Salad:
Toss kale with an even coat of olive oil and lemon juice. Season to taste with salt.

Plating:
Plate the Red Kale Salad with shaved pear, shaved carrot and Caramelized Pear. Evenly place brie and toasted hazelnuts. Drizzle with wildflower honey, and sprinkle the Caramelized Coffee Bean Powder.

"The Garden Of" Salanova Lettuce
fromage blanc, poppy seed, stone fruits, Eureka lemon honey, Marcona almonds, opal basil

Wine Pairing:
Arcadian Chardonnay Sleepy Hollow Vineyard
La Voix Here and Heaven Chardonnay, John Sebastiano Vineyard Sta. Rita Hills
Longoria Chardonnay Fe Ciega Vineyard, Sta. Rita Hills

Chef's Notes:
"The Garden Of" was the first farm that caught my eye at the farmers market when I arrived in Santa Barbara. We are lucky to have the Takikawa family farming here in our backyard. I'd never seen so many perfectly arranged heads of lettuce in my life that day at the market. The Salanova variety is approachable because it is similar to red leaf and butter lettuce. Visually, it is one of my favorite salads we've ever had on the menu. People are surprised to see the salad is one perfect head of lettuce prepared just for them. The nutty flavor of the poppy seeds brings out the complex flavors of the salad.

Prep Time:
1 hour preparation.

Special Equipment Needed:
cheesecloth, China cap (option: sieve double lined with cheesecloth), ice bath

Servings:
4

INGREDIENTS

Eureka Lemon Honey:
¾ cup wildflower honey (250 g)
2 Eureka lemons, zested
¼ tsp salt

Fromage Blanc:
2 cups whole milk (500 ml)
¼ cup each heavy cream and
  buttermilk (60 ml each)
1 T champagne vinegar (13 ml)
2 tsp fresh thyme, de-stemmed
½ tsp honey (3 g)
salt and pepper to taste

Poppy Seed Vinaigrette:
2 egg yolks (40 g)
1 tsp salt (3 g)
½ cup lemon juice (105 ml)
¼ cup honey (83 g)
¾ cup olive oil (157 ml)
½ cup grapeseed oil (107 ml)
1 T lemon zest (6 g)
½ cup poppy seeds (15 g), toasted,
  cooled
pinch citric acid

Marinated Stone Fruit:
1 ripe plum, 1 ripe apricot
sugar to taste
salt to taste
1 T olive oil (13 ml)
2 stems opal basil

Marcona Almonds:
3 T Marcona almonds (27 g)
1 tsp salt (3 g)
1 tsp olive oil (5 ml)

Garnish:
bachelor buttons, marigolds, opal basil
Marcona almonds
Marinated Stone Fruit, sliced
Eureka Lemon Honey

DIRECTIONS

Eureka Lemon Honey:
Bring all ingredients up to boil in a small saucepot and remove from the heat. Cool completely before serving.

Fromage Blanc:
Over low heat, bring milk and cream to 170°F. Stir in buttermilk and vinegar. Remove from heat for 30 minutes, allowing curds to form. Gently pour into China cap (option: sieve double lined with cheesecloth). When no whey is left dripping from the China cap or cloth, gently press mixture to remove all the whey. Place fromage blanc in bowl and mix together with thyme, honey, salt and pepper to taste, then chill over an ice bath. Adjust consistency with whey. Place in piping bag. The end result is creamy and spreadable.

Poppy Seed Vinaigrette:
In a Vitamix or high-powered blender combine egg yolks, salt, lemon juice and honey. Blend on high until emulsified. Pour grapeseed oil and olive oil in until completely incorporated. Pour into a bowl and fold in poppy seeds, lemon zest and citric acid.

Marinated Stone Fruit:
Split fruits in half. Scoop out pits. Slice into thin wedges. Toss in a bowl with a pinch of sugar and salt, olive oil and opal basil stems. Marinate for 15 minutes.

Marcona Almonds:
Toss almonds with olive oil and salt and bake on a sheet tray lined with parchment paper at 300°F for 10-12 minutes or until golden.

Plating:
Using a spoon, place tablespoon of Poppy Seed Vinaigrette around the rim of the plate. Pipe Fromage Blanc in center of plate. Toss a head of Salanova lettuce in olive oil, lemon juice and salt. Place the base of the lettuce on the Fromage Blanc. Pipe more Fromage Blanc throughout pockets of the lettuce. Place Marcona Almonds on the fromage blanc. Finish the dish with marinated stone fruits, edible flowers, opal basil and Eureka Lemon Honey.

Warm Rainbow Carrots
miso-carrot butter, toasted cashews, ginger pickled carrots, chili flake, mint

Wine Pairing:

Holus Bolus Blanc, Roussanne, Santa Maria Valley
Dragonette Grenache, John Sebastiano Vineyard, Santa Ynez Valley
Solomon Hills Chardonnay, Bien Nacido Estate, Santa Maria Valley

Alternative Pairing:

Ballast Point Brewing Company Pumpkin Down

Chef's Notes:

Taylor, my Executive Sous Chef, came to me and said, "Let's do salt-roasted carrots just like people do baked potatoes." They are moist and seasoned perfectly. For the miso-carrot butter, we cook carrots in carrot juice to intensify the flavor. The gremolata adds a surprising freshness and contrasting bitterness. When this is on the menu, it is a favorite both in the kitchen and in the dining room.

Prep Time:

1 ¼ hours, plus pickling

Special Equipment Needed:

mandoline, chinois (option: fine-meshed sieve), ice bath

Servings:

4

Editor's Note:

Note that this recipe uses white miso, which is sweeter and less salty than red miso.

INGREDIENTS

Ginger Pickled Carrots:
½ cup purple carrots (65 g), thinly sliced
½ cup red wine vinegar (115 ml)
1 T salt (9 g)
¼ cup sugar (50 g)
½ cup water (58 ml)
2 jalapeño chiles, split
1 tsp ginger powder (2 g)
¼ cup fresh ginger (25 g), peeled,
  finely chopped

Roasted Rainbow Carrots:
1 bunch large rainbow carrots, reserve
  tops
olive oil
salt

Carrot-Miso Butter:
3½ T butter (45 g)
2½ cups carrot (325 g), peeled, chopped
1 tsp salt (3 g)
2 T + 1 tsp sugar (30 g)
3 oz carrot juice (90 ml), may need extra
2 T white miso (40 g)

Carrot Top Gremolata:
1 garlic clove, chopped
olive oil
3 carrot tops, finely chopped
zest of 1 orange
¼ tsp salt

Toasted Cashews:
½ cup cashews (70 g)
salt to taste

Garnish:
several sprigs fresh mint and carrot tops

DIRECTIONS

Ginger Pickled Carrots:
Shave carrots thinly with a mandoline. Simmer red wine vinegar, salt, sugar, water, jalapeño, ginger powder and fresh ginger together for 10 minutes. Pour over carrots and marinate in the refrigerator for a minimum of 72 hours. Drain before use.

Roasted Rainbow Carrots:
Preheat the oven to 350°F. Cut carrot tops off, remove big stems and reserve for the gremolata. Toss carrots in olive oil. Make a ½" layer on parchment-lined sheet pan. Place carrots in an even layer on top of salt. Roast approximately 50-60 minutes or until knife tender.

Carrot-Miso Butter:
Melt butter in a rondeau or wide, deep skillet. Add carrots and cook gently for 10 minutes on low heat. Add salt, sugar, carrot juice, then cover and simmer until carrots are tender. While still warm transfer to blender. Add miso and blend until creamy and smooth. Adjust consistency with carrot juice if needed. Pass through a chinois or fine-meshed sieve and chill in a bowl inside an ice bath.

Carrot Top Gremolata:
Lightly sauté garlic in olive oil, until tender. Cool completely. Combine carrot tops, along with orange zest, salt and cooled garlic, in a mixing bowl.

Toasted Cashews;
Set oven to 300°F. Spread cashews on a baking sheet, then toast for 10-12 minutes or until aromatic. Toss evenly with salt, then cool completely.

Plating:
Plate the Roasted Rainbow Carrots and Ginger Pickled Carrots on a serving platter. Dot with Carrot-Miso Butter and Carrot Top Gremolata, then garnish with carrot tops, mint and cashews.

Rainbow carrots.
Next page: Tom Shepherd and crew pruning his peach orchard.

Roasted Beets and Burrata
pluot, toasted pistachios, hibiscus, mâche

Wine Pairing:

Whitcraft Santa Barbara County 4 Soils Pinot Noir
Riverbench Cork Jumper Blanc de Noirs
Presqu'ile Pinot Noir, Rim Rock Vineyard, Santa Maria Valley

Alternative Pairing:

Telegraph Brewing Company Reserve Wheat with Hibiscus

Chef's Notes:

Canned beets ruined this vegetable for most people, myself included. Beets are intimidating if you aren't already in love with them. This recipe should give you the confidence to prepare and appreciate beets in a new way. I enjoy how the hibiscus highlights the earthiness of the beet while adding floral notes and a sweet and sour finish.

Prep Time:

1 hour active preparation (plus 3 hours for baking and chilling)

Special Equipment Needed:

cheesecloth

Servings:

4

Editor's Note:

Dried hibiscus is available at specialty grocers. It is also sold under its Spanish name, *jamaica*.

INGREDIENTS

Hibiscus Vinaigrette:
¼ tsp black peppercorn
¼ teaspoon juniper berries
1 bay leaf
¼ cup dried hibiscus (30 g)
5 T red wine vinegar (65 ml)
¼ cup sugar (50 g)
¼ cup water (58 ml)
¼ vanilla bean, seeds only
1 tsp salt (3 g)
½ cup olive oil (105 ml)
1 tsp xanthan gum (6 g)

Roasted Beets:
2 T salt (19 g)
2 T ground black pepper (16 g)
6 T each red wine vinegar and extra
    virgin olive oil (78 ml each)
1 bunch of fresh thyme, de-stemmed
½ lb golden beets (226 g),
    cleaned, skins retained
½ lb red beets (226 g),
    cleaned, skins retained

Toasted Pistachios:
½ cup raw pistachios (55 g)
olive oil
salt

Mâche:
2 cups mâche (110 g)
salt to taste
olive oil
lemon

Garnishes:
½ lb burrata (226 g), sliced
1 pluot, sliced
1 persimmon, sliced
1 gold baby beet, shaved
1 red baby beet, shaved
1 Chioggia baby beet, shaved

DIRECTIONS

Hibiscus Vinaigrette:
Preheat the oven to 325°F. Spread peppercorn, juniper berries and bay leaf on baking sheet and bake for 12-15 minutes or until aromatic. Tie up in a square of cheesecloth to make a sachet, then place into a pot with hibiscus, vinegar, sugar, water, vanilla bean seeds and salt. Bring to a boil, then turn off and let steep and cool for 45 minutes. After removing sachet, blend in a Vitamix or high-powered blender until velvety smooth. Slowly add olive oil, with blender on low, in a steady stream until emulsified. Sprinkle in xanthan gum. Pass through a chinois. Chill over an ice bath. Adjust seasoning to taste.

Roasted Beets:
Preheat the oven to 350°F. Whisk salt, pepper, olive oil, vinegar and thyme in a mixing bowl. Place beets into a deep baking dish. Pour solution into the dish to a 1" level. Wrap dish tightly with foil. Bake for 60-90 minutes or until knife tender, adding water if necessary during baking. If the dish is too shallow, or the oven too hot, the beets will dry out too soon. Peel beets with a clean towel while still warm so the skin removes easily. Chill completely, then cut into bite-sized pieces.

Toasted Pistachios:
Set oven to 300°F. Coat pistachios evenly with olive oil and season with salt. Spread on a parchment-lined baking sheet and toast for 10-12 minutes, stirring occasionally. Let cool.

Mâche:
Lightly season mâche with lemon, olive oil and salt to taste.

Plating:
Sauce the plate with Hibiscus Vinaigrette. Toss the Roasted Beets in Hibiscus Vinaigrette and add to the plate. Place the burrata, pluot and persimmon slices and Mâche, then garnish with toasted pistachios and shaved beets.

Roasted Chioggia beets.

EARTHTRINE FARM

Robert Dautch of Earthtrine Farm, better known as B.D., has also been called "the organic alchemist" and the "farmer with a heart of gold." Considered a pioneer among organic growers selling produce at Santa Barbara farmers' markets, he first grew herbs and vegetables at his market garden in the late '70s. The garden was a homestead on Del Playa in Isla Vista. "We farmed three lots that were empty because of a building moratorium," he says, "dragging very long hoses from our house."

After moving north for co-op farming in the Sacramento Valley, helping supply Chez Panisse and other restaurants in the farm-to-table movement, B.D. returned to buy his Earthtrine Farm in the foothills of Carpinteria in 1986. The name comes from the astrological birth signs of his family—three earth signs that form a triangle said to be in the most harmonious of alignments.

In the late '90s, B.D. purchased 10 acres in Ojai. He still farms both sites, shuttling between the coastal farm, which is good for greens like lettuce, kale and cilantro, and Ojai, where temperature extremes boost the flavor of his oranges. In Ojai he also grows figs, summer vegetables and the aromatic herbs that are chefs' favorites. His market stand, where as many as six kinds of basil may be on display, is a treat for the senses.

B.D. claims he can't resist planting everything he likes and therefore grows more than 100 varieties of vegetables, fruits and flowers. His main crops are dozens of lettuces, bitter greens and his culinary herbs such as French tarragon, Persian mint, South American epazote and Thai basil. His personal favorites are thyme and parsley, excellent in "pretty much anything I cook."

"People love my little broccoli bunches," B.D. adds. "Also the surprises I bring—the weeds." A sign at his stand exhorts: "Go Wild. Eat Weeds!" Depending on the season, he might be selling nettles, purslane, amaranth, miner's lettuce, or lamb's quarters, used in soups and salads. "If you're going to live in harmony with nature, you have to eat weeds!" he says with enthusiasm.

Despite, or maybe because of, his long hours alone in the fields, B.D. likes to work alongside his crew at Earthtrine's three weekly markets (two in Santa Barbara, one in Ojai). People come by as much for his fresh organic produce as for the chance to say hello, talk recipes and bask in his cheerful optimism.

—Hilary Dole Klein

Central Coast Spring Vegetables
charred spring onions, romanesco, asparagus, pickled ramps, soft poached egg, Parmesan

Wine Pairing:

Habit Grüner Veltliner, Rancho Arroyo Perdidto Vineyard, Santa Ynez Valley
Combe Trousseau Stolpman Vineyards Ballard Canyon

Alternative Pairing:

The Apiary Rustique Mead

Chef's Notes:

As a chef, I am deeply connected to the seasons, and each one has a profound effect on me. As much as I love the earthiness of root vegetables delivered on dark winter days, I start dreaming of the more fragile vegetables that grow in the spring. I love to explore the versatility of each vegetable. I think this dish represents the bounty of our area in springtime. The egg adds luxuriousness, a counterpoint to the lean asparagus, romanesco and spring onions.

Prep Time:

40 minutes, plus pickled vegetables

Special Equipment Needed:

Silpat, grill, ice bath, immersion circulator (option: small pot), ice bath possible

Servings:

4 as a shared plate

Editor's Note:

You can poach the eggs, but the delicate, viscous texture of a 64°C sous vide egg is worth purchasing an immersion circulator. Make sure the water is up to temperature before adding the eggs, for proper timing.

INGREDIENTS

Pickled Ramps:
1 cup ramps (100 g)
½ cup red wine vinegar (115 ml)
¼ cup sugar (50 g)
1 T salt (9 g)
¼ cup water (58 ml)
1 tsp chile flake (2 g)

Parmesan Crisps:
1 cup Parmesan cheese (100 g), grated
black pepper and salt to taste

Parmesan Vinaigrette:
1 egg yolk (20 g)
1½ T Dijon mustard (23 g)
7 T champagne vinegar (90 ml)
½ tsp each salt and black pepper
1 cup Parmesan (120 g), small dice
approx. ¾ cup grapeseed oil (150 ml)

Spring Vegetables:
8 stalks asparagus
4 spring onions, cut in half lengthwise
½ head romanesco, cut into pieces
¼ head purple cauliflower, cut into
  florets
olive oil
lemon juice
salt to taste

Soft Poached Eggs:
4 eggs
white vinegar (if poaching)
olive oil
1 T chive (2 g), finely diced
black pepper and sea salt to taste

Garnish:
red watercress
2 baby carrots, shaved
2 breakfast radishes, shaved
10 each sugar snap peas, blanched
10 each fava beans, blanched
olive oil
lemon juice
salt

DIRECTIONS

Pickled Ramps:
Put ramps into a nonreactive bowl. Heat vinegar, sugar, salt chile flake and water to a simmer and pour over the ramps. Marinate in the refrigerator for a minimum of 72 hours. Drain before use.

Parmesan Crisps:
Preheat oven to 325°F. Spread an even ¼" layer of Parmesan on a sheet pan lined with a Silpat. Season evenly with black pepper and lightly with salt. Bake until cheese melts, 10-12 minutes, rotating three or four times. Cool completely, then break into shards. If not using immediately, wrap tightly with plastic.

Parmesan Vinaigrette:
In a blender, combine egg yolk, mustard, vinegar, salt and pepper. Slowly incorporate the Parmesan cheese until smooth. Slowly add oil in a thin stream with blender until emulsified, using water to adjust consistency if needed. The end result should be thick and creamy.

Spring Vegetables:
Coat asparagus and onions evenly with oil and salt, then grill until knife tender. Blanch romanesco and cauliflower individually until knife tender. To blanch: fill a 5-quart pot 80% with water. Season the water with salt until it tastes like the ocean. Bring to a boil, then transfer to an ice bath, stirring to speed up the cooling process. Drain through a colander when cooled. Evenly coat asparagus, onions, romanesco and cauliflower in olive oil. Season to taste with lemon juice and salt.

Soft Poached Eggs:
Heat water in a water bath with an immersion circulator to 64°C and cook eggs for 40-45 minutes. Once egg has set but yolk is still runny, drop the temperature to 58°C to stop the cooking process and hold the eggs. Or soft poach the egg using the classic method of using simmering water with a touch of vinegar. Cook 3 minutes, then remove with ladle. Season with olive oil, chives, black pepper and sea salt.

Plating:
Place a spoonful of Parmesan Vinaigrette on the plate and arrange the Spring Vegetables and Pickled Ramps on it. Lightly season shaved carrot, shaved radish, snap peas, fava beans with olive oil, lemon juice and salt to taste. Evenly distribute them around the plate. Finish with Soft Poached Egg, Parmesan Crisps and red watercress.

Spring Pea and Farro Risotto
sheep's milk feta, Niçoise olive crumble, pea shoots, Ojai Pixie tangerines, mint

Wine Pairing:

Piro Points West Pinot Noir, Santa Maria Valley
Tatomer Paragon Grüner Veltliner
Au Bon Climat Pinot Noir Knox Alexander, Santa Maria Valley

Alternative Pairing:

Ojai Valley Brewing White Pixie Ale

Chef's Notes:

Ojai Pixie tangerines were the impetus for this dish. This is an example of finding a local ingredient and developing an idea around it. The Ojai Pixie tangerine has the perfect balance of sweet and tart. I discovered how to dehydrate olives in San Francisco. I wanted to use them because of how interesting and crunchy they turn out. The farro becomes rich and creamy once you add the fresh peas and feta.

Prep Time:

2 hours

Special Equipment Needed:

ice bath, grill, China cap (option: fine-meshed sieve)

Servings:

2-4

INGREDIENTS

Niçoise Olive Crumble:
8 cups Niçoise olives, pitted (1 kg)

Fresh Spring Peas:
1 cup spring peas (130 g), from 1 lb
  (453 g) pea pods

Farro:
4 sprigs fresh thyme
1 cup whole-grain farro (180 g)
1 quart water (1 L)
2 tsp salt (6 g)
1 T olive oil (13 g)
½ cup feta cheese (75 g), crumbled
1 T butter (14 g)
2 T orange juice (25 ml)
½ bunch fresh mint, de-stemmed,
  chopped

Garnish:
1 cup pea shoots
1 bulb fennel, shaved thinly
1 Ojai Pixie tangerine, peeled and
  separated into segments
¼ cup feta cheese (40 g), crumbled

DIRECTIONS

Niçoise Olive Crumble:
Drain Niçoise olives, then soak in fresh water for 24 hours. Drain. Spread on a parchment-lined sheet pan and cook at 200°F for 24 hours until brittle and dry. Pulse in food processor just until coarsely chopped. If you go too far, the olives will release their oil and make a paste. No need to panic as this is also good.

Fresh Spring Peas:
Right before serving dish, blanch peas quickly in a large pot of salted water. To blanch: fill a 5-quart pot 80% with water and bring to a boil. Season the water with salt until it tastes like the ocean. Blanch the peas until tender. When cooked perfectly, peas should pop gently if pressed. Transfer to an ice bath to keep bright, vibrant color, stirring to speed up the cooling process. Drain through a colander when cooled.

Farro:
Preheat the oven to 325°F. Tie thyme together securely with twine. Spread the farro on a parchment-lined sheet tray and toast for 15 minutes or until aromatic. Bring water and salt to a rapid boil in a large pot, then add the thyme and toasted farro slowly—to avoid boil over. Turn down the heat to medium and cook approximately 30 minutes until the farro starts to burst like wild rice. Discard thyme sachet, then drain farro through a China cap or fine-meshed sieve.

Place farro in a small pot and drizzle with olive oil while hot, so oil is absorbed as it cools. Stir in feta and butter and cook over medium heat with enough water to prevent burning. Cook and stir until creamy and bound. Salt to taste, then fold in orange juice and Fresh Spring Peas.

Plating:
Place the Farro Risotto into a bowl. Sprinkle feta and Niçoise Olive Crumble across faro. Finish with tangerines, shaved fennel and pea shoots.

Spring peas.

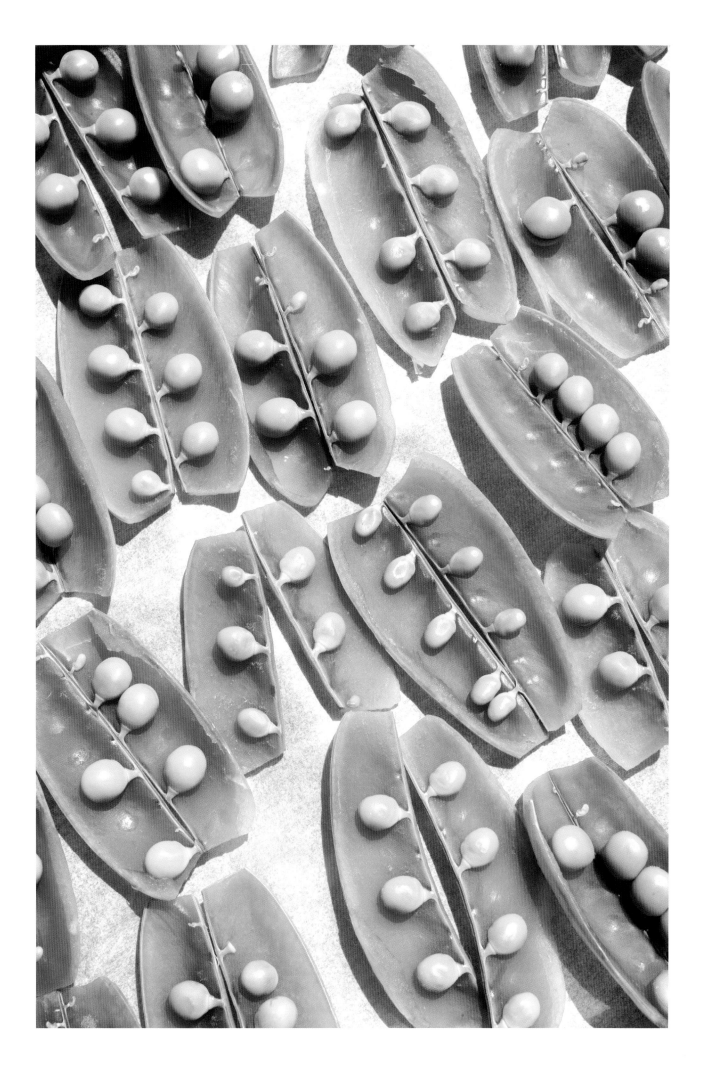

Caramelized Cauliflower Gratin
Gruyere, preserved lemon, chile flake, bacon breadcrumbs

Wine Pairing:

Longoria Pinot Grigio, Santa Ynez Valley
Au Bon Climat Pinot Gris (60%)/Pinot Blanc (40%), Santa Maria Valley
Hilliard Bruce SKY Pinot Noir, Sta. Rita Hills
Peake Ranch Pinot Noir, John Sebastiano Vineyard, Sta. Rita Hills

Alternative Pairing:

brewLAB Alliance Saison
Tahoe Mountain Brewing Company Provisions Rustic Multi-grain Saison

Chef's Notes:

Learning how to make bacon breadcrumbs was an epiphany for me. I knew we had to use them somewhere, and this take on a gratin really does them justice. I worked at an imported cheese counter while studying at college. I was obsessed with great cheeses. In 2005 I made a pilgrimage to Gruyere, Switzerland. I ate Gruyere cheese, tasted it, smelled it, to understand all its stages. I've never looked at Gruyere the same again, and it became a part of me. It is one of the best parts of this dish.

Prep Time:

1 hour active preparation, plus preserved lemon

Special Equipment Needed:

4 individual-sized cast iron serving kettles, chinois or fine-meshed sieve

Servings:

4

Editor's Note:

Extra bacon breadcrumbs can be stored in the freezer for future use.

INGREDIENTS

Preserved Lemon:
6 lemons
6 T salt (54 g)
4 T sugar (52 g)

Bacon Breadcrumbs:
1 loaf sourdough levain
1 lb slab bacon (453 g), finely diced
salt and black pepper to taste

Mornay Sauce:
3 T butter (42 g)
3 T all-purpose flour (23 g), sifted
2 cups milk (490 ml)
1 tsp salt (3 g)
½ tsp freshly ground black pepper
¾ cup freshly grated Gruyere (75 g)

Caramelized Cauliflower:
canola oil
1 head cauliflower, washed, cut into
  florets, patted dry
peel of 2 preserved lemons
salt, chile flake, lemon juice to taste

Garnish:
2 T fresh thyme (4 g), de-stemmed

DIRECTIONS

Preserved Lemon:
Cut lemons into quarters and coat evenly with the salt and sugar. Pack into preserving jar or nonreactive bowl, then seal the jar with the lid or cover bowl with plastic wrap. Let sit at room temperature—they will be ready for use in 4 weeks. Once ready, remove 8 lemon quarters and separate rind. Wash the rind, pat dry and dice finely.

Bacon Breadcrumbs:
Preheat oven to 250°F. Cut the loaf in 1" cubes, then spread them evenly on baking sheet. Toast for approximately 30 minutes or until completely dry. Cool, then blend in a food processor until a coarse powder.

In a sauté pan, render fat from bacon over medium heat, stirring occasionally to cook evenly. Remove with a spider or slotted spoon, drain on paper towels, then dice and reserve bacon for garnish. Add crumbs to remaining fat in pan and cook over low heat, stirring, until crumbs absorb the fat and are the consistency of wet sand. Season with salt and pepper. Spread in an even layer on a parchment-lined sheet pan to toast in the oven until light brown. Do not overcook or crumbs will burn when broiled.

Mornay Sauce:
Melt butter in a medium saucepan over low heat, then add flour and cook for 2 minutes, whisking constantly. Slowly pour milk into the butter-flour mixture, while whisking, then bring to a boil. Continue whisking and cooking for 1 minute or until thickened. Remove from heat, whisk in salt, pepper and Gruyere, adjusting consistency with milk if needed. The end result should be creamy and rich. Pass through a chinois or fine-meshed sieve. Keep warm.

Caramelized Cauliflower:
Heat cast iron pan over high heat and coat evenly with canola oil. Just before the oil smokes, add the dry cauliflower and cook until caramelized on all sides. Drain off fat and generously coat cauliflower with Mornay Sauce. Season with diced preserved lemon peel, salt, chile flake and lemon juice to taste.

Plating:
Divide the cauliflower between the four small cast-iron pots. Top with a generous portion of Bacon Breadcrumbs and broil under a salamander or on the top rack of oven broiler until golden brown. Garnish with fresh thyme and crispy diced bacon.

CHRIS THOMPSON

CHRIS THOMPSON HAS WILD, SUNBLEACHED hair, almost contained by his faded blue baseball cap. He is waiting for us as we pull over on the side of the dusty road, one worn brown leather boot crossed over the other as he leans against the car. It's a hot day in the Santa Ynez Valley, and the dry, dusty air, so different from the seaside climate we just left in Santa Barbara, is surprising. We step out of the air conditioning and into the sundrenched afternoon. Chris's red, sun-worn cheeks give away hours spent outside already today. Chris grows many types of crops, from onions to melons to tomatoes. In the shade of an oak tree, Chris fixes his piercing blue eyes out over his fields and begins to explain to us how to grow food the right way.

Chris Thompson's philosophy is centered on problem-solving, around keeping the big picture in mind and being as effective as possible with time and resources. "It's all about observation. Walking around, checking on things to see what's going on. I've trained myself to scan the fields, and I can see what's healthy and what's not healthy. When you work out here your whole life, you can just tell. The more you can simulate nature's diversity, the less chance there is that things will be out of balance."

It's exactly this large-scale sense of balance that informs most of Chris's farming. He uses soil analysis to determine any mineral deficiencies so he can remedy them. "The micronutrients are what give produce its flavor," he tells us. For example, he discovered that if you can add boron to the soil around tomato plants at just the right time, you can increase their calcium uptake and reduce the amount of rot and wasted plants. "You create a better quality product," he explains, matter-of-factly. Chris plants rows of flowers, sunflowers, zinnias and cosmos among his crops to attract bugs that will eat damaging larvae on his plants. He uses chisels, rollers, discs, plows and compaction meters to till his soil in a way that will work in conjunction with the naturally occurring compaction patterns. Chris puts out containers of water at the end of each row to attract crows, so they don't ruin his drip irrigation systems. He invented coyote-proof gopher traps and uses any spare space in his fields to grow dry beans and tomatillos, which his workers harvest and eat at most meals.

"Nature is programmed to reproduce," Chris tells us. "Even if the soil is missing all the iron, the tomato is still going to reproduce, but believe me, that tomato is gong to be seriously deficient in iron. If you don't maintain and monitor that, then you're putting out substandard food that doesn't have the flavor, the shelf life or the nutritional content it should. As a farmer, that's my job. Your primary source of health is what you eat. Not the pills you take, or the hospital; it's what you eat. When you have a plant that's full of all the right minerals and full of life, it wants to keep living. And then when you eat that, you want to keep living too."

Chris comes from a family of Danish farmers who have been farming in the Santa Ynez Valley for more than a hundred years. He learned a lot from them about crop rotations, operating machinery and the ins and outs of farming, but Chris has taught himself many of his innovative techniques. "I don't understand why all farmers don't do it this way. I do a lot of consulting to try and teach people, but I guess it just takes more time and effort and a lot more thought. I think farmers are sometimes thought of as stupid, or as hicks or something like that. But to work with nature and actually pull it off, that's science." Chris spends a lot of time studying, reading and keeping himself informed of new technologies and techniques to keep the flow of healthy, nutrient-rich plants coming.

"That's the one thing that I have some beef with chefs. I determine the variety, in a special medium, I purchase and start the seeds. I nurture that seedling. In the meantime I prepare the field with minerals, fertilizer. I plant that little seedling out, and I protect it from insects, I eliminate the competition of weeds and I feed it and water it until it's ready to harvest. Then I pick it at peak of harvest, and you guys doll it up with balsamic vinegar and get all the glory. And I don't dig it! It used to be that if you wanted to know how something is grown, you ask the farmer. That's the kind of relationship we're looking for." As Chris speaks, he looks directly at Jason and then over his fields. Jason kicks some dirt, and they both laugh with a little discomfort. "It's true though," Jason says. "One thing I've always said is that you guys make our jobs easier. If you produce a product that's perfect, or as close to perfect as it can be, then we really don't have to do much. Maybe we add sea salt and olive oil. But other than that, we don't have to do much to make it taste good. If it's a tomato, it should taste like a tomato." Chris fixes his gaze back on Jason and says, "And that's how it should be."

Chris's passion for this creation of life is evident as he walks us through the dusty rows of onions and melons, explaining his craft. The amount of work and attention to detail it takes to create a harvest of good food is humbling and infectious. Chris Thompson strikes this balance between quantity and quality through his constant search for the best and most sustainable methods and an endless curiosity. Before we leave, Jason talks with Chris about a seasonal menu, one that is as balanced as Chris's soil and that reflects the diversity of nature that is so important. With bunches of gigantic onions rolling around in the trunk, Jason quietly contemplates recipes all the way back to Santa Barbara.

—Annie Villanueva

Chris Thompson and Jason Paluska with a couple of onions.

From the Ocean

Yellowtail Hamachi Crudo
avocado mousse, pickled Fresno pepper, candied orange peel, kumquat, jicama

Wine Pairing:

Larner Vineyard and Winery Malvasia Bianca, Ballard Canyon
Palmina Larner Vineyard Malvasia Bianca, Santa Ynez Valley
Fiddlehead Cellars Hunnysuckle Sauvignon Blanc, Santa Ynez Valley
Verdad Wines Albariño, Sawyer Lindquist Vineyard

Alternative Pairing:

Captain Fatty's Craft Brewery Cucumber Calypso Sour

Chef's Notes:

My favorite fish to eat raw has always been yellowtail tuna. The richness and delicate texture are unlike anything else. It is always good. Pair this fish with just about anything.

Prep Time:

1 hour active preparation, plus pickling

Special Equipment Needed:

mandoline, ice bath

Servings:

4 as appetizer

Editor's Note:

Buy sashimi-grade fish and keep refrigerated or chilled.

INGREDIENTS

Pickled Fresno Peppers:
½ cup Fresno peppers, sliced (65 g)
½ cup champagne vinegar (115 ml)
1 T salt (9 g)
¼ cup sugar (50 g)
¼ cup water (58 ml)

Tangerine Vinaigrette:
1 cup + 3 T tangerince juice (250 ml)
2 T champagne vinegar (26 ml)
1 tsp salt (3 g)
¼ cup olive oil (50 ml)
1 tsp xanthan gum (2 g)

Candied Orange Peel:
1 cup navel orange peel (55 g),
  approximately 5 oranges
1 cup sugar (220 g)
water

Avocado Mousse:
2-3 ripe avocados (100 g)
2 tsp salt (6 g)
2 T fresh lime juice (26 ml)
1 tsp citric acid (2 g)
4 T olive oil (50 ml)

Yellowtail Hamachi:
4 oz sushi-grade hamachi (115 g)
  (option: sushi-grade tuna)
olive oil
salt

Garnish:
¼ cup red cabbage (32 g), sliced
¼ cup jicama (45 g), medium diced
2 kumquats, sliced
1 tangerine, segmented
cilantro, de-stemmed

DIRECTIONS

Pickled Fresno Peppers:
Place Fresno peppers into a nonreactive bowl. Heat vinegar, sugar, salt and water to a simmer and pour over the peppers. Marinate in the refrigerator for a minimum of 72 hours. Drain before use.

Tangerine Vinaigrette:
Combine tangerine juice, champagne vinegar and salt in a blender. Mix on high speed. Slowly stream in olive oil. Sprinkle in xanthan gum.

Candied Orange Peel:
Using a sharp peeler, remove peel from orange, remove pith and finely julienne the peel. Cover with cold water in a small pot and bring just to a boil, then remove from heat. Strain and repeat. Strain then add the sugar and 2 cups of water. Bring to a boil and strain. Cool in an even layer on a parchment-lined sheet pan.

Avocado Mousse:
Blend avocado, salt, lime juice and citric acid in a food processor. Slowly stream in olive oil and emulsify thoroughly. Pass through a chinois or fine-meshed sieve.

Yellowtail Hamachi:
Slice hamachi across the grain. In a bowl inside an ice bath, coat the slices with an even layer of olive oil and salt.

Plating:
Sauce the plate with Avocado Mousse. Season red cabbage and jicama with Tangerine Vinaigrette and salt. Place the hamachi slices in and around the cabbage. Garnish with sliced kumquat, tangerine segments, Pickled Fresno Peppers, cilantro leaves and Candied Orange Peel.

Medley of peppers.

SANTA BARBARA MARICULTURE COMPANY

Above: Bernard Friedman and Chef Jason Paluska harvesting mussels. Opposite: Bernard harvesting mussels.

WHEN ARE HOPE RANCH MUSSELS happy, healthy and ready to harvest? When they're "fat and edible," says Bernard Friedman, mussel farmer and owner of Santa Barbara Mariculture Company.

At a year old, his *Mytilus galloprovincialis*, also known as Mediterranean or chef's mussels, are at the peak of their plump, briny sweetness. Bernard hauls them out of his 25-acre open-ocean farm and onto his boat for processing and same-day delivery for select local markets and restaurants.

Two to six days a week, he's out to sea in a T-shirt, suspenders and fisherman's pants, the sun glinting off *Perseverance*, his 35-foot boat. His 7 a.m.-to-dusk gig seems idyllic.

Bernard was always one for boating and water sports. "But I was never into the food scene—I didn't know I would become a mussel farmer." In college he studied biology and worked as a commercial diver, harvesting mussels growing on oil rigs in the Santa Barbara Channel. The work fueled his interest in fisheries management and led him to his master's thesis: how to cultivate oysters on the rigs.

"Oysters grow themselves," he says. "But how to grow 100,000 pounds—that's where experience comes in. You have to learn how to grow 100 pounds first. I got to 100,000 after 12 years." After that, Bernard went out on his own, shifting his focus to mussels as a less expensive crop with more potential. His eco-friendly, sustainable methods do not deplete any of our valuable ocean resources.

On harvest days, he texts his customers at 7 a.m. for orders. By 8 a.m., they've texted back for 300 to 1,700 pounds each of his shiny blue-black filter-feeders, which grow on "fuzzy" ropes attached to 700-foot lines in nutrient-rich waters off Hope Ranch. He threads the ropes into his shipboard conveyor, which strips the mussels into a brushing machine that scrubs them for bagging, after which they go into drums of seawater. "Then we jam back to the dock to deliver them as fast as we can," he explains, for record keeping and client pickup at an FDA-approved distributor.

His boat fills at 3,500 pounds, and he averages about 20,000 pounds a month but has plans to scale up to 360,000 pounds when approved by the state. His thinking has always been, "Why can't we do this? I'm determined. That's how I live my life. That's how I run my business."

—Trish Reynales

Hope Ranch Mussels
Lark bouillabaisse, Jimmy Nardello peppers, charred scallion, navel orange, tarragon, sourdough levain

Wine Pairing:

Dragonette Sauvignon Blanc, Happy Canyon
Presqu'ile Sauvignon Blanc, Santa Barbara County
Lucas & Lewellen Estate Vineyards Rosé of Pinot Noir, Santa Barbara County
Vogelzang Vineyard Birdsong Sauvignon Blanc, Santa Ynez Valley

Alternative Pairing:

Telegraph Brewing Company Orange Pale Ale
Ballast Point Brewing Company Pineapple Sculpin

Chef's Notes:

We left the harbor before daylight, stumbling around in the dark. Bernard Friedman showed me how he farms the best mussels in the world right here in Santa Barbara. Creamy, plump, salty, sweet, delicate and yet explosive with flavor. You have to come to Santa Barbara to get them.

Prep Time:

1½ hours

Special Equipment Needed:

cheesecloth, cartouche

Servings:

4

Editor's Note:

Buy only mussels that are firmly closed and do not submerge them in water. Right before using, scrub them with a stiff brush and cut off the beards.

INGREDIENTS

Lark Bouillabaisse:
⅓ cup each onion, carrot, fennel bulb
  (60 g each), large dice
⅔ cup red bell pepper (100 g), large dice
1 tsp garlic (3 g), finely chopped
1 serrano chile, de-seeded
½ cup extra virgin olive oil (105 ml)
salt to taste
sachet:
  1 T orange peel (6 g)
  1 sprig fresh thyme
  1 sprig of fresh parsley
  2 sprigs fresh tarragon
  ½ tsp saffron
3½ cups water (800 ml)
½ cup sherry vinegar (115 ml)
orange juice, as needed

Jimmy Nardello and Shishito Peppers:
10 Jimmy Nardello peppers, de-
  stemmed
10 shishito peppers, de-stemmed
olive oil
salt to taste

Charred Scallions:
2 scallions
olive oil
salt to taste

Mussels:
½ cup white wine (115 ml)
2 lbs Hope Ranch mussels (906 g),
  clean and remove beards
1 T butter (14 g)
salt to taste

Garnish:
1 navel orange, segmented
¼ bunch tarragon, de-stemmed
¼ bunch parsley, de-stemmed
1 fennel bulb, shaved thinly
fennel fronds
wild fennel blossoms
slices of sourdough levain bread,
  grilled

DIRECTIONS

Lark Bouillabaisse:
Preheat oven to 400°F. Coat onion, carrot, fennel, bell pepper, garlic and chile evenly with extra virgin olive oil and salt. Arrange in one layer on a parchment-lined sheet tray and roast 30-40 minutes or until knife tender. Tie up the orange peel, thyme, parsley and tarragon in cheesecloth to make a sachet. Put sachet, roasted vegetables, water and vinegar into a large pot. Add saffron. Bring to a boil then simmer until reduced by half. Remove sachet. Blend vegetables and cooking water into a puree, then strain through a chinois or fine-meshed sieve. Season to taste with salt. Adjust consistency with fresh-squeezed orange juice. The end result should be between a broth and a soup. Keep warm.

Jimmy Nardello and Shishito Peppers:
Lightly coat peppers in a bowl with olive oil and salt. Grill until just tender.

Charred Scallions:
Coat scallions with olive oil then grill on both sides until nicely marked and tender. Chop and season with salt to taste.

Mussels:
Heat the wine and mussels in a pot over high heat and cover with a lid. Steam just until mussels open, then add Lark Bouillabaisse. When adding salt to taste, be aware the mussels have added salinity. Keep mussels in pot on low heat. Finish with butter. Turn off heat. Keep covered so mussels stay moist.

Plating:
Add Charred Scallions and half of the shaved fennel into the pot of warm mussels. Ladle Mussels and Lark Bouillabaisse into serving bowls. Evenly distribute Jimmy Nardello and Shishito Peppers and navel orange segments. Garnish with tarragon, parsley, shaved fennel, fennel fronds and fennel blossoms. Finish with slices of grilled bread.

California Oysters on the Half Shell
Early Girl tomato and strawberry granita, red shiso

Wine Pairing:

Alma Rosa El Jabalí Vineyard Brut Rosé, Sta. Rita Hills
Paul Lato Sauvignon Blanc, Le Jardin Secret Grimm's Bluff Vineyard
Fenetre Á Côte Pinot Gris, Sta. Rita Hills

Alternative Pairing:

Almanac Beer Company Dogpatch Strawberry Wild Ale

Chef's Notes:

When somebody asks me my favorite meal it has to be in 2008 at Ubuntu in
Napa. It is the restaurant that thrust chef Jeremy Fox into the limelight. I was
working in San Francisco and hadn't heard about it until my friend Tracy read
in the *New York Times* it was the next must-have meal. The most memorable dish
was a pizza that was made with a strawberry sofrito, in place of a classic tomato
marinara. I never realized how similar the flavors actually were. This idea has
always followed me since that meal. However, I hadn't combined these two
disassociated ingredients until now. The surprising and complementary pairing
works wonderfully. Bright, clean, tart, sweet and savory. I love it.

Prep Time:

15 minutes active preparation plus chill time

Special Equipment Needed:

juicer or chinois or fine-meshed sieve, crushed ice, oyster knife

Servings:

6 oysters

Editor's Note:

Buy only oysters that are firmly closed and keep them in the refrigerator or iced.

INGREDIENTS

Early Girl Tomato and Strawberry Granita:
1 lb ripe Early Girl tomatoes (453 g),
  de-stemmed
$\frac{1}{2}$ lb ripe strawberries (226 g),
  de-stemmed
approx. $\frac{1}{4}$ cup water (58 ml)
$1\frac{1}{2}$ T sugar (20 g)
approx. 1 tsp citric acid (4 g)
approx. 1 tsp salt (3 g)

Oysters on the Half Shell:
6 live oysters
crushed ice

Garnish:
red shiso leaves
finger limes

DIRECTIONS

Early Girl Tomato and Strawberry Granita:
Blend strawberries with tomatoes in batches, using a Vitamix or high-powered blender. Use just enough water to blend smoothly. Pass the juice through a chinois. Using a whisk, incorporate salt, sugar and citric acid. Taste for balance of flavors. Depending on the ripeness of your tomatoes and strawberries, you may need to adjust the level of sugar as well as citric acid. Pass the ingredients again through a chinois into a flat pan with sides roughly 3-5 inches deep. Place in freezer and scrape every 4 hours until a fluffy texture is achieved. No snowballs. (Note: reserve in the freezer until serving—the granita melts quickly.)

Oysters on the Half Shell:
Line a deep serving platter with crushed ice. Immediately before serving, remove the top shell of the oysters. Place the oysters on top of crushed ice or rock salt.

Plating:
Spoon a tablespoon of Early Girl Tomato and Strawberry Granita on each oyster, then garnish with red shiso and finger limes. Serve immediately.

Executive Chef Jason Paluska hard at work harvesting on Bernard's boat. Opposite: Bernard Friedman with freshly harvested local Hope Ranch oysters.

Fishing boats in Santa Barbara Harbor.

Citrus-Cured King Salmon
black pepper crème fraîche, yuzu vinaigrette, pickled shallot, dill, brioche, kumquats

Wine Pairing:

The Hilt Chardonnay Vanguard, Santa Barbara County
Domaine de la Côte Siren's Call Pinot Noir, Sta. Rita Hills
Zotovich Estate Rosé of Pinot Noir, Sta. Rita Hills
The Paring Rosé of Pinot Noir, Sta. Rita Hills

Alternative Pairing:

Libertine Brewing Company Edna Table Wild Saison

Chef's Notes:

Wild California King Salmon is one of the most important and delicious catches on the West Coast. It has a short season with high demand. When it is available, I always want to put it on the menu. This cure incorporates different varieties of citrus to lift the salmon to new heights.

Prep Time:

15 minutes active preparation plus 2 days for crème fraîche, 12-24 hours depending on the thickness of King Salmon fillet

Servings:

6-8

Editor's Note:

Use authentic buttermilk—a byproduct of churning butter—or cultured buttermilk with active bacterial culture for best results.

INGREDIENTS

Pickled Shallot:
1¼ cup shallot (150 g), peeled, sliced
  thinly
½ cup champagne vinegar (100 ml)
¼ cup sugar (50 g)
1 T salt (9 g)
½ cup water (115 ml)

Citrus-Cured King Salmon:
2 T coriander seed (12 g)
1 tsp each peppercorn and fennel seed
  (3 g each)
1 bunch fresh dill, chopped
½ bunch each fresh chives and
  tarragon, finely chopped
zest and juice of 1 each orange,
  grapefruit, lemon, lime
¾ cup firmly packed brown sugar (150 g)
1⅓ cup salt (175 g)
1 lb salmon fillet (453 g), de-skinned,
  deboned, cleaned of all bloodlines

Black Pepper Crème Fraîche:
1⅔ cup heavy cream (400 ml)
⅔ cup buttermilk (160 ml)

1½ tsp freshly ground black pepper (5 g)
1 tsp salt (3 g)

Yuzu Vinaigrette:
⅓ cup yuzu juice (70 ml)
2 T lime juice (26 ml)
2 tsp lemon juice (10 ml)
1 tsp each lime, lemon, orange zest
  (2 g each), finely chopped
1 tsp salt (3 g)
½ tsp sugar (2 g)
½ cup olive oil (100 ml)

Frisée Salad:
2 cups frisée (50 g)
Yuzu Vinaigrette
1 tsp salt (3 g)
3 T chive (9 g), finely chopped

Garnish:
3 T fresh dill (6 g), de-stemmed
2 T fresh tarragon (6 g), de-stemmed
4 kumquats, sliced
2 thick slices brioche, toasted
  option: bagel or English muffin

DIRECTIONS

Pickled Shallot:
Put shallots into a nonreactive bowl. Heat vinegar, sugar, salt and water to a simmer. Pour over the shallots. Marinate in the refrigerator for a minimum of 72 hours. Drain before use.

Citrus-Cured King Salmon:
Preheat oven to 325°F. Toast the coriander seed, peppercorn and fennel seed on a parchment lined sheet pan for 8-10 minutes or until aromatic. Cool completely. Grind in blender until smooth. In a nonreactive bowl, mix the ground spices thoroughly with dill, chives, tarragon, the zest and juice of an orange, grapefruit, lemon and lime, brown sugar and salt. Coat salmon evenly with spice mixture. Cover top of bowl with plastic wrap, then set in the refrigerator for 12-24 hours.

Cure is complete when the moisture is 50% removed and the fish has a firm "meaty" texture but not so dry that it has the consistency of beef jerky. Rinse and pat dry. If not using immediately, wrap in parchment, wrap in plastic and store in refrigerator until ready to serve. Slice thinly right before plating.

Black Pepper Crème Fraîche:
Whisk heavy cream and buttermilk together in a glass jar and leave at room temperature for 48 hours until firmed up.

Once ready whisk until stiff peaks form. Fold in black pepper and salt.

Yuzu Vinaigrette:
Place the yuzu, lime and lemon juices, lime, lemon and orange zest, salt and sugar in a bowl. Whisk until salt and sugar are dissolved, then whisk in olive oil.

Frisée Salad:
Toss the frisée in enough Yuzu Vinaigrette to coat evenly, season with salt, then sprinkle with chives.

Plating:
Arrange sliced salmon in ribbons across the serving plate. Make a quenelle of the Black Pepper Crème Fraîche and place to the side. Add Frisée Salad, then garnish with Pickled Shallot, dill, tarragon and kumquats. Serve with toasted brioche.

Hokkaido Scallop Crudo
melons, cucumber granita, black sesame cracker, borage, finger lime

Wine Pairing:

Cebada Vineyard Sparkling Blanc de Noirs
Solminer Dry Riesling, Santa Barbara County
Flying Goat Pinot Gris, Sierra Madre Vineyard, Santa Maria Valley
Babcock Pinot Gris Naughty Little Hillsides, Estate Grown, Sta. Rita Hills

Alternative Pairing:

Draughtsmen Ale Works Japanese Rice Lager

Chef's Notes:

Raw scallops will surprise you as they melt in your mouth. By freezing cucumber juice to make a granita you have the epitome of clean and fresh, a perfect complement to the creaminess of the scallop. Borage blossoms are both beautiful and surprisingly taste like cucumber and raw oyster. The bitterness of the black sesame cracker adds the correct balance.

Prep Time:

1 hour active preparation, plus 6 hours for chilling

Special Equipment Needed:

2 Silpats or 1 Silpat plus a drying rack, food scale, glass loaf pan, ice bath

Servings:

4 as shared plate

Editor's Note:

Buy high-quality scallops, take them home packed in ice and keep chilled at all times to retain their fine flavor and avoid any "fishy" odor. Squid ink can be purchased on Amazon and at some Asian and fish markets.

INGREDIENTS

Black Sesame Cracker:
1 cup black sesame seed (120 g)
6 egg whites (126 g)
2 T lemon juice (26 ml)
3 T water (45 ml)
1 tsp squid ink (7 ml)
½ cup powdered sugar (50 g)
½ tsp salt
white sesame seeds
nonstick cooking spray

Persian Cucumber Granita:
7 Persian cucumbers, peeled,
  de-seeded, chopped
⅓ cup water (80 ml)
4 T sugar (52 g)
3 T lime juice (39 ml)
pinch salt

Scallops:
4 diver scallops

Melon:
½ cup each watermelon, Ambrosia melon,
  honeydew (80 g each), cut into chunks
pinch chile flake
olive oil
lime juice and salt to taste

Garnish:
borage flowers
1 finger lime
Persian cucumber slices

DIRECTIONS

Black Sesame Cracker:
Preheat the oven to 325°F. Toast the black sesame seeds on a baking sheet for 10 minutes or until they just start to smell toasted, then remove from oven. Turn down the oven to 225°F. Put the warm sesame seeds, egg whites, lemon juice, water and squid ink in a blender and blend on medium speed. Add the powdered sugar and continue to blend on medium-high speed until a semi-smooth paste starts to form. The puree will not be completely smooth but needs to be smooth enough to spread thin. If the mixture becomes too thick for the blender, transfer to a bowl and mix thoroughly. Stir in salt.

Spray a Silpat lightly with cooking spray and place inside a baking sheet. Spread the paste thinly and evenly over the Silpat so it bakes consistently. (Tip: pour the paste into the center and using a rubber spatula held as flat to the surface as possible, spread the paste out from the center to the edges using a gentle circular motion.) For final flattening, pick up the baking sheet and holding it level, shake it gently until the paste smooths out. Sprinkle white sesame seeds on top and bake for 1-1½ hours or until crisp but not overcooked. Since the cracker is black, it is difficult to assess when it is crispy but not burned, so break off a corner to cool and taste. When crisp, remove from oven and immediately peel off the Silpat onto another Silpat or a rack sprayed with cooking spray. When cooled, break into shards and keep in an airtight container until served.

Persian Cucumber Granita:
Blend the cucumbers and water in a blender until smooth. Strain through a chinois or fine-meshed sieve and press down with a ladle to extract all the liquid. Weigh out 600 grams of the cucumber liquid. Add the sugar, lime juice and salt to the cucumber liquid and whisk until the sugar has dissolved, then pour into a glass loaf pan. Place in the freezer and scrape a fork through the granita down with a fork every 2 hours—this creates the light flaky texture. Break up any clumps with the end of the fork. Granita is ready in 6 hours.

Scallops:
Slice the scallops thinly crosswise, across the "grain" of the muscle. Reserve in a bowl inside a bowl of ice to keep chilled until serving.

Melon:
Toss melon with chile flake, olive oil, lemon juice and salt to taste.

Plating:
Season scallops evenly with olive oil and salt. Place the melon and cucumber across the plate then arrange the scallops across the melon. Add the borage, mint and Black Sesame Cracker. Squeeze the pulp out of the finger lime to garnish. Right before serving, add a scoop of Persian Cucumber Granita and serve immediately—the granita will melt quickly.

Caviar finger limes.

Cast Iron Roasted Arctic Char
caramelized cauliflower, golden raisins, pine nuts, preserved lime, salmon roe, mint pistou

Wine Pairing:

Aligoté Le Bon Climat, Clendenen Family, Santa Maria Valley
Habit Chenin Blanc, Santa Ynez Valley
Lutum Sanford & Benedict Chardonnay, Sta. Rita Hills
Melville Estate Pinot Noir Block M, Sta. Rita Hills

Alternative Pairing:

Calyx Gin & Tonic

Chef's Notes:

One of the greatest streets in San Francisco is Clement Street in the Richmond District. It is filled with the best ethnic restaurants in the city. Burma Superstar is worth the wait in line. Burmese cuisine is like nothing I had ever eaten before. It excited and inspired me. This dish is my ode to that fine institution.

Prep Time:

1 hour active preparation, plus 1 month for preserving lime

Special Equipment Needed:

cheesecloth, cartouche, chinois (option: fine-meshed sieve), cast iron skillet, ice bath

Servings:

4

Editor's Note:

If Arctic char is unavailable, substitute salmon.

INGREDIENTS

Preserved Lime Puree:
6 limes, quartered, de-seeded
6 T sea salt (90 g)
4 T sugar (52 g)

Pickled Curry Cauliflower:
½ head cauliflower (375 g), cut into florets
salt
sachet:
    5 star anise pods
    1 T whole cloves (4 g)
    3 bay leaves
    1 T peppercorns (8 g)
½ cup each white vinegar and
  champagne vinegar (105 ml each)
9 T sugar (117 g)
1 cup water (230 ml)
1 T curry powder (8 g)
½ tsp ground turmeric (4 g)

Cauliflower Puree:
1 head cauliflower (750 g)
approx. 2 cups heavy cream (480 ml)
salt to taste

Caramelized Cauliflower:
½ head cauliflower (375 g), cut in florets
canola oil
1 T butter (14 g)
2 sprigs fresh thyme, de-stemmed
salt to taste

Mint Pistou:
1 bunch fresh mint, de-stemmed
pinch chile flake
olive oil
salt to taste

Pine Nuts:
4 tsp pine nuts (14 g)

Clement Street Spice:
2 tsp ground cumin (6 g)
1 tsp each ground coriander, fennel,
  fenugreek, clove (3 g each)
2 bay leaves, 1 ground, 1 whole
1 tsp ground black pepper (3 g)

DIRECTIONS

Preserved Lime Puree:
Coat lime quarters evenly with the salt and sugar, then pack tightly in nonreactive bowl or canning jar. Leave at room temperature for 4 weeks, stirring every 24 hours. A white film may form; simply rinse before use. Remove any seeds. Measure limes with a measuring cup. Place in blender along with 1½ times the volume of water and blend on high speed until completely incorporated. Pass through a chinois or fine-meshed sieve.

Pickled Curry Cauliflower:
Steam cauliflower for 2 minutes. Season to taste with salt while still hot. Sachet: Preheat the oven to 325°F. Toast star anise and cloves on a sheet pan 8-10 minutes or until aromatic. Tie up in cheesecloth with bay leaves and peppercorns. Bring white vinegar, champagne vinegar, sachet, sugar, water, curry powder and turmeric to a boil and pour over cauliflower. Cover with a cartouche. When cool, let pickle in refrigerator for a minimum of 72 hours. Drain right before serving.

Cauliflower Puree:
Place cauliflower in a pot just larger than it is and cover with heavy cream to a level 80% up the side of the cauliflower. Simmer until knife tender, stirring occasionally. Let cool until safe to handle. Puree in a blender with enough of the cooking cream to create a pudding consistency. Cool, then pass through a chinois or fine-meshed sieve and season with salt to taste.

Caramelized Cauliflower:
Pat cauliflower dry. Caramelize cauliflower in hot cast iron skillet evenly coated with canola oil. Fold in butter and thyme once seared. Spread the cauliflower out flat on a towel-lined plate to cool. Season with salt to taste.

Mint Pistou:
Bring a large pot of water to a boil. Lightly season with salt. Blanch the mint until tender. When tender, leaves will disintegrate when rubbed between fingers. Shock in ice bath, then spin dry. Keep cold at all times, adding ice to the blender if needed. Puree in blender with chile flake and enough olive oil to make a paste. Transfer to a bowl over ice and season to taste with salt.

Pine Nuts:
Preheat oven to 300°F. Toast pine nuts for 10-12 minutes. Cool.

Clement Street Spice:
Whisk spices in a mixing bowl.

INGREDIENTS

Golden Raisins:
¾ cup golden raisins (124 g)
2 T each white verjus and white wine
  (26 ml each)
½ cup water (115 ml)

Roasted Arctic Char:
2 lb char fillets (1 kg)
canola oil
3 T butter (42 g)
sprig of fresh thyme, de-stemmed

Garnish:
olive oil
¼ cup Castelvetrano olives (30 g),
  sliced very thinly
1 tsp Preserved Lime Puree (above)
1 tsp fresh lime juice (13 ml)
1 oz salmon roe (28 g)
½ cup wild arugula (15 g)

DIRECTIONS

Golden Raisins:
Put the raisins, verjus, wine, water and Clement Street Spice in a small pot and bring to a boil. Pull off the heat and cover until raisins are rehydrated and plump. Discard bay leaf. Season to taste with salt.

Roasted Arctic Char:
Pat the fillets dry with paper towels. Sear skin-side down in a hot cast iron pan coated with canola oil, then turn down the heat and add butter and thyme. As butter melts, baste it over the top of the fish. Cook just until fish just slightly firms up.

Plating:
In a hot pan evenly coated with olive oil, heat Caramelized Cauliflower, olives and Golden Raisins until heated through. Finish with Preserved Lime Puree and fresh lime juice. Sauce Cauliflower Puree on plate. Place warmed vegetables across it. Place the Roasted Arctic Char on top. Garnish with Mint Pistou, salmon roe, Pickled Curry Cauliflower, pine nuts and arugula.

Executive Sous Chef Taylor Melonuk filleting fish.

Grilled Red Snapper

coconut and kaffir lime broth, mussels, clams, Granny Smith apple, crispy parsnip, Thai chile, cilantro

Wine Pairing:

Diatom Hamon Chardonnay, Sta. Rita Hills
Scar of the Sea Bien Nacido Vineyard Chardonnay, Santa Maria Valley
MaidenStoen Lafond Vineyard Riesling, Sta. Rita Hills

Alternative Pairing:

Figueroa Mountain Brewing Company Lizard's Mouth Imperial IPA
21st Amendment Brewery Down to Earth Session IPA

Chef's Notes:

I never had Thai food growing up in Tomball, Texas. The second I tried it I was addicted. How could you not be? It has the best combination of everything from flavors to texture to richness. My favorite ingredient in this dish after the fish is the green apple. It helps keep the dish balanced and fresh. Well, that's not entirely true. I also really like the fresh kaffir lime leaf chopped finely and sprinkled in and around. And if you are lucky enough to have one, zest a fresh kaffir lime onto the snapper.

Prep Time:

2 hours

Special Equipment Needed:

mandoline, deep fryer (option: cast iron skillet with thermometer), thermometer

Servings:

4

INGREDIENTS

Coconut and Kaffir Lime Broth:
canola oil
½ cup carrots (55 g), sliced
⅓ cup each shallots and green apple
  (50 g each), sliced
⅔ cup red onion (100 g), sliced
1½ T serrano chile (12 g), de-seeded, sliced
5 T galangal (50 g), peeled, grated
  (option: ginger)
2 T garlic (16 g), minced
1 T curry powder (8 g)
1 cup white wine (230 ml)
4¼ cups chicken stock (1 L)
1 coconut, milk only (approximately
  ½ cup or 110 ml)
sachet:
  2 bay leaves
  ½ lemongrass stalk
  kaffir lime leaf
  1 tsp each lemon, orange, lime
  peel (2 g each)
  4 tsp salt (11 g)
1 lb mussels (453 g)
1 lb clams (453 g)
½ cup white wine (105 ml)
1 Thai chile, sliced very thinly
1 T butter (14 g)

Crispy Parsnip:
canola oil
1 parsnip
salt

Steamed Parsnip and Carrot:
1 parsnip, cut into obliques
1 carrot, cut into obliques
olive oil and salt to taste

Frisée Salad:
1 Granny Smith apple, skin on, julienned
4 cups frisée (100 g)
1 red bell pepper, julienned
¼ bunch cilantro, de-stemmed
olive oil
lime juice and salt to taste

Grilled Red Snapper:
2-3 lb whole red snapper (1–1.5 kg),
  cleaned and filleted
olive oil
salt to taste

Garnish:
1 kaffir lime, zested
handful cilantro leaves, de-stemmed

DIRECTIONS

Coconut and Kaffir Lime Broth:
In a pan evenly coated with a thin layer of canola oil, sweat carrots, shallots, green apple, red onion, serrano chile, galangal and garlic over low heat until completely tender. Do not let vegetables brown. Stir in curry powder and cook for two minutes. Deglaze with wine and cook to sec—almost dry. Add chicken stock and coconut milk and reduce by ⅓ over medium heat. Remove from heat, add the sachet of bay leaf, lemongrass, kaffir lime, citrus peels and salt, then let steep for 1 hour. Discard sachet and puree mixture in blender. Strain through a fine-meshed sieve or chinois, then keep broth warm.

5 minutes before serving, add the mussels and clams to a hot pan. Immediately add white wine, then cover with lid to steam them open. Stir in broth, Thai chile and butter.

Crispy Parsnip:
Preheat canola oil in deep fryer to 300°F. (Option: use a cast iron skillet with thermometer.) Shave the parsnip on a mandoline. Fry parsnip until golden brown, then drain on paper towels and season with salt. The parsnip will crisp up out of the fryer.

Steamed Parsnip and Carrot:
Steam parsnip and carrot until knife tender. In a bowl, coat evenly with olive oil and salt to taste.

Frisée Salad:
Toss apple, frisée, red bell pepper and cilantro in olive oil, then season to taste with lime juice and salt. Tip: squeeze a bit of lime juice on the apple slices as you julienne them to prevent browning.

Grilled Red Snapper:
Pat snapper fillets dry with paper towels. Coat lightly with olive oil, season with salt, then place on hot grill skin-side down for 2 minutes, until evenly marked. Turn and cook on the other side for 2 minutes—cooking time will depend on thickness of fillets. (Tip: use the tip of a sharp knife to see the interior of the fish. When it has just turned opaque, remove from heat.)

Plating:
Plate Coconut and Kaffir Lime Broth with clams and mussels on the bottom of a large serving bowl, then add Steamed Parsnip and Carrot. Place Grilled Red Snapper on top with Frisée Salad. Zest kaffir lime over dish in an even layer and top with Crispy Parsnip and cilantro leaves.

Whole Grilled Branzino
spiced chickpeas, artichokes, grilled fennel, almond romesco, fritto misto

Wine Pairing:

Sandhi Bentrock Chardonnay, Sta. Rita Hills
Grassini Sauvignon Blanc Block 14, Happy Canyon
Storm Sauvignon Blanc, Presqu'ile Vineyard, Santa Maria Valley

Alternative Pairing:

Naughty Oak Brewing Company Chela Roja

Chef's Notes:

We decided to elevate "the whole fish" experience by cleaning it completely
and serving two beautiful fillets with the tail still attached. No bones, no head,
no mess. The ingredients here are clearly Mediterranean in inspiration, where
branzino (sea bass) is a celebrated fish. I first ate a deep-fried lemon when I was
23. It was powerful, memorable and honest. Just a slice of lemon dredged and
fried. I remember thinking, you can eat the whole thing? This dish was written
with that memory in mind. I love it because it is so "hearty" and yet still light
and refreshing.

Prep Time:

1½ hours active preparation, plus overnight soaking

Special Equipment Needed:

chinois (option: fine-meshed sieve), ice bath, deep fryer (option: cast iron skillet
with thermometer)

Servings:

4

INGREDIENTS

Spiced Chickpeas:
1 cup dry chickpeas (200 g)
1 T each ground coriander, cumin,
  fennel seed (8 g each)
mirepoix (per recipe pg. 272)
salt to taste

Almond Romesco:
1 cup almonds (140 g), sliced
canola oil
¾ cup shallot (90 g), sliced
1 T garlic (8 g), sliced
1½ cups piquillo peppers (230 g)
2 T smoked paprika (16 g)
½ tsp ground cumin
½ cup each white wine and sherry
  vinegar (105 ml each)
½ cup olive oil (100 ml)
salt to taste

Artichokes:
juice of ½ lemon
2 globe artichokes
olive oil
salt
4 sprigs fresh thyme
2 T garlic (16 g), sliced

Grilled Fennel and Spring Onion:
1 fennel bulb, fronds de-stemmed
4 spring onions
olive oil
salt to taste

Fritto Misto:
canola oil
1 Meyer lemon
1 fennel bulb
cornstarch
salt to taste

Roasted Almonds:
2 T sliced almonds (16 g)
olive oil
salt to taste

Grilled Branzino:
1 whole branzino
olive oil

Spiced Chickpeas:
1 T butter (14 g)
½ cup spinach (37 g)

Garnish:
fennel fronds

DIRECTIONS

Spiced Chickpeas:
Soak chickpeas overnight. Preheat oven to 325°F. Toast coriander, cumin and fennel seed on a sheet pan 8-10 minutes or until aromatic. Cool. Blend to a fine powder. Add to pot along with mirepoix and enough water to cover. Bring to a boil, then simmer. Cover until chickpeas are tender. Season with salt. Cool. Remove mirepoix. Drain chickpeas and reserve liquid.

Almond Romesco:
Boil almonds in large pot of water until tender, then drain. Evenly coat a pan with canola oil. Over low heat, sweat shallot and garlic until translucent. Add piquillo peppers and cook until tender. Stir in paprika and cumin and cook until fragrant. Deglaze with wine and vinegar. Add almonds and cook until almost dry. Mix in blender with enough water to spin freely. Add olive oil slowly to emulsify. Blend until completely smooth. Season with salt. Pass through chinois and cool over ice.

Artichokes:
Quarter artichokes, trim ends and remove thistle and place in bowl of lemon water. Drain, pat dry. Coat evenly with olive oil. Season with salt. Place in a pot of cold water and bring to boil. Simmer, add thyme and garlic, cover and cook until knife tender. Keep warm.

Grilled Fennel and Spring Onion:
Cut fennel in half lengthwise and remove fibrous core. Simmer in lightly seasoned water until knife tender, then drain and pat dry with paper towels. Grill until evenly marked, then toss in oil and salt. Cool, then dice. Toss spring onion in olive oil and salt. Char on grill until knife tender. Set aside.

Fritto Misto:
Heat canola oil in deep fryer to 325°F. Thinly slice lemon horizontally. Remove all seeds. Thinly shave fennel, reserving fronds. Toss lemon and fennel bulb in cornstarch. Add to deep fryer in one batch—the shaved fennel will form a "nest". Fry until crispy and season with salt.

Roasted Almonds:
Preheat oven to 300°F. Coat almonds with coat of olive oil and season with salt. Spread across a parchment-lined baking sheet, then toast for 10-12 minutes or until golden. Cool.

Grilled Branzino:
Fillet branzino so there are no pin bones and tail is still attached to both fillets. Brush with oil and grill skin-side down for 1½ minutes, then turn 90° and grill to create crosshatch marking. Flip and cook 3-4 minutes or until the fish begins to firm up. The flesh should be rosy to bright white when cooked. Brush with olive oil before plating.

Spiced Chickpeas:
In a sauté pan, add chickpeas along with just enough chickpea cooking liquid to heat through. Add butter to glaze. Fold in spinach and Grilled Fennel. Season with salt and lemon juice.

Plating:
Sauce the serving platter with Almond Romesco. Spoon Spiced Chickpeas and lay Grilled Branzino on top. Arrange the Fritto Misto and the artichokes around the fish. Garnish with Grilled Spring Onion, fennel fronds and Roasted Almonds.

Dungeness Crab Gnocchi
chorizo crumb, Castelvetrano olives, navel orange, lobster roe, cilantro

Wine Pairing:
Solminer Grüner Veltliner, Santa Ynez Valley
Flying Goat Brut Cuvée, Santa Barbara County
Kunin Wines Stolpman Viognier, Ballard Canyon

Chef's Notes:
The Parisian technique for making gnocchi is fast and efficient. The texture is decadent because is it slightly poached and simmered in butter. The chorizo crumb gives crunch and meatiness without overpowering the crab. Lobster roe is worth finding because it makes the dish taste as if you've added a spoonful of the ocean.

Prep Time:
2 hours active preparation

Special Equipment Needed:
large piping bag with a 1" tip (#3), cooking twine, tamis (option: fine-meshed sieve), ice bath

Servings:
4-6

Editor's Note:
Call your local seafood purveyor for lobster roe.

INGREDIENTS

Parisian Gnocchi:
1 cup milk (245 ml)
½ cup butter (112 g)
1 T Dijon mustard (15 g)
2 cups sifted all-purpose flour (250 g)
3 eggs (135 g)
1 tsp salt (3 g)
1 T fresh parsley (5 g each), de-stemmed,
  finely chopped
1 T tarragon (2 g each), de-stemmed,
  finely chopped
4 tsp lemon zest (8 g), finely chopped

Chorizo Crumb:
1 lb brioche (453 g)
½ lb chorizo (226 g), finely diced
salt to taste

Beurre Blanc:
1 cup white wine (230 ml)
½ tsp salt
1 shallot, sliced
pinch freshly ground black pepper
1 sprig fresh thyme, de-stemmed,
  chopped fine
¾ cup heavy cream (180 ml)
2 cups + 3 T butter (270 g)

Gnocchi and Dungeness Crab:
1 tsp lobster roe (5 g)
1½ cups chicken stock (345 ml)
4 cups gnocchi (above)
1 lb crab meat (453 g)
salt to taste

Garnish:
several Castelvetrano olives, pitted,
  sliced
½ navel orange, segments
cilantro

DIRECTIONS

Parisian Gnocchi:
In a large pot, combine milk, butter and mustard over low heat. When butter melts, stir in the flour all at once and whisk briskly until a thick batter forms. Scrape into the bowl of a stand mixer and let cool to lukewarm. With the paddle attachment, mix in eggs, one by one, on low speed. Mix thoroughly between each egg. When the batter is thick and bound, add salt, parsley, tarragon and lemon zest. (Note: the batter should be stiff but workable. If it seems too soft, add a small amount of flour. If the batter is not stiff enough, the gnocchi will fall apart.) Place into a large piping bag with a 1" tip (#3).

Bring a large pot of lightly salted water to a simmer. Tightly tie a string from one handle of the pot to the other (as tight as a guitar string). Pipe gnocchi into simmering water, cutting off each gnocchi on the string. Cook in batches for approximately 3-5 minutes or until cooked through but tender. Don't crowd the pot, as gnocchi will rise to the surface. Drain on a towel-lined sheet tray.

Chorizo Crumb:
Preheat oven to 250°F. Cut the bread into 1" cubes, then spread evenly on baking sheet. Toast for approximately 30 minutes or until completely dry. Cool. Blend in a food processor until a powder.

In a sauté pan over medium low heat, cook the chorizo until crispy. Remove from fat and cool. Blend in a food processor. Set aside. Add bread crumbs to chorizo fat and cook over low heat, stirring until crumbs absorb the fat and are the consistency of wet sand. Spread in an even layer on a parchment-lined sheet tray to toast in the oven at 300°F until golden brown. Fold in chopped chorizo. Salt to taste.

Beurre Blanc:
In a saucepot, reduce the white wine, salt, shallot, pepper and thyme until almost dry. Add the cream and reduce to sauce consistency. Emulsify butter in batches by constantly whisking over low heat. Pass through chinois. Keep warm.

Gnocchi and Dungeness Crab:
Pass the lobster roe through a tamis or fine-meshed sieve into a bowl inside an ice bath. In a large sauté pan, heat the gnocchi in chicken stock over gentle heat. Fold in crab meat and lobster roe. Add enough Beurre Blanc to glaze crab meat and gnocchi evenly. Salt to taste. Adjust acidity with fresh lemon juice.

Plating:
Place Gnocchi and Dungeness Crab into serving bowl. Spoon Chorizo Crumb evenly over gnocchi. Finish with Castelvetrano olives, orange segments and cilantro.

Executive Sous Chef Taylor Melonuk making Parisian gnocchi, using string across top of pot to cut off each piece.

Grilled Spanish Octopus
zucchini, fingerling potato, coriander-lime yogurt, pickled carrot, pineapple, tequila

Wine Pairing:

Dragonette Happy Canyon Rosé
Palmina Vermentino, Santa Ynez Valley
Ampelos Vineyard and Cellars Santa Barbara County Viognier
Kimsey White Blend, Ballard Canyon

Alternative Pairing:

Island Brewing Company Tropical Lager
Uinta Brewing Coriander Salt Ready Set Gose

Chef's Notes:

I majored in Hotel and Restaurant Management at the University of Houston. One elective course was to take a cruise from Galveston to Belize to get credit for the semester. I discovered fried chicken with habanero hot sauce and pineapples on this trip. This is a tropical and spicy dish that I wanted to re-create with octopus. This method allows you to slow cook it to add depth of flavor, until just tender. Make sure your grill is screaming hot so you can char it quickly. Serve immediately while it is hot and crunchy.

Prep Time:

2 hours of active preparation, plus pickled carrots

Special Equipment Needed:

Cryovac® and immersion circulator (option: oven), ice bath

Servings:

4

Editor's Note:

The octopus you buy will likely be already cleaned and frozen—saving you the first steps of preparation for this recipe. Slow-cooking yields a very tender octopus.

INGREDIENTS

Pickled Carrot:
1 T salt (9 g)
½ cup carrots (65 g), sliced
¼ cup sugar (50 g)
½ cup red wine vinegar (115 ml)
  (note: use champagne vinegar if
  carrots are yellow)
¼ cup water (58 ml)

Pineapple-Habanero Gastrique:
1⅓ cup pineapple (150 g) peeled, cut
  into obliques
olive oil
salt
2 T shallots (16 g), diced
1 T habanero chile (8 g), de-seeded, diced
4 tsp firmly packed brown sugar (17 g)
½ cup lemon juice (105 ml)
½ cup glucose (167 g) (option: corn
  syrup)

Compressed Pineapple:
¼ pineapple
3 T tequila (40 ml)

Coriander-Lime Yogurt:
1 cup Greek yogurt (235 g)
1 lime, zest and juice reserved
1 tsp ground clove (3 g)
1¾ tsp each ground coriander and
  fennel seeds (5 g each)
2 tsp salt (6 g)

Vegetables:
12 fingerling potatoes
olive oil
salt
canola oil
1 zucchini, cut into obliques
lime juice to taste

Grilled Octopus:
6 lb octopus (2.7 kg)
enough olive oil to cover octopus
½ bunch each fresh rosemary,
tarragon and thyme
1 navel orange, split

Garnish:
¼ bunch fresh cilantro, de-stemmed
zest of 1 lime
1 habanero chile, de-seeded, sliced

DIRECTIONS

Pickled Carrot:
Lightly salt carrots in nonreactive bowl. Heat wine vinegar, sugar, salt and water to a simmer, then pour over the carrots. Marinate for a minimum of 72 hours. Drain before use.

Pineapple-Habanero Gastrique:
Toss pineapple in olive oil, season with salt, then grill until tender. Sauté shallots and habanero in a sauté pan evenly coated with olive oil until tender and translucent. Season with brown sugar and a pinch of salt, then deglaze with lemon juice. Add glucose (option: corn syrup), then reduce over medium heat until slow bubbles form. Place all ingredients into a blender and combine until completely smooth, then cool in a bowl inside an ice bath. (Note: the finished consistency should be that of maple syrup.)

Compressed Pineapple:
Peel and remove core of pineapple, then cut into lengthwise planks. Put into a Cryovac® bag with tequila. Remove air with the vacuum sealer, then place bag in refrigerator overnight to infuse. (Option: place pineapple and tequila in nonreactive bowl, seal with plastic wrap and let marinate in refrigerator overnight. Stir occasionally to marinate evenly.) Cut into 1" cubes, then lay flat on towel to drain.

Coriander-Lime Yogurt:
Mix yogurt, lime zest, lime juice, clove, coriander, fennel and salt together.

Vegetables:
Preheat oven to 375°F. Evenly coat potatoes with olive oil and season with salt. Place cut-side down on a parchment-lined baking sheet and roast until knife tender. Halve potatoes lengthwise. Coat a hot sauté pan with an even layer of canola oil and caramelize the cut sides of the potatoes. Fold in zucchini and cook until tender. Season with lime juice and salt to taste.

Grilled Octopus:
Freeze octopus to tenderize, then thaw in refrigerator overnight. Preheat water bath with immersion circulator to 77°C or oven to 200°F. Remove and discard beak, eyes and brain if your octopus was sold intact, then cut off the arms and butterfly the bulb. Place in baking dish and cover with olive oil, rosemary, tarragon, thyme and orange peel. Braise for 5-6 hours or until knife tender, turning occasionally (if cooking sous vide, seal octopus in bag with herbs). Octopus will shrink considerably during cooking to approximately ⅓ the original volume. 10 minutes before serving drain and grill octopus until heated through and nicely charred. Toss in Pineapple-Habanero Gastrique.

Plating:
Spread the Coriander-Lime Yogurt across the plate. Add the zucchini and potatoes. Place glazed Grilled Octopus and Compressed Pineapple over vegetables. Finish with Pickled Carrot, cilantro, sliced habanero and lime zest.

Herb-Roasted Diver Scallops
ruby red grapefruit, Manila clams, celery, fingerling potatoes, Thai basil

Wine Pairing:

Kunin Pape Star Blonde, Santa Ynez Valley
Habit Chenin Blanc, Jurassic Park Vineyard, Santa Ynez Valley
Ampelos Santa Barbara County Viognier
Qupé Roussanne Bien Nacido Hillside Estate, Santa Maria Valley

Alternative Pairing:

BarrelHouse Brew Company Sunny Daze Citrus Blonde

Chef's Notes:

Step one: buy yourself a cast iron pan you will have for the rest of your life. Make sure you get your hands on one before you start this dish. Cook everything in it. It is the best way to sear a scallop. This dish is based on my love of grapefruit. My grandparents lived in McAllen, Texas, on the Mexican border. If you have ever wondered where ruby red grapefruit comes from, this is the place.

Prep Time:

1 hour, plus pickling

Special Equipment Needed:

ice bath, cast iron skillet

Servings:

2-4

INGREDIENTS

Pickled Fresno Peppers:
1 cup Fresno peppers (130 g), sliced thinly
½ cup red wine vinegar (115 ml)
¼ cup (50 g) sugar
1 T salt (9 g)
¼ cup water (58 ml)

Thai Basil Puree:
½ lb fresh basil (225 g), de-stemmed
olive oil
salt to taste

Celery:
2 stalks celery, thinly sliced on the bias

Fingerling Potatoes:
½ lb fingerling potatoes (225 g), cut
  into obliques
2 sprigs fresh thyme
2 tsp salt (6 g)

Grapefruit Beurre Blanc with Clams:
1 large grapefruit, measure 1 cup of
  the juice (210 ml)
½ cup butter (112 g)
pinch salt

Manilla Clams:
6 Manila clams, cleaned
¼ cup white wine (58 ml)
sliced chives

Herb-Roasted Diver Scallops:
4 large diver scallops (U/10)
canola oil
¼ cup butter (56 g)
2 sprigs fresh thyme

Garnish:
grapefruit segments
fresh Thai basil leaves
celery hearts

DIRECTIONS

Pickled Fresno Peppers:
Place Fresno peppers into a nonreactive bowl. Heat vinegar, sugar, salt and water to a simmer and pour over the peppers. Marinate in the refrigerator for a minimum of 72 hours. Drain before use.

Thai Basil Puree:
Fill a 5-quart pot 80% with water and bring to a boil. Season the water with salt until it tastes like the ocean. Blanch the basil until tender. Test by removing a leaf. It should disintegrate when rubbed between fingers. Once tender, transfer basil to an ice bath, stirring to speed up the cooling process, then spin dry. Puree in a Vitamix or high-powered blender with a couple ice cubes and enough olive oil to create a pudding-like consistency. Pass through a chinois. Season to taste with salt.

Celery:
Blanch and shock the celery, then drain.

Fingerling Potatoes:
In a medium-sized pot, cover the potatoes with cold water. Add thyme and bring to a boil. Add salt, then turn heat down to simmer. Cook until potatoes are knife tender, then drain and remove thyme.

Grapefruit Beurre Blanc with Clams:
Juice the grapefruit and measure 1 cup juice (210 g), saving the rest. Reduce by half over medium heat. Remove pot from heat, add salt and butter and whisk until a rich butter sauce forms.

Manilla Clams:
Place clams in a pot over high heat. Add wine, cover with lid and steam until clams open up. Turn off heat, fold in beurre blanc, celery and potatoes. Finish with chives and a splash of fresh grapefruit juice to taste.

Herb-Roasted Diver Scallops:
Pat scallops dry. Coat cast iron skillet with canola oil and heat until the oil starts to smoke. Sear one side of the scallops until evenly caramelized. Turn down heat to low and add butter and thyme. Baste the melted butter over the scallops just to warm through.

Plating:
Sauce the plate with Thai Basil Puree. Gently position scallops. Arrange clams, celery and fingerling potatoes around the scallops. Garnish with grapefruit segments, Thai basil, celery hearts and Pickled Fresno Peppers.

Passing winter storm, Hendry's Beach.

From the Ranch

Steak Tartare
red garnet yam chips, red wine salt, chimichurri, chile flake, lemon zest

Wine Pairing:

Ken Brown La Encantada Vineyard Pinot Noir, Sta. Rita Hills
JCR Vineyard Pommard 5 Pinot Noir, Santa Barbara County
Alma Rosa Barrel Select Pinot Noir, Sta. Rita Hills

Alternative Pairing:

Firestone Walker Brewing Company Luponic Distortion No. 002

Chef's Notes:

Steak tartare is one the most under appreciated dishes out there. I absolutely love a rare steak, or better yet, a juicy rare burger. When buying meat, always seek out the highest quality. I don't like to add much more than a little salt, pepper and diced shallot to the ground steak. The crispy yam chips add a surprising sweetness, and the spicy chimichurri completes this dish.

Prep Time:

1½ hours

Special Equipment Needed:

Silpat, deep fryer, mandoline or meat grinder (option: slice by hand), ice bath, 3" ring mold

Servings:

1-2

INGREDIENTS

Red Wine Sea Salt:
½ cup sel gris
red wine

Chimichurri Aioli:
2 T cumin (16 g)
2 T coriander seed (12 g)
2 T chile flake (6 g)
1 egg yolk (20 g)
4 tsp Dijon mustard (25 g)
½ tsp salt
3 T sherry vinegar (40 ml)
4 T cilantro (24 g), chopped with stems
2 T parsley (10 g), chopped with stems
approx. ¾ cup grapeseed oil (160 g)

Red Garnet Yam Chips:
canola oil
1 red garnet yam

Spice Blend:
1 tsp salt (3 g)
1 T chile flake (3 g)
1 tsp Aleppo pepper (3 g)

Steak Tartare:
4 oz ground prime hanger steak (115 g)
  (option: beef tenderloin)
1 tsp olive oil (5 ml)
1 T shallots (10 g), peeled, chopped
½ tsp salt
1 tsp freshly ground black pepper (3 g)

Garnish:
parsley and cilantro leaves, de-
  stemmed
zest of ½ lemon
Red Wine Sea Salt

DIRECTIONS

Red Wine Sea Salt:
Preheat oven to 200°F (with fan on if you have a convection oven). Combine sel gris with just enough red wine to create the consistency of wet sand. Layer evenly on a Silpat on a baking sheet and dehydrate in oven for 24 hours or until completely dry. Cool and scrape into a small bowl. If the dried salt has clumped together, press gently with the back of a large spoon or mortar and pestle to break up lumps.

Chimichurri Aioli:
Preheat oven to 325°F. Toast cumin, coriander and chile flake on a sheet pan 8-10 minutes or until aromatic. Cool completely, then blend into a fine powder. Blend in egg yolk, Dijon mustard, salt and sherry vinegar, then add cilantro and parsley and blend until smooth. With blender on low, add grapeseed oil in a thin, even stream until emulsified. Adjust consistency with water to make a thick but pourable aioli.

Red Garnet Yam Chips:
Heat canola oil in deep fryer to 300°F. Shave yams into rounds with mandoline or slice thinly by hand. Fry in batches until golden brown, turning occasionally to cook evenly. Drain on paper towels or rack.

Spice Blend:
Blend salt, chile flake and Aleppo pepper. Coat chips evenly with Spice Blend while hot so they absorb the flavor.

Steak Tartare:
Grind hanger steak or hand chop, and then put in a bowl over an ice bath. Mix in the olive oil, shallots, salt and pepper. Press into a ring mold.

Plating:
Sauce the serving platter with Chimichurri Aioli. Place the ring mold on a 4" square of parchment and press the Steak Tartare firmly into it. Slide your hand under the parchment and transport the ring mold to the platter. Carefully upend the round of Steak Tartare onto the platter, then slide the ring mold off the tartare. Add spiced Sweet Potato Chips and garnish with parsley, cilantro, lemon zest and Red Wine Sea Salt.

Herbs at Santa Barbara Farmers Market.

Duck Liver and Belgian Waffles
sherry maple gelée, duck fat roasted pecans, spicy kumquat marmalade, pickled nameko mushrooms

Wine Pairing:

Ojai Vineyard Kick On Ranch Riesling, Los Alamos Valley
Riverbench Cork Jumper Blanc de Blancs, Santa Maria Valley

Alternative Pairing:

Draughtsman Aleworks Extra Pale Ale
The Bruery Mischief Belgian-style Ale

Chef's Notes:

I love duck liver mousse. It is full of flavor with a hint of gaminess that I find irresistible. It has been on our menu in some form or another since the beginning. This has to be my favorite rendition. Make sure to eat this while the waffle is piping hot so the mousse melts like butter.

Prep Time:

2½ hours active preparation, plus 72 hours for pickling

Special Equipment Needed:

ice bath, chinois (option: fine-meshed sieve), 4" x 6" terrine, blowtorch (option: tongs over a flame), food scale, candy thermometer, Belgian waffle iron

Servings:

4

Editor's Note:

Keep the raw duck liver chilled in a bowl over an ice bath or in the refrigerator before use. If necessary, substitute chicken liver for duck liver and beech mushrooms for nameko mushrooms.

INGREDIENTS

Pickled Nameko Mushrooms:
½ cup nameko mushrooms (25 g),
  base removed
½ cup cider vinegar (105 ml)
¼ cup sugar (50 g)
1 T salt (9 g)
¼ cup water (58 ml)

Duck Liver Mousse:
½ lb duck liver (226 g)
milk
canola oil
⅓ cups shallots (50 g), sliced
2 tsp garlic (6 g), sliced
4 tsp bourbon (20 ml)
1 tsp salt (3 g)
pinch pink salt
5 T butter (70 g), softened
3 T crème fraîche (42 g)

Sherry Maple Gelée:
1 cinnamon stick
1 star anise pod
½ cup maple syrup (150 ml)
⅓ cup sherry vinegar (76 ml)
1 T fish sauce (12 ml)
1 T fresh thyme (3 g)
1 bay leaf
2 tsp maple sugar (10 g)
1 T salt (9 g)
gelatin 2% total weight

Spicy Kumquat Marmalade:
2 cups kumquats, quartered and
  de-seeded (600 g)
10 T sugar (130 g)
½ cup glucose or corn syrup (160 g)
pectin mixture:
  3 T sugar (39 g)
  2 tsp granulated pectin (6 g)
  1 tsp cayenne pepper (2 g)
  1 tsp salt (3 g)

Duck Fat Roasted Pecans:
¼ cup pecans (30 g)
duck fat
salt

Belgian Waffles:
1 pkg active dry yeast or (3 g) instant yeast
½ cup warm water (115 ml)
2 cups milk (490 ml)
½ cup butter (112 g), melted
2 tsp salt (6 g)
1 tsp sugar (5 g)
2 cups + 2 T all-purpose flour (265 g)
spray olive oil or pan spray
2 eggs (90 g), beaten
pinch baking soda

Garnish:
Shaved persimmon, watercress, frisée,
olive oil, lemon and Maldon Sea Salt

DIRECTIONS

Pickled Nameko Mushrooms:
Put mushrooms into a nonreactive bowl. Heat vinegar, sugar, salt and water to a simmer, then pour over mushrooms. Marinate in the refrigerator for a minimum of 72 hours. Drain before use.

Duck Liver Mousse:
Soak liver overnight in the refrigerator in enough milk to cover, then drain, rinse and pat dry with paper towels. Reserve in the refrigerator until ready to use. Line terrine with food-grade plastic wrap. Sear liver to medium rare in hot pan evenly coated with canola oil, set aside, then add shallots and garlic to the same pan and sweat until translucent over medium low heat until completely tender. Deglaze pan with bourbon, then scrape into bowl inside ice bath to chill. Place mixture and livers into a Vitamix or high-powered blender and puree with salt, pink salt, butter and crème fraîche. Pass mousse through a chinois or fine-meshed sieve into a bowl inside an ice bath. Transfer mousse mixture to the terrine. Chill thoroughly (about 4 hours) before capping with gelée. 5 minutes before serving, slice into 2" portions.

Sherry Maple Gelée:
Burn the cinnamon and star anise with a blowtorch in a dry sauté pan (or hold with tongs over a flame). Bring cinnamon, star anise, maple syrup, vinegar, fish sauce, thyme, bay leaf, maple sugar and salt to a simmer. Turn off heat and let steep for 15 minutes before straining and weighing. Weigh out 2% of this number in gelatin. Bloom in a small container with just enough ice water to cover, then stir into warm maple mixture to dissolve. Pour over Duck Liver Mousse and chill through, approximately 2 hours.

Spicy Kumquat Marmalade:
Combine kumquats with first measurement of sugar and glucose over low heat, stirring with a rubber spatula. Whisk together the second measurement of sugar and pectin in a dry bowl, then whisk into the pot. Using a candy thermometer, cook to 220°F (104°C). Once thickened, bubbles will be thick and slow. Transfer into a bowl set inside a bowl of ice. When completely cold, fold in cayenne pepper and salt.

Duck Fat Roasted Pecans:
Preheat oven to 300°F. Coat pecans evenly with duck fat and place on parchment-lined sheet pan. Cook 10-12 minutes or until toasted. Season to taste with salt.

Belgian Waffles:
Proof yeast in the warm water only if using active dry yeast; instant yeast doesn't need proofing. Whisk together with milk and butter. In a separate bowl, whisk together salt, sugar and flour, then fold into the liquid just until mixed. Batter may be lumpy. Rest overnight in the refrigerator. 30 minutes prior to serving, preheat Belgian waffle iron and lightly spray with oil. Whisk in beaten eggs and baking soda. Using approximately ½ cup at a time, cook waffles until golden brown.

Plating:
Plate a 2" slice of Duck Liver Mousse. Sprinkle with Maldon Sea Salt. Place waffles on one end with a small ramekin of Spicy Kumquat Marmalade. Arrange the Pickled Nameko Mushrooms and Duck Fat Roasted Pecans around the Duck Liver. Garnish with lightly dressed frisée, shaved persimmon and watercress.

Kumquats.

Herb-Crusted Bone Marrow
Aleppo pepper buttermilk biscuits, Campari and grapefruit marmalade

Wine Pairing:

Chanin Chardonnay Sanford & Benedict Vineyard, Sta. Rita Hills
Lutum Pinot Noir Rinconada Vineyards, Sta. Rita Hills
Combe Trousseau, Ballard Canyon

Alternative Pairing:

Russian River Brewing Company Blind Pig IPA

Chef's Notes:

Biscuits, fresh out of the oven, are easily one of my all-time favorite foods. A little smear of butter and fresh jam is all you need. Roasted bone marrow is the world's greatest butter. The bitter peel from the grapefruit along with the Campari really makes this an exciting dish.

Prep Time:

40 minutes active preparation, plus brining

Special Equipment Needed:

candy thermometer, ice bath

Servings:

4

Editor's Note:

Ask your butcher to cut the marrow bones in half lengthwise.

INGREDIENTS

Bone Marrow:
1 lb marrow bones (453 g), split
  lengthwise
salt

Candied Grapefruit Peel:
1 cup grapefruit peel (55 g),
  approx. 3 grapefruits
1 cup sugar (220 g)
water

Grapefruit-Campari Marmalade:
2 ruby red grapefruit (300 g pulp)
6 T sugar (80 g)
¼ cup glucose or corn syrup (80 g)
pectin mixture:
  4 tsp sugar (20 g)
  1 tsp pectin (4 g)
2 tsp Aleppo pepper (6 g)
3 T Campari (40 ml)
1 tsp salt (3 g)

Aleppo Pepper Buttermilk Biscuits:
2 cups all-purpose flour (250 g)
1½ tsp baking soda (7 g)
1 tsp baking powder (4 g)
1 T sugar (13 g)
2 tsp salt (6 g)
10½ T cold butter (150 g)
1⅓ cup buttermilk (300 ml)
2 tsp Aleppo pepper (6 g)
7 tsp fresh thyme (12 g), chopped
2 tsp black pepper (4 g)

Garnish:
chervil, picked
chives, sliced
tarragon, picked

DIRECTIONS

Bone Marrow:
Soak bones in the refrigerator for 48 hours in enough lightly salted ice water to cover. Water-to-salt ratio should be 10 parts water to 1 part salt. Replace the salted water periodically until the water is clear. Drain and pat dry. (Tip: soaking removes the "taste of gnarly barnyard.") Half an hour before serving, preheat the oven to 425°F. Place marrow bones on parchment-lined sheet pan and roast for 10-15 minutes until marrow is hot but not melted. (Tip: stab a paring knife in the marrow to see if it is tender, then touch the tip of knife to see if the marrow is hot all the way through.)

Candied Grapefruit Peel:
Using a sharp peeler, remove peel from grapefruit, remove pith and finely julienne the peel. Cover with cold water in a small pot and bring just to a boil, then remove from heat. Strain and repeat. Strain then add the sugar and 2 cups of water. Bring to a boil and strain. Cool in an even layer on a parchment-lined sheet pan.

Grapefruit-Campari Marmalade:
Using a sharp peeler, remove grapefruit peel, all of the pith, membranes and seeds but save as much flesh as you can. Combine grapefruit flesh with first measure of sugar and glucose over low heat, stirring with a rubber spatula. Whisk together the second measure of sugar and pectin in a separate bowl, then whisk into the sugar/glucose. Using a candy thermometer, cook this mixture to 220°F. (Note: once thickened, slow, thick bubbles form.) Transfer in to a bowl set inside a bowl of ice. When completely cold, fold in Aleppo pepper, Campari, Candied Grapefruit Peel and salt.

Aleppo Pepper Buttermilk Biscuits:
Whisk together flour, baking soda, baking powder, sugar and salt. Add half the butter and cut in, using a pastry cutter or by pulsing in a food processor, until mixture is the size of gravel. Add remaining butter and cut in to pea size. Fold in buttermilk, Aleppo pepper, thyme and black pepper and mix just until dough comes together. Do not overwork. Turn mixture out onto a parchment-lined sheet pan, then press flat to 1½ inch thick. Chill until cold enough to cut.

Preheat the oven to 425°F (can bake with bone marrow). Cut rounds with #50 round cutter (approx. 2"). Re-press any trim and re-cut, placing biscuits on a parchment-lined sheet tray 2" apart. Bake until golden brown, about 15 minutes.

Plating:
Plate bone marrow and sauce Grapefruit-Campari Marmalade over the marrow. Cover with chervil, chives and tarragon. Place Aleppo Pepper Buttermilk Biscuits alongside.

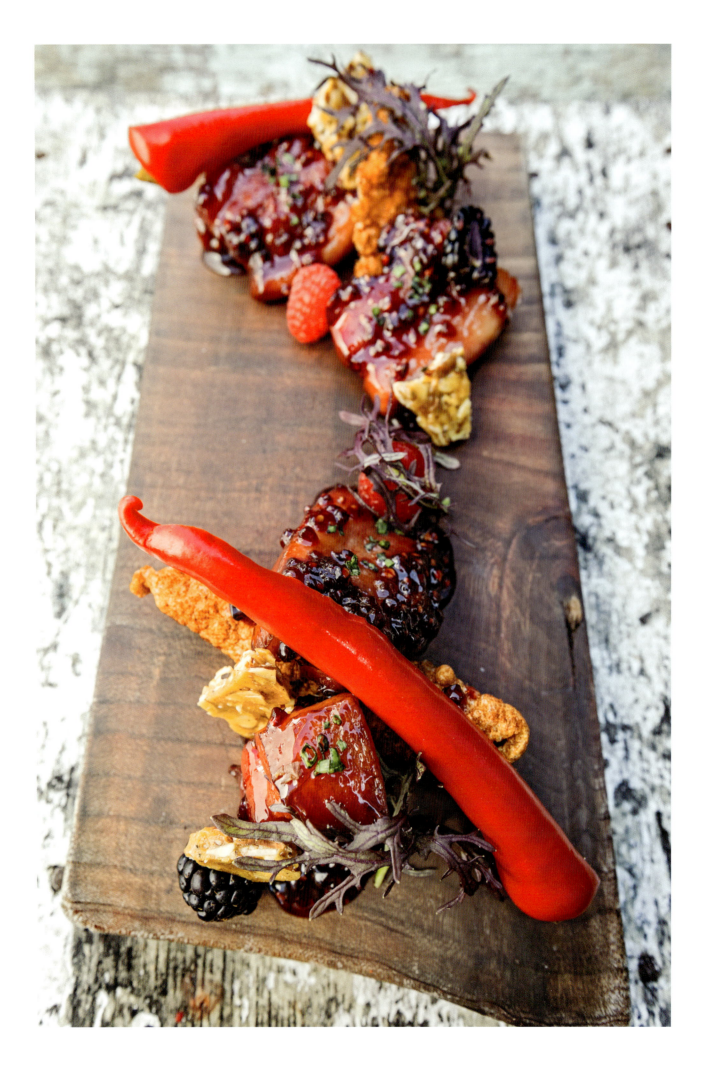

Smoked Pork Belly
roasted blackberry gastrique, almond brittle, pickled corno di toro peppers, chicharron

Wine Pairing:

Tyler Pinot Noir La Rinconada, Sta. Rita Hills
Potek Kick On Ranch Riesling, Los Alamos Valley
Melville Winery Estate Syrah, Sta. Rita Hills

Alternative Pairing:

Topa Topa Brewing Company Gadabout Oatmeal Stout

Chef's Notes:

I've finally figured out how to cook pork belly perfectly. There are a lot of ways to do it. This is the most rewarding of all. They say patience is a virtue. This dish takes a minimum of four days to prepare. Hang in there. It is a three-day cure. A two-hour smoke. A 12-hour braise and 12 hours to press. Two minutes to fry. Then you are just moments from my favorite bite of all time.

Prep Time:

2 hours active preparation, plus curing, smoking, marinating, braising, chilling

Special Equipment Needed:

smoker with oak chips, deep fryer (option: cast iron skillet with thermometer), ice bath, 2 Silpats

Servings:

8-10

Editor's Note:

Never smoke directly over flames; pork belly will burn.

INGREDIENTS

Pork Belly:

cure

  7 T fennel seed (48 g)

  10 star anise pods (28 g)

  2 garlic cloves

  4 T coriander seed (24 g)

  1 T chile flake (3 g)

  5 tsp yellow mustard seed (10 g)

  1 cup salt (130 g)

  $\frac{1}{2}$ tsp pink salt

  $\frac{1}{2}$ cup sugar (100 g)

2 lb pork belly (906 g)

approx. 4 cups duck fat (800 g)

canola oil

Chicharron:

1 lb pork skin (453 g)

$\frac{1}{4}$ bunch thyme

$\frac{1}{2}$ head garlic

chicken stock to cover, approx. 3 cups

chile mixture:

  $\frac{1}{4}$ cup ancho chile powder (15 g)

  $1\frac{1}{2}$ tsp cayenne (4 g)

  $\frac{1}{2}$ tsp citric acid

  $\frac{1}{2}$ tsp salt

Pickled Corno di Toro Peppers:

$\frac{1}{2}$ cup corno di toro peppers (50 g)

$\frac{1}{2}$ cup red wine vinegar (115 ml)

$\frac{1}{4}$ cup sugar (50 g)

1 T salt (9 g)

$\frac{1}{4}$ cup water (58 ml)

Roasted Blackberry Gastrique:

5 cups blackberries (750 g)

olive oil

2 T sugar (26 g)

2 T red wine vinegar (28 ml)

2 T red verjus (25 ml) or substitute

  more red wine vinegar

$1\frac{1}{2}$ tsp salt (4 g)

DIRECTIONS

Pork Belly:

Preheat oven to 325°F. Toast fennel, star anise, garlic, coriander, chile and mustard seed on a sheet pan for 10-12 minutes or until aromatic and evenly toasted, stirring occasionally to prevent burning. Cool. Grind in a blender. Mix with salt, pink salt and sugar in a mixing bowl with a whisk. Gently score the pork belly, making an even crosshatch pattern (see pg. 250). Coat the pork belly in the dry cure. Wrap and marinate in the refrigerator for 72 hours, checking every 12 hours to ensure meat is evenly coated.

Rinse thoroughly, then pat dry. Smoke gently over oak for an hour, rotating every 20 minutes for even smoking. Melt duck fat over low heat just until it melts and is pourable. Place smoked pork belly in a close-fitting baking pan and cover with melted duck fat (budget option: part canola). Braise in a 175°F oven for 12 hours. (Tip: if 200°F is the lowest setting on your oven, braise at this temperature for 5-6 hours or until knife tender.) Remove pork belly and let cool. (Tip: cool, strain and store duck fat in the refrigerator for future use.) Wrap the pork in plastic wrap, place a weighted container on top to compress it, then refrigerate overnight.

10 minutes before serving, heat a deep fryer or cast iron skillet filled with canola oil to 375°F. Remove pork skin, cut meat into individual portions. Deep fry meat for 2 minutes. Glaze with Blackberry Gastrique at room temperature.

Chicharron:

Preheat oven to 250°F. Place skins, thyme and garlic in a baking dish and cover with chicken stock. Bake for 4 hours or until skins are knife tender. Remove skins and place on parchment-lined baking sheet. When cool, trim excess fat from skin.

Turn down oven to 200°F and turn on fan. Dehydrate skins in oven until completely dry—this could take 24 hours. Grind the ancho chile, cayenne, citric acid and salt together. Heat canola oil in a deep fryer to 400°F (option: cast iron skillet with thermometer) and cook skins until crispy. Drain and season evenly with chile mixture. (Tip: chile mixture is spicy, so test a chicharron with spice mixture before seasoning the batch.)

Pickled Corno di Toro Peppers:

Halve peppers lengthwise, remove seeds but keep stems on. Place into a pickling jar or nonreactive bowl. Heat vinegar, sugar, salt and water to a simmer, then pour over the peppers. Marinate for a minimum of 72 hours. Drain before use.

Roasted Blackberry Gastrique:

Toss berries in oil, then place in a baking pan and blister under the salamander or on top rack of broiler. Berries will bubble and release juice; stir to blister evenly. Remove from oven. Meanwhile, melt the sugar across the bottom of a large pot over low heat, to make a caramel. Watch carefully, adjusting the heat so the sugar melts but does not burn. When sugar is melted, immediately deglaze the pot with vinegar and verjus. Stir in the blackberries and salt, then reduce slowly until the gastrique coats the back of a spoon. Cool to room temperature.

INGREDIENTS

Almond Brittle:
1½ cups almonds (200 g), toasted
½ cup butter (112 g)
½ cup sugar (100 g)
¼ cup water (58 ml)
2¼ T glucose (45 g) or corn syrup
1 tsp salt (3 g)
1 tsp freshly ground black pepper (3 g)
1 tsp baking soda (5 g)

Garnish:
1 T chives (6 g), finely diced
¼ cup each fresh blackberries and
  raspberries (25 g each)
mustard greens

DIRECTIONS

Almond Brittle:
Preheat oven to 300°F. Place almonds on a parchment-lined sheet pan and bake until evenly toasted, stirring occasionally. Keep almonds warm. Melt butter in a large pot, then stir in the sugar, water and glucose. Boil mixture and continue to cook until it becomes a golden caramel color—approximately 10 minutes after it begins bubbling and foaming. Watch the mixture carefully. Once it starts to turn golden, it will rapidly reach the caramel color. Immediately add salt, pepper and baking soda, then stir in almonds and turn out on a Silpat. Cover with a second Silpat and gently smooth the top using an oven mitt. Work quickly as the brittle will set up fast. Do not let any part of the hot brittle touch your bare hands—it will burn. When cool, break into shards.

Plating:
Plate Pork Belly glazed with Roasted Blackberry Gastrique. Arrange the Pickled Corno di Toro Peppers, Almond Brittle, Chicharron and mustard greens. Garnish with chives, fresh blackberries and fresh raspberries.

Slow-Cooked Superior Farms Lamb Ribs
medjool date caramel, salsa verde, crushed pistachios, fennel pollen

Wine Pairing:

A Tribute to Grace Grenache, Vie Caprice Vineyard, Santa Ynez Valley
Au Bon Climat Pinot Noir Le Bauge Au-dessus, Santa Maria Valley
Fiddlehead Cellars Pinot Noir Seven Twenty Eight, Fiddlestix Vineyard
Pence Unum, Estate Pinot Noir, Sta. Rita Hills

Alternative Pairing:

Hollister Brewing Company White Fuzz Blonde Ale

Chef's Notes:

You won't see these back home at The Rib Tickler, my favorite spot in my
hometown. I actually had lamb ribs for the first time in New York City. They
erased every memory of all the smoked pork ribs I'd eaten prior. They were that
good. The secret ingredient here is the date caramel made with oranges and
sherry vinegar. Also, the herbaceous salsa verde becomes especially rich with the
addition of the roasted lamb fat. Remember to cook your ribs on a rack so the
fat drips cleanly off.

Prep Time:

6 hours active preparation, plus marinade, plus 6 hours roasting

Special Equipment Needed:

chinois (option: fine-meshed sieve)

Servings:

4-6

INGREDIENTS

Lamb Ribs:
2 racks lamb ribs
3 T fennel seed (18 g)
3 T cumin seed (18 g)
2 T each ground cinnamon and
  paprika (16 g each)
1 T cayenne pepper (8 g)
1 tsp pink salt (6 g)
3 T salt (29 g)
1⅓ cups firmly packed dark brown
  sugar (280 g)

Medjool Date Caramel:
1 cup medjool dates (150 g), pitted
¼ cup sherry vinegar (58 ml)
pinch salt
1" strip of orange peel, pith removed
juice from approximately 4 oranges
  (440 ml juice)

Salsa Verde:
1 T coriander seed (6 g)
¼ bunch each fresh mint and
  tarragon, de-stemmed, chopped
¼ bunch each fresh cilantro and
  parsley, chopped with stems
1 fennel frond, de-stemmed, chopped
2 tsp chile flake (6 g)
approx. ¾ cup lamb fat or
  olive oil (160 ml)

Toasted Pistachios:
1 cup pistachios (140 g)

Garnish:
fennel pollen
nasturtium leaves
marigold blossoms
carrot tops

DIRECTIONS

Lamb Ribs:
Clean lamb ribs and pat dry with paper towels. Grind fennel and cumin seed in a blender. Combine with cinnamon, paprika, cayenne, pink salt, salt and brown sugar. Coat the ribs evenly with spice mixture. Wrap and refrigerate for 12 hours. Preheat oven to 180°F (or 200°F if lowest setting). Place lamb ribs on a roasting rack on a parchment-lined sheet tray and cook for 4-6 hours. The ribs should be tender enough that the bone could be easily removed. Let rest for 10 minutes before carving. Save all of the lamb fat for the salsa verde.

Medjool Date Caramel:
Put pitted dates, sherry vinegar, salt, orange peel and ⅔ of the juice in a small pot, cover and simmer for 30 minutes or until dates are soft. Puree in a blender with enough orange juice to create a thick but pourable consistency. Strain through a chinois or fine-meshed sieve.

Salsa Verde:
Preheat oven to 325°F. Toast coriander seed for 8-10 minutes on a sheet tray. Cool and grind. Chop mint, tarragon, cilantro, parsley and fennel fronds. Add enough lamb fat or olive oil to bind into a chunky salsa. Stir in coriander and chile flake. Season to taste with salt.

Toasted Pistachios:
Toast pistachios at 300°F for 10-12 minutes. Cool. Crush into large pieces.

Plating:
Using tongs, plate the lamb ribs in a balanced stack, then glaze them with Medjool Date Caramel. Add Salsa Verde and toasted pistachios and garnish with carrot tops, marigold blossoms and nasturtium leaves. Sprinkle an even layer of fennel pollen to finish the dish.

Edible Santa Barbara flowers.

Crispy Suckling Pig Confit
quince, braised red cabbage, whiskey pickled jalapeño, crispy pig ears

Wine Pairing:
Stirm Kick On Vineyard Eolian Riesling, Santa Barbara County
Amplify Wines Muscat, Wind Willow Vineyard, Santa Barbara County
Potek Tierra Alta Grenache, Ballard Canyon

Alternative Pairing:
Breaker Bourbon on the rocks

Chef's Notes:
This recipe is not for the faint of heart or a cook pressed for time! It requires a lot of space and effort. We first butcher the pig, separating it into eight manageable parts and go from there. The steps are not difficult to follow but there are many so you have to be really engaged with the process all along the way. For me, it's totally worth it because the end result is amazing.

Prep Time:
1 hour active preparation plus brining, braising, pickling, baking and chilling

Special Equipment Needed:
plenty of space in your refrigerator, high-sided baking pans (#600 hotel pans), 2 rondeau pans, 2 full-sized sheet trays, latex gloves, deep fryer (option: cast iron skillet with thermometer)

Servings:
20

Editor's Note:
A sectioned 11-pound suckling pig should fit in most home ovens, but remember to have ample space in your refrigerator for curing it. Order the suckling pig from your butcher or online.

INGREDIENTS

Suckling Pig:
11 lbs suckling pig (5 kg), sectioned
1½ cups fennel seeds (160 g)
1 cup star anise pods (45 g)
½ cup cinnamon (30 g)
1¼ cups coriander seed (100 g)
3 T chile flake (10 g)
6 T black pepper (54 g)
4 cups salt (500 g)
2½ cups sugar (500 g)
1 tsp pink salt (6 g)
approx. 6 quarts duck fat (6 L)
approx. 1 quart canola oil if not
    using 100% duck fat (1 L)

Pickled Watermelon Radish:
2 lbs watermelon radish (906 g),
    halved, sliced
3½ cups red wine vinegar (805 ml)
2 cups sugar (400 g)
1¾ cups water (402 ml)
11 T salt (107 g)

Whiskey Pickled Jalapeño:
1 lb jalapeños (452 g), sliced
¾ cup + 2 T Bulleit Bourbon (226 ml)
¾ cup + 2 T cider vinegar (226 ml)
1 cup honey (340 g)
1 cup apple juice (248 ml)
salt to taste

Bacon-Braised Red Cabbage:
4 large red onions (2 kg), chopped
8 cloves garlic, finely chopped
6½ lb bacon lardons (3 kg)
4 jalapeño chiles (25 g), sliced into
    rounds with seeds
12 heads red cabbage, cored,
    finely julienned
½ gallon apple juice (2 L)
4¼ cups red wine vinegar (1 L)
1 gallon red wine (4 L)
3 T salt (29 g)
sachet (separated in 2 bundles):
    10 tsp coriander seed (20 g)
    17 tsp caraway seed (40 g)
    7½ tsp black peppercorn (20 g)
    10 tsp whole allspice (20 g)
    10 bay leaves (dry or fresh)

Pork Jus:
5 lb ham hocks (2.25 kg)

DIRECTIONS

Suckling Pig:
Preheat oven to 325°F. Place fennel seeds, star anise, cloves, coriander, chile flake and mustard seeds on a parchment-lined baking sheet, then bake for 8-10 minutes or until evenly toasted and aromatic. Let cool completely before grinding in a Vitamix or high-powered blender. Mix with salt and sugar in a mixing bowl with a whisk, then coat the sectioned pig in the dry cure. Wrap in food-safe bags and refrigerate for 36 hours, checking every 6 hours for even coating of seasoning.

Rinse pig sections thoroughly and pat dry. Preheat oven to 225°F. Place pork in baking dish and cover with duck fat then with foil. (Option: use half duck fat, half canola oil.) Bake until knife tender and meat is falling off the bone. Let cool. Remove all bones and separate from the skin. (Editor's note: suckling pig bones make great Christmas gifts.) Place outer skin down on a parchment-lined ½ sheet tray, then press the meat onto the skin to form a ½" layer. Cover with another sheet of parchment, then another sheet tray. Compact meat by pressing on the top tray. Refrigerate for 24 hours, pressing occasionally to form a "meat block" that you can slice into portions.

Pickled Watermelon Radish:
Put watermelon radish into a nonreactive food-safe container. Heat vinegar, sugar, salt and water to a simmer, then pour over the watermelon radish. Marinate for a minimum of 72 hours. Drain before use.

Whiskey Pickled Jalapeño:
Place sliced jalapeño peppers into a nonreactive bowl. Heat vinegar, honey, apple juice, bourbon and salt to a simmer and pour over the peppers. Marinate in the refrigerator for a minimum of 72 hours. Drain before use.

Bacon-Braised Red Cabbage:
In two large rondeau pans (wide, deep skillets), pour enough canola oil to lightly cover the surface area of each. Once the oil starts to rapidly smoke, distribute the bacon equally between both pans, careful not to overcrowd. The objective is to get the bacon crispy as possible and to cook the remaining ingredients in the bacon fat. Once all of the bacon is crispy, remove and pour into a perforated hotel pan with a deep hotel pan below it to catch the fat. Utilizing all of the rendered bacon fat, sweat the onions, garlic and jalapeño until completely tender. Do not get color on the vegetables. Add a sachet into each rondeau. Once tender, add the cabbage and cook for an additional 5 minutes. Use the salt to season each layer, noting that by the end of the process you may need to adjust the seasoning. Add the red wine vinegar and reduce to just before dry. At this point cut out a cartouche to fit each rondeau. Add the apple juice and wine, cover and cook slowly until the cabbage is completely tender.

Pork Jus:
Braise the ham hocks in chicken and veal stock, thyme and garlic until tender, either on the stove over low heat

INGREDIENTS

8½ quarts chicken stock (8 L)
4¼ quarts veal stock (4 L)
2 bunches fresh thyme
4 heads garlic, halved horizontally
3 T red wine vinegar (42 ml)

Quince Butter:
2 lbs fresh quince (906 g), rinsed, peeled,
  fibrous core removed and roughly
  chopped
1 lb butter (453 g)
1½ tsp salt (4 g)
1 cup + 2 T granulated sugar (225 g)
2 T apple cider vinegar (25 ml)
1 each vanilla bean, split
sachet:
  2 cinnamon sticks
  5 each long pepper pods
  3 each bay leaves

Crispy Pig Ears:
sachet wrapped in cheesecloth:
  1 sprig of thyme
  4 bay leaves
  15 black peppercorns
  10 star anise pods
  2 heads of garlic, split horizontally
½ cup canola oil (105 ml)
1 onion, peeled, quartered
2 stalks celery, roughly chopped
2 carrots, peeled, roughly chopped
8½ quarts chicken stock (8 L)
1 T salt (9 g)
1 lb cleaned pig ears (453 g), cleaned of
  all hair and dirt
cornstarch
salt
black pepper

Garnish:
cilantro

DIRECTIONS

or wrapped with aluminum foil and baked at 325°F for approximately 2 hours or until tender. Reserve the ham hocks for another use. Strain the cooking liquid and reduce down to a sauce consistency.

Quince Butter:
Melt butter in a saucepot large enough to hold 1 gallon over medium heat. Once the butter begins to slowly brown, whisk gently so that the butter solids do not stick to the bottom. Add quince, sachet, sugar and salt. Cover and cook on low heat, stirring occasionally with a wooden spoon until completely tender. Deglaze with cider vinegar and use wooden spoon to remove any of the quince that has stuck to the edges of the pot. Remove sachet and add scraped vanilla bean. Pour all contents into a blender and blend on high for 3 minutes. Pass through a chinois or fine mesh sieve. Quickly ice down in a stainless steel bowl; set in ice. Use a rubber spatula and spin the bowl to release as much steam as possible. Double-check seasoning of sugar and salt. Quince on the greener side will need more sugar than the recipe calls for.

Crispy Pig Ears:
Gather a stockpot that will be able to hold 2 gallons of liquid. Add canola oil, turn the flame on high and wait until it begins to smoke. Add mirepoix and caramelize until fragrant and tender. Deglaze with all of your chicken stock, add the salt and submerge the ears and sachet. Cover with a lid and cook on low heat, or the equivalent of 300°F in an oven, until you can stab the ears with a knife and feel little to no resistance. Once tender, remove from the heat and take off the lid. Let them rest in the warm liquid until room temperature or when cool enough to handle. Put on a pair of latex gloves and remove each ear with a wide slotted spoon. Lay on a full-sized commercial sheet tray lined with parchment. Once all the ears have been placed on parchment and cleaned of food bits that might have stuck to the ears. Next they need to be pressed. Cover with a sheet of parchment paper, as well as a full sheet tray and place onto a flat surface in the refrigerator. Evenly distribute 15-20 lbs of weight across the top sheet tray in order to press the ears. This process will last 24 hours minimum. The more evenly they are pressed, the easier they will be to julienne evenly. The next step is to remove any excess gelatin from the ears and julienne in thin strips. Dredge simply in cornstarch and deep-fry at 375°F until golden brown. Drain onto paper towels to soak up excess fryer oil. Season with salt to taste and freshly cracked black pepper.

Plating:
10 minutes before serving, sear each portion skin-side down in a hot cast iron pan evenly coated with canola oil until the skin is crispy as a cracker and the meat is heated through. As it cooks, baste the rendered fat from the skin back over the meat. Serve skin side up.

Place Bacon-Braised Red Cabbage on plate. Arrange seared Suckling Pig above cabbage to elevate it from the plate. Add a spoonful of Quince Butter, Pickled Watermelon Radish and Whiskey Pickled Jalapeño. Sauce the plate with Pork Jus. Finish with Crispy Pig Ears and cilantro.

Marinated and Grilled Hanger Steak
charred broccoli, Calabrian chile, crispy shallots, mint

Wine Pairing:

Stolpman Vineyards Syrah Angeli, Ballard Canyon
Frequency Artist Series GSM, Santa Barbara County
SAMsARA Syrah, Santa Barbara County
Ken Brown Thompson Vineyard Syrah, Santa Barbara County

Alternative Pairing:

Topa Topa Brewing Company Common Lager (Steam Beer)

Chef's Notes:

The grill is my favorite place to cook. This dish has a true familiarity about it by pairing beef with broccoli but the Calabrian chile and mint provide a piquant twist. I like to blanch the broccoli ahead of time so that it is nice and tender when it comes off the grill. Let your broccoli marinate in the Calabrian chile vinaigrette so it soaks up a ton of flavor.

Prep Time:

45 minutes active preparation, plus marinating

Special Equipment Needed:

grill, deep fryer (option: cast iron skillet with thermometer)

Servings:

4

Editor's Note:

Calabrian chiles can be found in Italian specialty stores.

INGREDIENTS

Hanger Steak:
1½ tsp coriander seed (4 g)
½ bunch fresh parsley, chopped with stems
1 clove garlic
1 sprig fresh thyme
1 cup olive oil (210 ml) or more
1½ lb hanger steak (680 g)
salt

Crispy Shallots:
4 shallots, shaved thin
milk
canola oil
corn starch
salt to taste

Charred Broccoli in Calabrian Chile Vinaigrette:
½ tsp honey (3 g)
1 tsp salt (3 g)
1 tsp lime juice (4 ml)
1½ T sherry vinegar (20 ml)
3 T Calabrian oil (40 ml) (option: chile oil)
3 T olive oil (40 ml)
¼ cup Calabrian chile (30 g), sliced
¾ cup piquillo peppers (90 g), julienned
1 T garlic (8 g), minced
1 head broccoli, cut into large florets
salt to taste

Garnish:
fresh mint leaves

DIRECTIONS

Hanger Steak:
Preheat oven to 325°F. Toast the coriander seed on a sheet tray for 8-10 minutes. Remove and let cool. Blend coriander, parsley, garlic, thyme and oil in a blender until the consistency of a pesto, adding more olive oil if necessary. (Tip: do not overheat the blender, as it will cook the marinade.) Coat the steak with the marinade, cover, then place in the refrigerator for 72 hours, turning every 12 hours. Remove and let sit at room temperature for 30 minutes to temper steak. Season evenly with salt.

Grill steak to medium-rare over high heat, approximately 1½ minutes per side. Let rest 5 minutes, then slice against the grain.

Crispy Shallots:
Place shallots in nonreactive bowl and cover with milk. Soak for 1 hour, then drain on paper towels. Preheat deep fryer filled with canola oil to 325°F. (Option: use a cast iron skillet with thermometer.) Coat shallots with cornstarch and deep-fry until golden brown. Drain on paper towels and season to taste with salt.

Charred Broccoli in Calabrian Chile Vinaigrette:

Combine honey, salt, lime juice and sherry vinegar. Whisk in Calabrian oil and olive oil, then fold in sliced Calabrian chile, piquillo peppers and garlic. Taste for salt, acidity and heat and adjust if necessary. Blanch and shock broccoli, then dry. To blanch: fill a 5-quart pot 80% with water and bring to a boil. Season the water with salt until it tastes like the ocean. Blanch the broccoli until tender. Transfer to an ice bath when cooked, stirring to speed up the cooling process. Drain through a colander when cooled. Grill until evenly marked, then evenly coat in vinaigrette.

Plating:
Place the Charred Broccoli in Calabrian Chile Vinaigrette across the plate. Arrange the Hanger Steak above the Charred Croccoli. Garnish with Crispy Shallots and mint.

Shallots.

Crispy Duck Leg Confit
chai spiced kabocha squash, young turnips, satsuma tangerine, vanilla gastrique, crispy sage

Wine Pairing:

Palmina Nebbiolo, Santa Barbara County
Stirm Los Chuchaquis Gabilan Blanc
Chanin Pinot Noir, Sanford and Benedict Vineyard, Sta. Rita Hilla
Au Bon Climat Nebbiolo "Punta Exclamitiva", Santa Maria Valley

Alternative Pairing:

High West Campfire Whiskey

Chef's Notes:

I'm a chai spice addict. I got hooked in coffee shops when I was in high school. The chai spice blend reminds me of fall baking spices like you find in pumpkin pie. I love the contrast between the crispy duck leg and the roasted yet creamy kabocha squash. The sharpness in the vanilla gastrique plays a vital role in balancing this dish.

Prep Time:

1½ hours active preparation, plus 6 hours curing and braising

Special Equipment Needed:

blowtorch (option: open flame on stove), chinois (option: fine-meshed sieve), 2 ice baths, 5-gallon pot or larger, cast iron skillet, deep fryer (option: cast iron skillet with thermometer)

Servings:

4

Editor's Note:

Duck fat is expensive, but it can be reused—strain and refrigerate. The solids will sink to the bottom and separate from the pure duck fat.

INGREDIENTS

Chai Spice:
2 sticks cinnamon
2 pieces star anise
2 T cardamom seeds (16 g)
2½ tsp each allspice and clove (5 g
  each)
1 tsp ground ginger (2 g)
1 tsp black pepper (3 g)
2 tsp grated nutmeg (5 g)
(Note: use 1 tsp if grinding fresh
  nutmeg)

Duck Leg Cure:
1 lb salt (453 g)
1 bunch each fresh parsley and thyme,
  tough stems removed
1 head garlic, skin removed
8 duck legs

Vanilla Sage Gastrique:
¾ cup glucose (240 g), (option corn syrup)
1 cup + 2 T champagne vinegar (236
  ml)
3 T fresh sage (15 g), chopped with stems
¼ tsp salt
½ whole vanilla bean, scraped
½ stick of burnt cinnamon

Duck Confit:
1 gal duck fat (4 L) (option: use half
  canola oil)

Crispy Sage:
¼ cup fresh sage leaves (20 g)
canola oil
salt to taste

Vegetables:
2 young turnips, peeled, split
½ kabocha squash, sliced, skin-on
3 T olive oil (40 ml)
1 tsp Chai Spice (2 g)
1 T Vanilla Sage Gastrique (16 ml)
1 tsp lemon juice (5 ml)
salt and sugar to taste

Garnish:
1 satsuma tangerine, divided into
  segments

DIRECTIONS

Chai Spice:
Burn the star anise and the cinnamon for both the Chai Spice and Vanilla Sage Gastrique with a blowtorch in a dry sauté pan (or hold with tongs over a flame). Preheat oven to 325°F. Toast the rest of the chai spices on a sheet pan for 8-10 minutes or until aromatic. Cool completely. Blend 2 sticks cinnamon, 2 pieces star anise, toasted cardamom, allspice, clove, ginger, black pepper and nutmeg into dust.

Duck Leg Cure:
Blend salt, parsley, thyme, garlic and salt in food processor. Pack onto duck legs, wrap and refrigerate for 3 hours.

Vanilla Sage Gastrique:
Combine glucose, vinegar, sage, salt, vanilla bean and cinnamon in a saucepot. Reduce to syrup over low heat, just until it coats the back of a spoon. The gastrique will reduce in 2-3 minutes; do not boil. (If it makes a thick coat on the back of a spoon, you have reduced it too long, and it will likely harden when cooled.) Strain through a chinois or fine-meshed sieve, then cool in a bowl inside an ice bath.

Duck Confit:
Preheat oven to 200°F. Rinse legs thoroughly and pat dry with paper towels. Place in baking dish and cover with duck fat, tightly wrapped with foil, then braise for 3-4 hours just until knife tender. (Tip: duck is done when the bone is loose enough to be twisted out of the meat but the meat is not falling off the bone. Do not debone duck legs.) Heat a cast iron skillet over medium high heat, then coat evenly with canola oil. Pat legs dry with paper towels. Place skin-side down and sear for 2 minutes on low heat until golden brown. Coat with Vanilla Gastrique, saving 1 T to finish vegetables.

Crispy Sage:
Heat canola oil in a deep fryer to 300°F. (Option: use a cast iron skillet plus a thermometer.) Fry sage leaves in batches until crispy. Each leaf will bubble when it hits the hot oil; when bubbles stop, the leaf is done. Drain on paper towels and season with salt.

Vegetables:
To blanch the turnips: fill a 5-quart pot 80% with water, season with salt until it tastes like the ocean, bring to a boil, then cook turnips until tender. Transfer to an ice bath when cooked, stirring to speed up the cooling process. Drain in a colander when cooled. Turn oven up to 375°F. Coat kabocha evenly with olive oil, salt and sugar. Roast for 30 minutes or until tender. Cool completely. In a sauté pan evenly coated with olive oil, combine kabocha and turnips with Chai Spice and heat until caramelized on all sides. Finish with Vanilla Sage Gastrique and lemon juice.

Plating:
Arrange the vegetables on the serving platter. Place the duck legs on top. Garnish with Crispy Sage and tangerine segments.

Handmade Pappardelle with Goat Confit
Maitake mushrooms, Midnight Moon goat Gouda, juniper berry, Black Mission figs

Wine Pairing:

Roark Wine Company Malbec, Santa Ynez Valley
Star Lane Vineyard Merlot, Santa Ynez Valley
Lumen Pinot Noir, Sierra Madre Vineyard, Santa Maria Valley

Chef's Notes:

How do I convince you to try goat? There are so many countries that rely on goat. The United States is not one of them. This recipe should win you over. At The Lark we bring in whole goats so that you get a chance to try a little bit of everything. Cypress Grove Dairy Farm, out of Humbolt County, makes Midnight Moon goat Gouda that is perfect with this dish because of how tangy and creamy it is. It melts into the warm pasta. Chickweed is an uncommon ingredient but a perfect addition because it brings a clean and grassy finish to this earthy dish.

Prep Time:

2½ hours active preparation, plus brining and baking

Special Equipment Needed:

spice grinder, pasta maker

Servings:

4-6

Editor's Note:

Goat can be purchased online or in some farmers' markets and butcher shops.

INGREDIENTS

Goat Confit:
brine:
  1 cup salt (130 g)
  5 tsp pink salt (30 g)
  10 T brown sugar (130 g), firmly-
    packed
  1⅓ gallon warm water (5 L)
  mirepoix (per recipe pg. 272)
  ½ bunch each fresh thyme, parsley,
    rosemary, oregano
  2 heads garlic, split laterally
4-6 lb loin or shoulder of goat
  (approx. 2 kg), bone-in
1 gallon duck fat (1760 g)
  (budget option: use half canola oil)

Goat Spice Blend:
  10 tsp coriander (20 g)
  4 tsp allspice (10 g)
  5 tsp black pepper (10 g)
  2 T juniper berry (10 g)
  2 bay leaves

Pappardelle Pasta:
1 cup semolina flour (150 g), sifted,
  plus extra for dusting
1 cup "00" flour (150 g), sifted
20 egg yolks (400 g)
salt

Beurre Blanc:
14 T white wine (200 ml)
½ tsp salt
1 shallot, sliced
pinch freshly ground black pepper
1 sprig fresh thyme
1 cup heavy cream (200 ml)
2 cups + 3 T butter (270 g)

Caramelized Mushrooms:
1 lb Maitake mushrooms (453 g), halved
olive oil
salt to taste

Garnish:
4 oz Midnight Moon cheese (115 g)
4 fresh black figs, halved
¼ cup chickweed (9 g)
several leaves flowering kale
1 tsp Goat Spice Blend

DIRECTIONS

Goat Confit:
Dissolve salt, pink salt and sugar into warm water in a 6-quart or larger pot. Add mirepoix, thyme, parsley, rosemary, oregano and garlic. Chill completely. Add goat shoulder. Brine for 48 hours in the refrigerator. Preheat oven to 250°F. Drain goat, pat dry with paper towels and cover completely with duck fat (or duck fat and oil). Bake for 5-6 hours or until meat is falling off the bone. Cool and remove meat. (Note: strain duck fat into a container and reserve in the refrigerator for future use.) Pick into bite-sized pieces.

Goat Spice Blend:
Preheat the oven to 325°F. Toast all spices on parchment-lined sheet tray for 8-10 minutes, then cool. Put into a blender and blend until ground evenly.

Pappardelle Pasta:
In large mixer, mix the two flours together, then add the egg yolks. Mix with bread hook until the dough comes together. Portion into four equal pieces, wrap in plastic and let rest 30 minutes. Unwrap, then roll in batches in a pasta roller, starting at the widest setting. Roll at widest setting several times, until pasta is smooth and pliable, folding and pressing the edges into the center to create a rectangular pasta sheet. Roll the pasta sheet down to 2.5 setting on an electric pasta machine, or approximately 1/16th of an inch. Dust with 00 flour if the pasta is sticky. Cut pasta sheets into 9.5" pieces and dust liberally with semolina. Slice each portioned sheet into ¾" wide noodles. Dust a sheet pan with semolina and loosely bundle each batch of noodles on the pan. Cover with plastic wrap until ready to use. Cook until al dente in a large stockpot of boiling water lightly seasoned with salt.

Beurre Blanc:
In a saucepan, reduce the white wine, salt, shallot, pepper and thyme over low heat until almost dry. Add the cream and reduce to sauce consistency—when it coats the back of a spoon. Over low heat, whisk in the butter until emulsified, then strain.

Caramelized Mushrooms:
Coat a sauté pan evenly with olive oil. Turn on high heat. Once oil is smoking, sear mushrooms cut side down until deep golden brown and cooked through. Season with salt. Remove from pan.

Plating:
Combine pasta with Beurre Blanc over low heat. Fold in Caramelized Mushrooms, goat confit and Goat Spice Blend. Garnish with shaved Midnight Moon, figs, chickweed and flowering kale.

Fresh handmade pappardelle pasta.

Pomegranate Glazed Double-Cut Pork Chop
black-eyed pea and pork sausage cassoulet, poblano chile, rainbow chard

Wine Pairing:

The Hilt Pinot Noir, Sta. Rita Hills
Tatomer Kick-On Ranch Riesling, Santa Barbara County
Amy & Peter Made This Pinot Noir, Sta. Rita Hills
Santa Barbara Winery Primitivo, Santa Ynez Valley

Alternative Pairing:

Almanac Beer Co. Valley of the Heart's Delight, Barrel Sour Blonde
Cutler's Artisan Spirits 33 Straight Bourbon Whiskey

Chef's Notes:

Black-eyed peas and pork chops aren't fancy and never need to be. I do, however, love the sour and sweet bite of pomegranate, which grows in backyards all over Santa Barbara. It adds vitality and piquancy to a seemingly simple dish.

Prep Time:

½ hour active preparation (plus 24 hours for brining)

Special Equipment Needed:

grill

Servings:

2-4

INGREDIENTS

Pork Chop:
brine:
  6 T salt (50 g)
  1½ tsp pink salt (9 g)
  3 T brown sugar (39 g), firmly packed
  5½ cups warm water (1.25 L)
  1 tsp whole peppercorns (3 g)
  mirepoix (half of recipe pg. 272)
  2 sprigs fresh thyme
2 double-cut pork chops

Brown Butter Breadcrumbs:
¼ loaf sourdough levain, cubed
¼ pound Brown Butter
pinch salt and black pepper

Pomegranate Glaze:
3 T champagne vinegar (39 ml)
2 T glucose (40 g) (option: corn syrup)
5 T pomegranate juice (95 ml)
½ cup pomegranate molasses (150 g)

Pork Sausage:
1 T fresh chives (6 g), diced
1 T fennel seed (8 g)
3 cloves garlic (6 g), peeled
4 T white wine (56 ml)
½ tsp ground pepper
1 T salt (9 g)
1 tsp pink salt (6 g)
½ tsp chile flake
1 pound pork butt (453 g), ground

Black-eyed Pea and Pork Sausage Cassoulet:
1 cup black-eyed peas (180 g)
½ lb ham hocks (276 g)
1 jalapeño, sliced
mirepoix (half of recipe pg. 272)
2 poblano chiles, grilled, de-seeded,
  skin removed
2 T butter (28 g)

Sautéed Rainbow Chard:
1 bunch rainbow chard, de-stemmed
olive oil and salt to taste

Garnish:
⅓ cup pomegranate seeds (45 g)
1 T fresh chives (6 g), sliced

DIRECTIONS

Pork Chop:
Dissolve salt, pink salt and sugar in warm water, using a whisk in a 6-quart or larger pot. Add mirepoix, peppercorns and thyme. Cool completely. Add pork chops. Brine chops in the refrigerator for 24 hours.

15 minutes before serving, drain and pat dry with paper towels. Grill over low heat for 4 minutes, then flip and cook for 1 minute. Continue flipping and cooking for 1 minute until chops are done: firm to the touch or internal temperature of 145°F. Glaze with Pomegranate Glaze.

Brown Butter Breadcrumbs:
Preheat oven to 250°F. Toast bread cubes for 25-30 minutes or until dry, rotating the pan occasionally. Cool, then blend in a food processor until powder consistency.

Turn oven up to 300°F. In a sauté pan, add brown butter (see recipe pg. 45), breadcrumbs and pinch of salt and black pepper. Cook over low heat, stirring occasionally, until the consistency of wet sand. Spread in an even layer on a parchment-lined sheet pan and toast in the oven 5-8 minutes, until just light brown. (Tip: do not brown too much or breadcrumbs will burn when used on top of the cassoulet.)

Pomegranate Glaze:
Bring vinegar, glucose, juice and molasses to a boil, then simmer until the mixture coats the back of a spoon. Let cool to room temperature for proper viscosity.

Pork Sausage:
Lightly toast the fennel on a sheet pan in the 325°F for 8-10 minutes or until aromatic. Cool and grind fine. At the same time, wrap garlic in foil and roast in oven until tender. Let cool. Mix fennel and garlic, with wine, pepper, salt, pink salt and chile flake in a stand mixer bowl. Add ground pork, then paddle on low speed or mix thoroughly by hand. Cook in sauté pan over low heat until just cooked through.

Black-eyed Pea and Pork Sausage Cassoulet:
In a large pot, add the black-eyed peas, ham hocks, jalapeño, mirepoix and water to cover. Bring to a boil, then simmer for 2 hours or until tender, stirring occasionally. If needed, add water to maintain level at least halfway up the ham hocks. When done, season with salt to taste and cool the pot in an ice bath. Pull the hocks, shred the meat and fold back in, then drain the peas/hocks and place in mixing bowl. Fold in grilled poblano, butter, cooked Pork Sausage and chives. Adjust seasonings to taste and keep warm. 10 minutes before serving, place 2-4 servings into an ovenproof serving bowl, then top with Brown Butter Breadcrumbs. Broil for 30 seconds under salamander or broiler on top rack. (Tip: watch closely to avoid burning breadcrumbs.)

Sautéed Rainbow Chard:
Sauté chard in olive oil until tender, then season to taste with salt.

Plating:
Plate the Sautéed Rainbow Chard and glazed pork chops. Garnish with fresh pomegranate seeds and chives. Serve with a bowl of Black-eyed Pea and Pork Sausage Cassoulet.

Rainbow Swiss chard.

RANCHO SAN JULIAN BEEF

Elizabeth Poett and Austin Campbell, Rancho San Julian.

"THE NUMBER ONE RULE OF cattle ranching: Always leave a gate exactly how you found it," says Elizabeth Poett, grower of Rancho San Julian beef in Lompoc. Scooping her cowboy-booted toddler, Jack, onto her hip while gripping a Corona in the other hand, she slips through the gate and heads to the family ranch house. For nearly two centuries, Elizabeth's family of De la Guerras and Dibblees and Poetts have been working San Julian ranchland in the western Santa Ynez Mountains. Her great-great-great-grandfather José de la Guerra, comandante of Santa Barbara's Presidio, started the cattle operation in 1837, initially to raise beef to feed his soldiers.

Born and raised on the ranch, Elizabeth was mentored by her father, Jim Poett, one of the first producers of organic beef in California. San Julian cattle, bred from Angus bulls and free of hormones and antibiotics, roam free on 14,000 acres. Elizabeth joined the business in 2006, winning acclaim for her beautifully marbled, 100% grass-fed meat. Her highly coveted beef is fed only oat hay and the grass from the hills on which the cattle live.

Growing up as the 7th generation of her ranching family, Elizabeth had other plans for her future. She left Lompoc for college in the Midwest, then tried her hand at film production and screenwriting in New York and Los Angeles. Fate intervened when she met her future husband, Austin Campbell, a Santa Barbara rancher, at a cattle branding. It was at a time, she says, when her "interests just started to shift" back toward food and meat production and to returning home to carry on the family tradition.

"Sometimes you have to go away to really realize how lucky you are," Elizabeth says, her blue eyes alight.

As a rancher, wife and mother, she's keen to preserve the family legacy and support the valley's emphasis on land and community. Along with San Julian beef, she raises heritage turkeys. The ranch produces organic lavender, harvests honey and produces biodynamically farmed vegetables under the stewardship of Chris Thompson. "We want to bring everything food-related to people that the ranch can provide," Elizabeth says of this historic land.

—Annie Villanueva

Grilled Ribeye with Smoked Tomato
roasted shishito peppers, summer pole beans, Yukon potato puree, charred lettuce

Wine Pairing:

Star Lane Cabernet Sauvignon, Star Lane Vineyard, Happy Canyon
Jonata El Desafio de Jonata, Santa Ynez Valley
Koehler Mourvèdre, Santa Ynez Valley
Martian Ranch & Vineyard, Parallax Mourvèdre, Santa Barbara County
Grassini Family Vineyards Cabernet Sauvignon, Happy Canyon

Alternative Pairing:

Sierra Nevada Summerfest Crisp Lager
Deschutes Brewery Mirror Pond Pale Ale

Chef's Notes:

Summer is my favorite time of the year. Peppers, tomatoes, basil, eggplant, beans, squash, corn, stone fruit—it is all ripe and alive. Have you ever stuck your head into a full-grown tomato plant and just smelled how good it is? That is summer to me. If you love steak, then you are an automatic fan of grilled ribeye. Eat it on its own or cooked with freshly picked vegetables, hopefully from your own backyard or your local farmers' market. The Yukon potato puree is a classic French standard that is time-consuming but delicious.

Prep Time:

2 hours active preparation (approximately 7 hours total, including smoking)

Special Equipment Needed:

hot smoker (option: grill), 8 oz oak chips, chinois (option: fine-meshed sieve), ice bath, immersion blender (option: food processor), spice grinder

Servings:

2

INGREDIENTS

Smoked Tomato Base:
1½ lb ripe tomatoes (680 g)
10 bay leaves
2 T red wine vinegar (28 ml)
½ cup whole cherry tomatoes (75 g)
3 T smoked paprika (22 g)
salt to taste

Smoked Tomato Beurre Blanc:
14 T white wine (200 ml)
½ tsp salt
½ shallot, sliced
pinch black pepper
2 sprigs fresh thyme, de-stemmed
10 T butter (142 g)

Infused Cream:
2⅓ cups cream (537 ml)
1 head garlic, cut in half horizontally
3 sprigs fresh thyme
2 T black peppercorn (16 g)

Yukon Potato Puree:
1 lb Yukon potato (453 g), peeled
1 T salt (9 g), or to taste
1 cup butter (224 g), cold, diced
Infused Cream

Ribeye Pepper Blend:
5 T black peppercorn (50 g)
1½ T white peppercorn (14 g)
1 T Sichuan peppercorn (8 g)
4 T coriander (24 g)
12 oz ribeye steak (340 g)

DIRECTIONS

Smoked Tomato Base:
Soak oak wood chips in water for 20 minutes. Drain and ignite chips in hot smoker. Smoke tomatoes until tender, catching all juices. (Option: use your grill. Burn your briquettes or wood until they are embers with no active flames. Seal chips in foil pouch and poke holes in the top, then place on embers. Place the whole tomatoes directly on the grill with a drip pan containing 2 cups of water underneath. Smoke until tomatoes are soft, turning halfway through. Tomatoes may soften and drip into drip pan.) Save smoked cherry tomatoes to garnish.

Put the tomatoes and smoky tomato water from the drip pan into a large bowl. Strain through a chinois or fine-meshed sieve into a large pot, then add bay leaves. Reduce over medium low heat until tomatoes are like a runny tomato paste—when a spoon is dragged across the bottom of the pot, tomato mixture will take a moment before filling in the gap. Remove bay leaves, then add red wine vinegar and salt to taste.

Smoked Tomato Beurre Blanc:
In a saucepan, reduce the white wine, salt, shallot, pepper and thyme until almost dry. Whisk in the Smoked Tomato Base, paprika and red wine vinegar. Over low heat, whisk in the butter until emulsified. Strain through a chinois. Keep warm until serving.

Infused Cream:
Mix cream, garlic, thyme and peppercorn in a small pot. Turn the heat on low and let infuse for 30 minutes. Do not boil. Strain cream though chinois or fine-meshed sieve.

Yukon Potato Puree:
Cut potatoes into uniform 1" pieces. Cover with water to cover plus 4" above their top and bring to a boil. Add the salt, then turn the heat to medium-low and cook until knife tender. Drain, add butter and Infused Cream, then mash with a potato masher. Blend with an immersion blender until smooth, adding cream as necessary. (Option: whip in food processor in batches until smooth and fluffy—however, immersion blender works best.) Strain through a chinois or fine-meshed sieve, then season to taste with salt. Keep warm until serving.

Ribeye Pepper Blend:
Grind the three types of peppercorns and coriander until powdered, then coat the ribeye. Grill approximately 1½ minutes on each side until cooked medium-rare. Let ribeye sit for 3 minutes, then slice against the grain into ½" slices.

INGREDIENTS

Vegetables:
1 cup each haricot verts and yellow
  wax beans (150 g each)
1 cup shishito peppers or Padrón
  peppers (125 g)
3 Japanese eggplant, split lengthwise
olive oil

½ head romaine lettuce, split lengthwise
salt and lemon juice to taste

DIRECTIONS

Vegetables:
Blanch, then shock the haricot verts and yellow wax beans, then drain. To blanch: fill a 5-quart pot 80% with water and bring to a boil. Season the water with salt until it tastes like the ocean. Blanch the beans until tender. Transfer to an ice bath when cooked, stirring to speed up the cooling process. Drain through a colander when cooled. Sauté shishito peppers in hot pan evenly coated with olive oil until blistered. Add haricot verts and wax beans and cook briefly to heat through. Season to taste with salt.

Evenly coat romaine with olive oil and salt. Repeat with eggplant. Grill each until charred and tender. Toss with lemon juice to finish.

Plating:
Plate Yukon Gold Puree. Evenly arrange sliced ribeye. Place haricot verts, wax beans, peppers, and eggplant around ribeye. Garnish with smoked cherry tomatoes, grilled romaine and Smoked Tomato Beurre Blanc.

Heirloom cherry tomatoes.

Black Garlic Glazed Lamb Shank
harissa spiced fall vegetables, almond and pomegranate chutney, charred orange and Kalamata yogurt, grilled flatbread

Wine Pairing:

Happy Canyon Vineyard Piocho Bordeaux Red Blend
Longoria Blues Cuvée, Santa Barbara County
Lafond Winery Pinot Noir, Pommard Clone, Lafond Vineyard, Sta. Rita Hills
Westerly Wines, Westerly Red, Happy Canyon

Alternative Pairing:

Telegraph Brewing Company Stock Porter
M. Special Dozer Special American Brown Ale

Chef's Notes:

My first chef at Salt House in San Francisco loved North African cuisine, and I grew to love it too. This dish is not a wallflower. It is a little savage. It belongs at a big family feast. This is the only dish that requires two servers to bring it to the table at the restaurant. Shred the lamb and get a little bit of each ingredient in the flatbread for the perfect combination.

Prep Time:

2 hours plus brining and braising

Special Equipment Needed:

tamis (option: fine-meshed sieve), ice bath, microplane

Servings:

4 as a shared plate

INGREDIENTS

Lamb Shank:
brine:
  3 cups salt (390 g)
  1¼ cups brown sugar (250 g), firmly packed
  1⅓ gal water (5 L)
  1 T whole peppercorns (8 g)
  mirepoix (per recipe pg. 272)
  1 bunch fresh thyme
  1 bunch fresh parsley
2 lamb shanks
canola oil
1 bottle white wine (750 ml)
Lamb Stock (below)

Lamb Stock:
5 lb lamb neck bones (2.25 kg)
mirepoix (2x recipe pg. 272)
1 bottle white wine (750 ml)
2 heads garlic, cut horizontally
4 sprigs fresh rosemary
1 cup tomato paste (250 g)

Black Garlic Lamb Jus:
1 head fermented black garlic
2 T red wine vinegar (28 ml)
salt

Almond and Pomegranate Chutney:
1 cup almonds (135 g), sliced
1 cup pomegranate molasses (320 g)
2 cups pomegranate juice (420 ml)
1 cup red wine (230 ml)
2 sprigs fresh thyme, de-stemmed
½ cup sugar (100 g)
1 cup pomegranate seeds (150 g)

Charred Orange and Kalamata Yogurt:
1 orange (ripe and sweet)
olive oil
salt
½ cup Kalamata olives (75 g), pitted,
  chopped
2 cups plain unsweetened Greek
  yogurt (500 ml)
5 sprigs of fresh thyme, de-stemmed,
  chopped

DIRECTIONS

Lamb Shank:
Dissolve salt and sugar with warm water using a whisk in a 6-quart or larger pot. Add peppercorns, mirepoix, thyme and parsley. Cool completely. Add the lamb shanks, then brine for 24 hours in the refrigerator. In the meantime, make the Lamb Stock (below). After 24 hours, drain and pat shanks dry with paper towels. Discard the rest.

Season shanks with salt. Sear on all sides in a large pot evenly coated with canola oil, then remove. Caramelize mirepoix in the same pot, then deglaze with white wine and add Lamb Stock. Reduce liquid by half. Put lamb into a deep baking dish along with the mirepoix mixture and reduced Lamb Stock. Either braise on the stove over low heat or wrap tightly with aluminum foil and bake at 300°F for approximately 8 hours or until tender. Cool lamb in braising liquid. Remove shanks, strain and reserve braising liquid.

Lamb Stock:
Preheat the oven to 375°F. Arrange bones in one layer on sheet pan and roast 40 minutes, until caramelized. Pour lamb fat into a stockpot and caramelize the mirepoix in it, then deglaze with white wine. Add the roasted bones, garlic and rosemary, then add 4 L or more of water to cover completely. Whisk in tomato paste. Bring to a boil, then turn down heat and simmer on low for 5-7 hours or until liquid is reduced to ¼ the original volume. Cool and strain stock; discard bones and used mirepoix. Store in refrigerator if you are not using it immediately.

Black Garlic Lamb Jus:
In a saucepot bring Lamb Stock to a boil. Reduce to sauce consistency. Pass the fermented garlic through a tamis or fine-meshed sieve. Add the garlic and red wine vinegar to finish Lamb Jus. Pass through chinois and keep warm.

Almond and Pomegranate Chutney:
Preheat the oven to 300°F. Spread almonds on a baking sheet and toast 10-12 minutes until golden brown. Remove and let cool. In a pot large enough so the mixture does not boil over, reduce the pomegranate molasses, juice, red wine, thyme and sugar slowly until a sauce consistency. Then cool over an ice bath. Fold in the toasted almonds and pomegranate seeds right before serving.

Charred Orange and Kalamata Yogurt:
Slice the whole orange horizontally, then season slices evenly with olive oil and salt. Grill on both sides, then remove all seeds. Blend with Kalamata olives in a food processor until smooth. Transfer contents to a mixing bowl. Fold in yogurt and thyme. Salt to taste.

INGREDIENTS

Harissa Paste:
½ head garlic, cut in half horizontally
2 T fennel seeds (14 g)
2 T cumin seeds (16 g)
7½ tsp coriander seeds (15 g)
1½ T black peppercorns (10 g)
½ onion, cleaned and cut in half
canola oil
1 cup each dried ancho and guajillo
  chiles (50 g each)
½ cup each dried chipotle and chile
  de arbol chiles (25 g each)
1½ T garlic, grated on microplane (12 g)
2 tsp cayenne (4 g)
¾ cup olive oil (150 ml)
salt and lemon juice to taste

Root Vegetables and Swiss Chard:
canola oil
1 sunchoke, peeled, cut into obliques
1 each peeled, turnip, carrot,
  rutabaga, cut into obliques
1 bunch rainbow Swiss chard, de-
stemmed, julienned

Grilled Flatbread:
½ cup warm water (115 ml)
½ tsp instant yeast or 1 tsp active yeast
1½ cups sifted flour (225 g), plus
  extra for dusting
½ tsp salt
canola oil
olive oil and salt to taste

Garnish:
lamb braising liquid
2 T butter (28 g)
fresh lemon juice
cilantro
mint
salt to taste

DIRECTIONS

Harissa Paste:
Preheat the oven to 300°F. Wrap the garlic halves in foil and bake for 45 minutes. Let cool, then squeeze roasted garlic out and reserve. Spread fennel, cumin, coriander and black peppercorns on a baking sheet. Toast for 10-12 minutes, until aromatic. Cool and grind seeds together.

Cook both sides of each onion half on the flattop or in a hot sauté pan evenly coated with canola oil. Put in a bowl with ancho, guajillo, chipotle and chile de arbol with enough hot water to cover. Let stand for at least 30 minutes.

Remove most of the chile seeds for a spicy harissa; reserve seeds and blend in extra at the end to taste for fiery harissa. In a blender, combine onion, chiles, roasted garlic, toasted spices, raw garlic grated on microplane, cayenne and olive oil and blend until smooth, using just enough water to create a puree. Season to taste with salt and lemon juice. Pass through a chinois.

Root Vegetables and Swiss Chard:
Pour canola oil to 1" depth in a deep pot and heat to 300°F. Fry the sunchoke until golden brown. Steam the turnip, carrot and rutabaga until knife tender, then drain and cool. In a separate sauté pan over medium heat, add all the Root Vegetables with just enough braising liquid to heat them through. Glaze with butter and finish with fresh lemon juice, Harissa Paste and salt to taste. Fold in julienned rainbow Swiss chard.

Grilled Flatbread:
Whisk water and yeast together in a stand mixer bowl. Add flour and salt and mix with dough hook on low speed for 6-7 minutes. The dough will pull away from the sides and form a ball but still be soft to the touch. Cover bowl with plastic wrap and let dough proof for 30 minutes, then cut into 4 equal portions with a dough cutter or knife. The dough can be stretched by hand, like pizza dough or rolled out on a lightly floured prep surface. Grill the flatbread approximately 2 minutes, until it bubbles and puffs up. Flip and cook on the other side until browned. Finish with olive oil and salt.

Plating:
Preheat the oven to 400°F. In a sauté pan, add the cooked shanks and roast in the oven for 3-4 minutes, basting continuously with Black Garlic Lamb Jus until completely glazed. Place the Black Garlic Glazed Lamb Shanks and harissa spiced vegetables on a platter. Spoon Almond and Pomegranate Chutney over the lamb shank and then sprinkle fresh cilantro and mint. Serve with Charred Orange and Kalamata Yogurt and Grilled Flatbread.

Bone Marrow Crusted Beef Cheeks
winter root vegetables, caramelized oyster mushrooms, grilled leeks, red wine pickled shallots, horseradish

Wine Pairing:

Solminer Blaufränkisch deLanda Vineyard, Santa Barbara County
Lo-Fi Gamay Noir/Pinot Noir, Santa Barbara County
Santa Barbara Winery Lagrein, Joughin Vineyard, Santa Barbara County
Potek Winery Kimsey Syrah, Ballard Canyon

Alternative Pairing:

North Coast Brewing Company Old Rasputin Stout

Chef's Notes:

If you've never eaten beef cheeks, biting into one with spicy marrow crust should convert you into a full-fledged beef cheek disciple. By far one of our favorites from our fall menu, this dish encapsulates all of the that season's greatest hits. I assure you the effort is worth every minute.

Prep Time:

3 hours active preparation, plus soaking bones and making pickles

Special Equipment Needed:

ice bath, 10-quart stockpot, 1-oz ladle, large rack, chinois (option: fine-meshed sieve), grill

Servings:

4

Editor's Note:

You will need 1 bottle of full-bodied red wine for this recipe, divided between the pickled shallots, red wine salt, beef cheeks and beef cheek jus.

INGREDIENTS

Veal Stock:
5 lb veal bones (2.27 kg)
mirepoix (2x recipe pg. 272)
1 head garlic, cut horizontally
6 sprigs fresh thyme
1 cup tomato paste (250 g)

Bone Marrow Crust:
3 lb marrow bones (1.4 kg)
salt
$\frac{1}{4}$ cup marrow fat (50 g), from bones
  or butter (if rendered marrow fat
  doesn't yield $\frac{1}{4}$ cup)
1 loaf brioche
1 cup onion (150 g), finely chopped
2 tsp garlic (6 g), finely chopped
1 tsp salt (3 g)
2 T white wine (26 ml)
1 T fresh thyme (5 g), de-stemmed,
  finely chopped
4 tsp fresh horseradish root (20 g), grated
olive oil, if necessary
salt and black pepper to taste

Red Wine Pickled Shallots:
3 shallots, thinly sliced
7 T each red wine vinegar and red
  wine (98 ml each)
$\frac{1}{4}$ cup sugar (50 g)
1 T salt (9 g)
$\frac{1}{4}$ cup water (58 ml)

Red Wine Sea Salt:
$\frac{1}{2}$ cup sel gris
red wine

DIRECTIONS

Veal Stock:
Preheat the oven to 400°F. Place the bones on a baking sheet in one layer and roast for 40 minutes or until caramelized. Place in large stockpot, cover with water and bring to a boil. Discard water, cover with fresh water and boil again. Skim off any impurities, then lower heat to simmer and whisk in tomato paste. Cook for 8 hours, then add mirepoix, garlic and thyme and simmer another 4 hours. Skim off the fat and foam with a ladle as it cooks. Let cool and strain stock. Discard all solids.

Bone Marrow Crust:
Soak marrow bones in salted water for 3 days, in the refrigerator. (Note: water-to-salt ratio should be 10 parts water to 1 part salt.) Replace the salted water periodically until the water is clear.

Preheat oven to 400°F. Drain and pat dry marrow bones, then place in a bowl that sits inside a larger bowl of ice. Remove bones and any bone fragments, leaving only the marrow. Roughly chop the bone marrow into pieces no bigger than the size of a corn kernel and return to bowl.

Place empty bones in one layer on a rack inside a baking sheet and bake for 30 minutes. Strain the fat into a measuring cup and reserve. If the measurement is less than $\frac{1}{4}$ cup, add butter to complete the ratio. Turn oven down to 275°F. Slice brioche into 1" cubes, then spread on a baking sheet and toast for 45 minutes, rotating every 15 minutes until lightly golden. (Note: the cubes must be evenly dehydrated and only lightly golden. Too much color and they will burn in final step of recipe. Rub a cube between your fingers to test—when dry, it will crumble completely.) Cool completely. Blend the brioche cubes in a food processor to a coarse powder. Sweat onions and garlic together in the marrow fat over medium low heat until completely tender. Once translucent, season with salt, deglaze with white wine, then fold in thyme and horseradish. Combine toasted crumbs with fat/onion/garlic mixture in a large mixing bowl and work with a spatula until the consistency is that of a moist piecrust. Add olive oil if it feels too brittle or dry. Season to taste with salt and pepper. Line a $\frac{1}{3}$-size hotel pan or 9" x 9" baking dish with parchment. Press marrow crust into dish and place another weighted pan on top to compress. Refrigerate to set, then slice Bone Marrow Crust into $\frac{1}{4}$"-thick slices and reserve in the refrigerator.

Red Wine Pickled Shallots:
Put the shallots into a nonreactive bowl. Heat vinegar, red wine, sugar, salt and water just below a simmer, then pour over the shallots. Marinate for a minimum of 72 hours. Drain before use.

Red Wine Sea Salt:
Preheat oven to 200°F (with fan on if you have a convection oven). Combine sel gris with just enough red wine to create the consistency of wet sand. Layer evenly on a Silpat on a baking sheet and dehydrate in oven for 24 hours or until completely dry. Cool and scrape into a small bowl. If the dried salt has clumped together, press gently with the back of a large spoon or mortar and pestle to break up lumps.

INGREDIENTS

Beef Cheeks:
1 lb beef cheeks (453 g)
salt
canola oil
mirepoix (per recipe pg. 272)
⅔ bottle red wine (500 ml)
approx. 4 cups veal stock (1 L)

Beef Cheek Jus:
1 T red wine vinegar (14 ml)
2 T red wine (28 ml)
1 bunch fresh thyme
1 head garlic, cut horizontally

Roasted Carrots:
4 baby rainbow carrots
2 T olive oil (26 ml)
1 tsp salt (3 g)

Rutabaga and Carrot Puree:
½ rutabaga, peeled, large dice
1 large carrot, peeled, large dice
approx. 2 cups heavy cream (480 ml)
salt to taste

Pan-Roasted Rutabaga:
½ rutabaga, peeled, large dice
olive oil
salt and lemon juice to taste

Grilled Leeks:
1 leek, sliced
olive oil
salt
approx. 1 cup white wine (230 ml)
1 sprig fresh thyme
salt and lemon juice to taste

Caramelized Oyster Mushrooms:
4 cups oyster mushrooms (100 g)
canola oil
2 T butter (28 g)
½ bunch fresh thyme
salt

DIRECTIONS

Beef Cheeks:
Remove the silver skin from the beef cheeks and pat cheeks dry with paper towels. Season evenly with salt. Heat a large pot evenly coated with canola oil until it rapidly smokes (oil will slowly start to produce smoke as it gets hot; when the smoke is released in volume, it is hot enough to develop an evenly seared crust on the cheeks). Sear cheeks on all sides, then remove. Turn down the heat to medium high and caramelize the mirepoix, then deglaze with wine and reduce the liquid volume by half. Add the beef cheeks and enough veal stock to cover. Either braise on the stove over low heat or wrap with aluminum foil and bake at 325°F for 1½–2 hours or until tender. Let cool in braising liquid. Reserve the braising liquid for Beef Cheek Jus.

Beef Cheek Jus:
Strain the braising liquid from beef cheeks into a pot. Reduce down to a sauce consistency over medium high heat, skimming off fat with a 1-oz ladle. Strain through a chinois or fine-meshed sieve into a saucepot. Add red wine vinegar, 2 T red wine, thyme and garlic and steep for 15 minutes. Strain again and adjust seasoning, if necessary.

Roasted Carrots:
Preheat oven to 350°F. Wash and peel carrots, reserving carrot tops. Toss carrots evenly in olive oil and salt. Roast until knife tender on a parchment-lined baking sheet.

Rutabaga and Carrot Puree:
Place rutabaga and carrots in a saucepot and cover with cream. Over low heat, simmer until knife tender. Use a slotted spoon or spider to transfer the cooked vegetables to a blender. Puree to a pudding consistency, adjusting with warm cream as necessary. Pass through chinois or fine-meshed sieve, then salt to taste.

Pan-Roasted Rutabaga:
Steam rutabaga until knife tender. Coat evenly with olive oil and season with salt, then let cool. Add olive oil to a sauté pan. Add rutabaga until caramelized on all sides. Season to taste with salt and lemon juice.

Grilled Leeks:
Preheat oven to 300°F. Evenly coat leek with olive oil and season with salt. Place in baking dish with thyme and cover halfway up with white wine. Wrap with foil and bake until knife tender. Grill until evenly marked, then season to taste with salt and lemon juice.

Caramelized Oyster Mushrooms:
Wash and dry mushrooms. Separate them, cutting very large pieces in half. Sauté in a smoking-hot pan evenly coated with canola oil until caramelized. (Note: mushrooms will cook down to approximately 1 cup.) Drain off all oil, then finish with butter, thyme and salt to taste. Drain off excess butter, then lay out evenly on a rack to cool.

INGREDIENTS

Garnish:
reserved carrot tops, de-stemmed
olive oil
lemon juice and salt to taste
fresh horseradish

DIRECTIONS

Plating:

Put the beef cheeks in a sauté pan and baste with the Beef Cheek Jus under a salamander or broiler set to 500°F. Heat the cheeks all the way through and create an even glaze with the sauce by spooning over the top. Remove from the salamander or broiler and cover with slices of Bone Marrow Crust. Broil until golden brown.

Coat reserved carrot tops lightly but evenly with olive oil. Season to taste with lemon juice and salt.

Sauce the serving plate with Rutabaga and Carrot Puree. Next plate Roasted Carrots, Pan-Roasted Rutabaga, Grilled Leeks and Caramelized Oyster Mushrooms. Arrange Beef Cheeks on top. Garnish with Red Wine Pickled Shallots, fresh horseradish, dressed carrot tops and a pinch of Red Wine Salt.

Skyler Gamble, General Manager, picking up an order in the kitchen. Opposite: oyster mushrooms.

Roasted California Chicken
black pepper grits, grilled sweet corn, jalapeño, ham hock, pickled okra, chicken jus

Wine Pairing:

Fess Parker Rodney's Vineyard Syrah, Santa Barbara County
Sandhi Mt. Carmel Pinot Noir, Sta. Rita Hills
Carr Vineyards & Winery Cabarnet Franc, Santa Ynez Valley
Arcadian Fiddlestix Vineyard Sta. Rita Hills Pinot Noir

Alternative Pairing:

21st Amendment Brewery El Sully Mexican-Style Lager

Chef's Notes:

My Nana lived in a ranch house in the middle of nowhere in Brazoria, Texas. When I visited as a kid, she served me true Southern grits. That memory opened a door to my dedication to her. These are all of her favorite ingredients on one plate.

Prep Time:

1½ hours active preparation plus prep including air-drying

Special Equipment Needed:

drying rack, China cap or colander, chinois (option: fine-meshed sieve), grill

Servings:

4-6

INGREDIENTS

Roasted California Chicken:
1 organic, free-range chicken
3 cups salt (390 g)
1¼ cups brown sugar (260 g),
 firmly packed
½ gallon water (2 L)
4 tsp whole peppercorns (10 g)
mirepoix (per recipe pg. 272)
1 bunch each fresh thyme and parsley

Pickled Okra:
10 whole okra (130 g)
½ cup champagne vinegar (105 ml)
1 T salt (9 g)
¼ cup sugar (50 g)
¼ cup water (58 ml)
1 T mustard seed (4 g)
1 T chile flake (3 g)

Ham Hock:
½ lb ham hock (227 g)
1 sprig fresh thyme
water

Chicken Jus:
4 lb chicken carcasses (1.8 kg)
canola oil
1 cup water (230 ml)
mirepoix (per recipe pg. 272)
1 head garlic, split
2 cups + 10 T white wine (600 ml)
⅓ cup sherry vinegar (76 ml)
2½ quarts chicken stock (2.4 L)
5 cups veal stock (1.2 L)
pork stock reserved from cooking
 Ham Hock
sachet:
 ½ bunch each fresh thyme and
 parsley

DIRECTIONS

Roasted California Chicken:
Dissolve salt and sugar in water, using a whisk and add peppercorns, mirepoix, thyme, parsley and butchered chicken. Brine the chicken in the refrigerator for 4 hours. Then drain, pat dry with paper towels and place chicken on a rack. Air-dry in the refrigerator for 72 hours.

Preheat the oven to 425°F. Bake the chicken for approximately 25-30 minutes or until browned and juices run clear (internal temperature of 160°F). Remove from the oven, and let it rest for 6 minutes before carving.

Pickled Okra:
Place okra into a nonreactive bowl. Heat the vinegar, salt, mustard seed, chile flake, sugar and water to a simmer and pour over the okra. Marinate in the refrigerator for a minimum of 72 hours. Drain before use.

Ham Hock:
Preheat the oven to 300°F. Cover the ham hock in water in a baking dish. Add thyme and bake for 3 hours until tender. Remove and reserve meat, reserve cooking liquid for Chicken Jus. Refrigerate meat, if needed, then rewarm 10 minutes before serving.

Chicken Jus:
Pat the chicken carcasses dry. Heat a large rondeau or large deep skillet evenly coated with canola oil to the smoke point, but do not burn the oil. Very carefully using tongs, place as many carcasses as will fit evenly in one layer. Brown evenly on all sides. Reserve and add remaining carcasses in batches, maintaining medium high heat.

Once all chicken has been browned, turn off heat. Carefully deglaze pan with 1 cup water. (Caution: this process will produce a quantity of dangerous steam.) Once the water has evaporated, brown the caramelized chicken carcasses a second time, one by one, developing a very deep chicken flavor.

Remove chicken carcasses from the pot and add mirepoix. Caramelize completely and add garlic and cook until it is softened. Deglaze with wine and sherry vinegar. Add carcasses, chicken stock, veal stock and reserved Ham Hock cooking liquid. Add water, if necessary, to cover carcasses. Simmer for 4-6 hours or until liquid volume is reduced by half. Remove and discard chicken carcasses. Strain contents through a china cap into a clean pot, pressing on the chicken carcasses to extract all liquid. Strain again through a chinois into a clean pot.

Continue to reduce to a velvety sauce consistency. Pass through a chinois (or sieve) 3 times, not pressing the solids through, just swirling the chinois and rinsing after each pass. Tie up fresh thyme and parsley in a sachet and add to stock. Keep warm until serving. (Tip: if you need to reserve the jus, chill in a bowl inside an ice bath, then refrigerate and reheat before serving.) Discard sachet before use.

INGREDIENTS

Black Pepper Grits:
2 cups chicken stock (460 ml)
2 cups water (460 ml))
2 tsp salt (6 g)
1 cup white polenta (160 g)
1 T black pepper (7 g)
4 T butter (56 g)
4½ oz mascarpone (127 g)

Grilled Sweet Corn:
1 corn on the cob
olive oil and salt to taste

Garnish:
1 T fresh jalapeño (3 g), sliced
5 T fresh chives (10 g), sliced
chicken stock
Ham Hock
Chicken Jus
1 T butter (14 g)
5 raw okra, sliced
olive oil, lemon juice and salt to taste
dandelion and mustard greens

DIRECTIONS

Black Pepper Grits:
Bring the stock, water and salt to a boil in a large pot. Pour the polenta in slowly, in a stream, whisking to incorporate it fully. Cook over medium heat for 30-45 minutes, whisking every 5 minutes. If polenta begins to set up before the grains are tender, add more water. When tender, fold in the pepper, butter and mascarpone. Keep warm until serving.

Grilled Sweet Corn:
Evenly coat corn with olive oil and season lightly with salt. Grill, cool, then cut kernels off cob.

Plating:
Quenelle the Black Pepper Grits and lay the Roasted California Chicken on top. In a saucepot warm corn kernels, raw okra, sliced jalapeño and Ham Hock with chicken stock and butter, until evenly glazed. Finish with lemon juice, salt and chives. Plate succotash in and around the chicken. Sauce the plate generously with Chicken Jus. Finish with lightly seasoned dandelion and mustard greens.

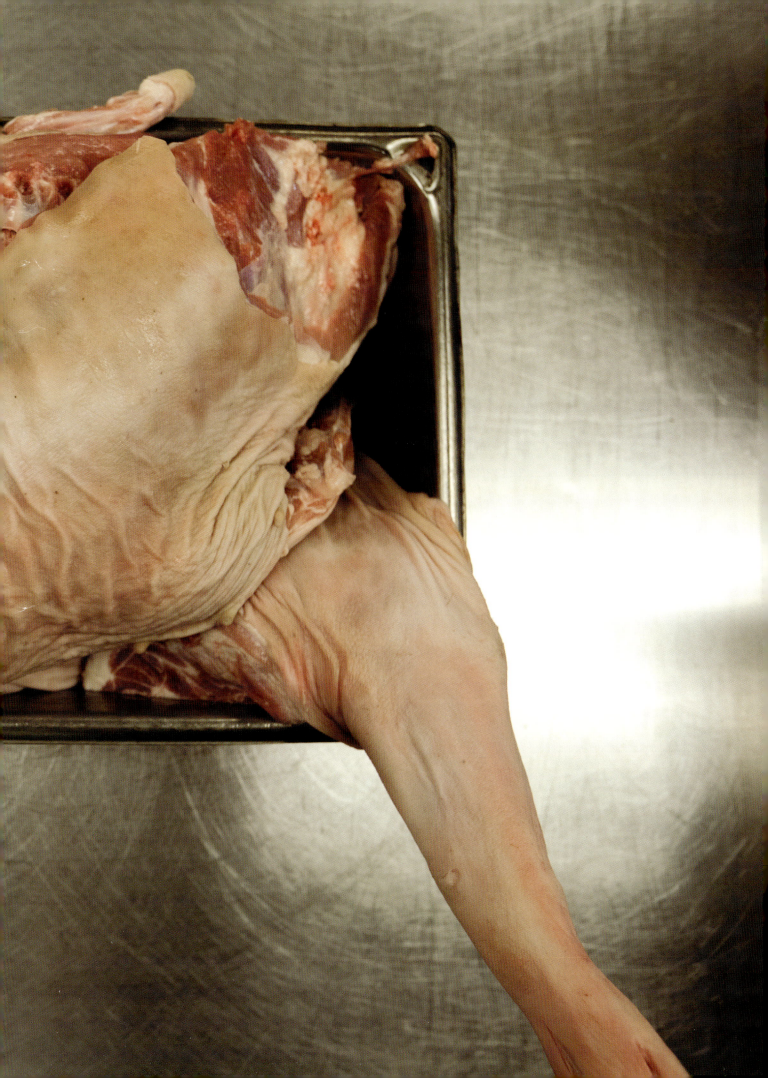

Porchetta di Testa

Wine Pairing:

Stolpman Sangio degli Angeli Sangiovese
Palmina Cortese, Cascina Cortese Vineyard, Santa Ynez Valley
Andrew Murray Vineyards Syrah, Tous Les Jours, Santa Ynez Valley
Buttonwood Winery & Vineyard, Cabernet Franc, Santa Ynez Valley

Alternative Pairing:

Ojai Valley Brewery Chapparal Sage Ale

Chef's Notes:

It is worth all the time and patience you have to do this right and not cut corners. We are very proud to serve this at The Lark. This is all about my respect for the pig and making sure everything is used. Chris Cosentino, the chef at a few of my favorite restaurants in San Francisco, inspired me to try this project. And I'm calling it a project rather than just a recipe. He started a butcher shop called Boccalone that I visited. He featured all sorts of bizarre cuts of cured meat you usually don't see. After I tried his version, I knew I wanted to one day create my own Porchetta di Testa. I proudly served chef Cosentino my version when he showed up to our communal table unannounced, and he told me it was delicious. I was nervous, self-conscious and relieved. My best advice when tackling this dish is to continue to reread the recipe until it makes complete sense.

Prep Time:

Five days minimum.

Special Equipment Needed:

several cotton kitchen towels, large nonskid cutting board, blowtorch, razor blade, boning knife, finely woven cheesecloth, butcher's twine, Cryovac® machine and bag or turkey brining bag, immersion circulator if available, 38-quart or larger stockpot, ice bath, Silpat

Servings:

10

Editor's Note:

Use a sharp and flexible boning knife. The cheesecloth needs to be finely woven to be sturdy enough to shape and contain the roulade. You can find this online or at gourmet kitchen stores.

INGREDIENTS

Porchetta di Testa:
whole Niman Ranch pig head
9⅓ T salt (75 g)
2 tsp pink salt (12 g)
zest of 12 lemons
1 cup chile flake (50 g)
1 bunch each fresh thyme, rosemary,
    oregano, parsley, stems separated
1 head garlic
2 cups Calabrian chile oil (400 ml)

DIRECTIONS

Porchetta di Testa:
Note on deboning the head: have dry kitchen towels on hand to mop up any juice and keep the head and surface dry to avoid the knife slipping. For best safety, use a sharp boning knife. Clean out the ears, nose and any crevices. Use a razor blade as a tool, if needed. Examine the nose and behind the ears very carefully to remove every speck of hair and dirt. Clean the head meticulously by using a blowtorch to remove hair. Sanitize the surface by running the flame over an area, but do not burn the skin. Wipe every inch with a cloth towel to insure all parts are impeccably clean.

Put a clean towel on top of a large nonskid cutting board and place the head upside down so the eyes are facing the cutting board and the snout is facing you. Take a sharp boning knife and cut the skin from the neck to the tip of the jaw, splitting the jaw skin in half. Start to work the end of the boning knife between the skin and the skull, gradually peeling the skin away from the head. Flip it over and continue to work the end of the knife along the bone, leaving the cheek meat attached to the skin. When the skin is almost detached, you can set the head on its neck and peel the skin away like a mask, cutting it away from the snout. The ears should be part of the skin, and the skin will be one homogeneous piece with no holes in it other than the eyeholes. Reserve the skull for stock. Check for membranes in the face-side of the skin and remove any you find; they will look like sweetbreads. There will be pockets of meat left on the skull: for instance, behind the jaw, behind the eyes and on the back of the head. Cut out and reserve all these bits, including the tongue, reserving in a bowl inside an ice bath. Remove the cartilage in the base of the tongue and use it with the skull to make Pork Stock below.

Lay out carved head on a clean work surface skin-side down. Season meat bits, tongue and the meat-side of the skin evenly with pink salt, then salt. Place the tongue on top of the snout— the back of the tongue will fit into the "pocket" at the end of the snout. Arrange the other meat bits in an even layer. Fold the ears into the eyeholes. In a blender, combine the zest, chile flake, thyme, rosemary, oregano, garlic, parsley and chile oil into a paste. Coat the meat side of the skin with a thick, even layer of herb paste. With the snout facing down, roll up left to right.

To keep the roulade together and shape it into as perfect a cylinder as possible, you will be wrapping it in fine-meshed cheesecloth, trussing it with twine. The goal of all these processes is to shape the roulade and keep it symmetrical. Cheesecloth purchased in a grocery store is often very loosely woven and not strong enough to keep the roulade together, so you may need to purchase finely woven (grade #50 or higher) cheesecloth from a gourmet shop or online. The cheesecloth needs to be at least 6" wider than the length of the roulade so each end can be tied securely with twine. Center the roulade on the end of the cheesecloth, then roll up tightly at least two turns. Tie up one end (call this end A) with a short piece of twine, snuggling the knot up as close as possible to the end of the meat. Tie up the other end (call this end B) with the end of a 4' piece of twine. Pick up the roulade by grabbing the cheesecloth extending from end B. Let the roulade hang down. With your other hand, wrap the twine around and around the

INGREDIENTS

DIRECTIONS

knot, cinching it tight, until you have a dozen or more turns of twine on the end. (See photo for illustration.) Knot the two ends of the twine tightly.

Turn the roulade 180 degrees and remove the short piece of twine from end A. Knot the end of a 4' piece of twine to it, snugging the knot as close to the end of the meat as possible. Hold end A up by the end of the cheesecloth and wrap a dozen or more turns of twine around the knot, cinching the twine tight. Knot the two ends of the twine tightly. Truss the wrapped roulade with twine to keep the cylindrical shape of the roulade. Reserve in the refrigerator until stock is ready.

For sous vide: vacuum pack roulade in a Cryovac® bag with cold pork stock and cook it in a water bath, with the immersion circulator set at 85°C (185°F), for 12-16 hours. For the home cook: simmer in pork stock at 185°F until very tender. Roulade is done when it releases gently when you push it, like the surface of a water balloon when pressed. If it still feels firm when you push on it, continue cooking. When done, cool in an ice bath for 90 minutes, turning every 15 minutes. If the roulade was in a Cryovac® bag, keep it in the bag to chill—if roulade was simmered without a bag, place it into a turkey brining bag, seal completely, then place in ice bath.

Remove roulade from bag separating any excess stock. Rewrap with several rounds of plastic, rolling up to make it as symmetrical as possible. Tie off and cinch both ends with twine. Seal again in a Cryovac® bag or brining bag. Submerge in ice bath for 24 hours, replacing ice as it melts and rotating the roulade occasionally. (This creates a round roulade without the flat bottom created when chilled on a flat surface.) Remove wrap and slice thinly into sheets.

Pork Stock:
pig skull
$1^{1}/_{2}$ x mirepoix
 (recipe pg. 272)
stems from thyme, rosemary and
 oregano above

Pork Stock:
Preheat the oven to 375°F. Pat the cleaned pig skull dry and roast in the oven for one hour. In a large pot, cover pig skull with water and add mirepoix. Simmer for 4 hours. Remove pig skull. Strain stock and chill in a bowl over an ice bath to reserve.

Pickled Maple Mustard Seeds:
approx. 2 cups maple syrup (600 ml)
$3^{1}/_{2}$ cups champagne vinegar (800 ml)
$1^{3}/_{4}$ cups water (402 ml)
1 T maple sugar (13 g)
6 cups whole yellow mustard seeds (400 g)
6 cups whole black mustard seeds (400 g)
salt to taste

Pickled Maple Mustard Seeds:
Bring maple syrup, champagne vinegar, water and maple sugar to a boil. Pour over the mustard seeds in a nonreactive bowl. Salt to taste and let marinate for a minimum of 72 hours.

Red Wine Sea Salt:
$^{1}/_{2}$ cup sel gris
red wine

Red Wine Sea Salt:
Preheat oven to 200°F (with fan on if you have a convection oven). Combine sel gris with just enough red wine to create the consistency of wet sand. Layer evenly on a Silpat on a baking sheet and dehydrate in oven for 24 hours or until completely dry. Cool and scrape into a small bowl. If the dried salt has clumped together, press gently with the back of a large spoon or mortar and pestle to break up lumps.

INGREDIENTS

Suggested Garnish:
1 bunch watercress, de-stemmed
3 breakfast radishes, shaved thinly
grilled sourdough levain
Calabrian chile oil

DIRECTIONS

Suggested Plating:
Cut parchment into sheets to receive individual roulade slices. Thinly slice the roulade, placing each slice onto a sheet of parchment. Plate a slice of roulade by picking up a sheet underneath and upending it onto the plate, then repeat with 2 more slices. Add dollop of Pickled Maple Mustard Seeds, sprinkle of Red Wine Sea Salt and slice of grilled sourdough levain. Garnish with watercress and radishes. Drizzle with Calabrian chile oil.

Ingredients for preparing Porchetta di Testa paste. Opposite: roulade.

 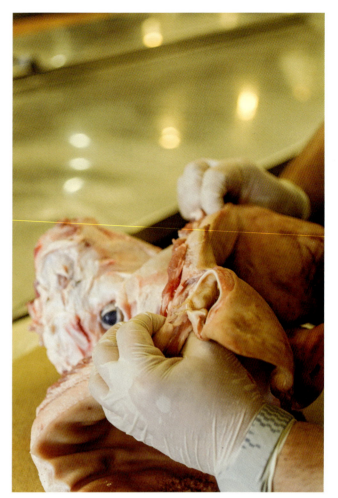

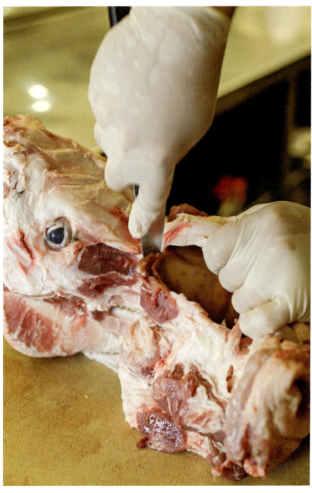 

The Basics

Brining & Curing

BRINING & CURING

Executive Sous Chef Taylor Melonuk cutting pork chops from rack of pork that has brined for 24 hours.

BRINING ADDS COMPLEX FLAVORS WHILE keeping meat tender and moist. Our kitchen philosophy is to always achieve as much flavor as possible, 100% of the time. People often ask what the secret ingredient to our roasted chicken is. It isn't an ingredient. It is a process. Brining or curing in our kitchen takes food to another level and gives true depth of flavor. With your first bite, you will see that mirepoix and the addition of aromatics change everything. There is never a question as to why you would brine and air-dry chickens. We do it because we want a juicy, flavor-packed bite, with crispy skin.

In most cases salt and sugar start the process, along with chopped vegetables and herbs in plenty of liquid. In this book we provide a variety of brining and curing recipes that work tremendously well in our kitchen. From the dry curing of pork belly and lamb ribs to the brining of pork chops, lamb shanks, venison or chicken, many years of recipe development, testing and refinement reside in these pages. Feel free to adjust a recipe to incorporate your own preference for citrus, herbs or spices in order to enhance a dish and make it more of your own.

HOW TO CURE PORK BELLY.

START WITH A SHARP KNIFE. Pat the pork belly dry completely so it is easy to handle.

USING THE LENGTH OF THE knife, not the tip, score the pork belly diagonally in both directions (like a crosshatch) to allow cure to absorb evenly.

EVENLY SLICE THE BELLY INTO three sections, making it easier to handle and allowing surface area for the dry cure to penetrate. Using the tip of your knife on the skin side, gently pierce the skin in the thickest areas to create as many openings in the pork belly for the cure to be absorbed.

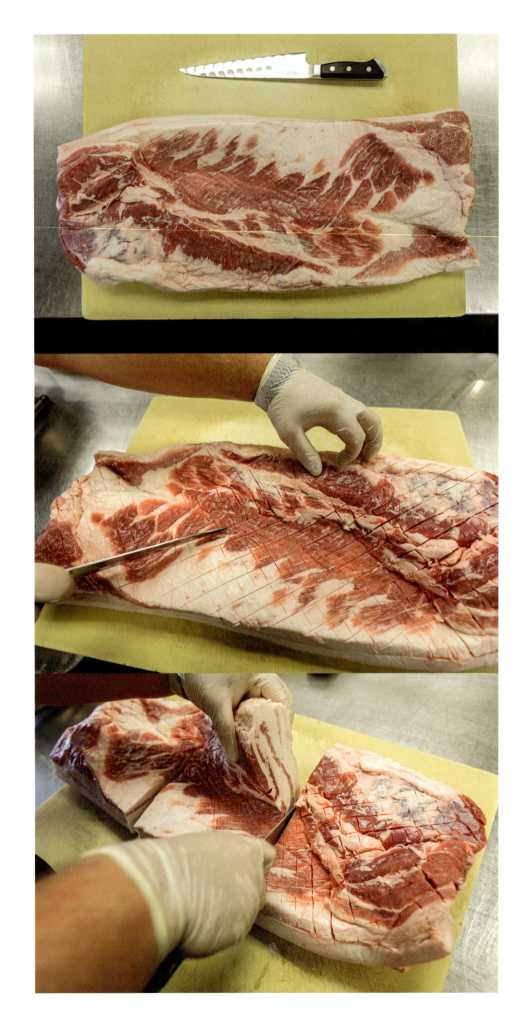

PREHEAT OVEN TO 325°F. EVENLY toast fennel, star anise, garlic, coriander, chile and mustard seed on a sheet pan for 12-15 minutes or until aromatic, stirring occasionally to prevent burning.. Let cool, then grind in a mortar and pestle.

MIX WITH SALT, PINK SALT and sugar in a mixing bowl with a whisk. Coat the pork belly in the dry cure. Wrap and marinate in the refrigerator for 72 hours, checking every 12 hours to ensure meat is evenly coated.

AFTER 72 HOURS, RINSE PORK belly, pat dry and it is ready to smoke.

The Basics

Pickling & Fermenting

PICKLING & FERMENTING

Pickling heirloom green tomatoes. Opposite: selection of pickled vegetables.

I'D GROWN UP THINKING PICKLES were what we bought from neighborhood gas stations that were room temperature, neon green and sealed in a bag with explosively concentrated brine. At one point during my break from culinary school in 2006, I made my way to Manhattan. I'd heard about a hot new place called Momofuku. Jars of pickles lined the countertop, and I ordered the house pickles on the menu. This simple dish came out with 12 varietes, all pickled differently.

How were they *that* good? I remember romanesco, rainbow carrot, cauliflower, daikon radish, onions, pole beans and more. I was amazed. They all had a different feel. David Chang had figured it out.

Pickling is amazingly simple and yet yields complex flavors. The recipes in this cookbook are written to enhance the true nature of each ingredient. Chef Berthold in San Francisco taught me the magic ratio of 2-1-1: two parts vinegar, one part sugar, one part water. It is a universal recipe for the balance of flavor.

Here is an example. We find a vegetable or fruit on hand that doesn't have a home on our menu, and we want to preserve it. Cippolini onions made the cut one day.

"Hey, JP," Serge asked. "What do you want to do with all these cippos left over from our last chicken set?"

"I think they'd be delicious on our new grilled eggplant dish," I said. So just like that, it happens. We quarter the peeled onions. We create a quick solution of champagne vinegar, sugar, water and a little salt. We bring the solution up to a boil and pour it over the onions. Easy as that. And it is back on the menu.

When I create a new dish, I almost always add a pickled element. I love what pickled vegetables bring out. A long time ago, my dad got a recipe for pickled okra, and I remember year-round it was in our fridge. It sounds obviously Southern, but okra sure does grow nicely in the hot, humid climate. Today most fruits and all vegetables will find themselves in a tangy solution in my kitchen.

WHY MAKE HOT SAUCES? BECAUSE you can capture the essence of summer in a bottle to enjoy year-round. Fermentation is a preservation method for food and a way to develop new flavors and attractive qualities for an ingredient we are already using. Lacto-fermentation is the oldest form of food preservation. Using only salt, water and a vegetable, the brine creates an anaerobic environment where only lactobacillus bacteria survive. This is what we want because lactobacillus bacteria act as a preservative to keep harmful bacteria from forming.

Habanero Fireball Hot Sauce is simple to prepare. First, use a sharp knife and be sure to wear gloves when working with chiles. Slice fresh habaneros into halves and place in a nonreactive container. Some people prefer to remove the seeds. Make enough brine (water and dissolved salt) to completely immerse the slices. Cover the container with folded parchment paper and let it sit at room temperature. Stir occasionally. Don't worry if you see mold start to develop. The mold is fine and part of the fermentation process. As long as there is enough salt in the brine and the chiles remain covered, it is doing exactly what it is supposed to be doing. Just scrape the mold off. And remember to stir the mixture. After two weeks strain the peppers from the brine and add two simple ingredients, salt and distilled white wine vinegar because its sharp flavor adds to the hot sauce. Consistency is very important. If it is too thick, it will be too intense. If too thin, it will have little impact. Our Habanero Fireball Hot Sauce captures the fiery essence of the chile while also being tasty and a fine addition to many a dish.

You've got to be a pretty big fan of heat for this one. I gave it a bad name on purpose because when you say it out loud, you realize it's going to light you up and make your nose run. "Habanero Fireball" is, however, delicious and easy to make. Remember to wear gloves and don't accidentally touch your special parts or eyes while making it.

1 lb habanero (453 g), sliced, no stems
3 T salt (24 g or 5% of raw habanero weight)
½ cup white wine vinegar (112 ml)

Coat peppers evenly with salt and let sit at room temperature for one day. Cover completely with water and store covered in a dark environment for two weeks. Keep at room temperature (75°F) and stir daily. After two weeks, blend in a Vitamix or high-powered blender with vinegar for it to spin smoothly. Adjust consistency with water used to ferment habanero peppers. Pass through a chinois. You can store this hot sauce for months in the refrigerator. But why would you? Use it daily. It goes with nearly every meal.

Fermenting habanero chiles. Opposite: a bottle of Habanero Fireball Hot Sauce.

The Basics

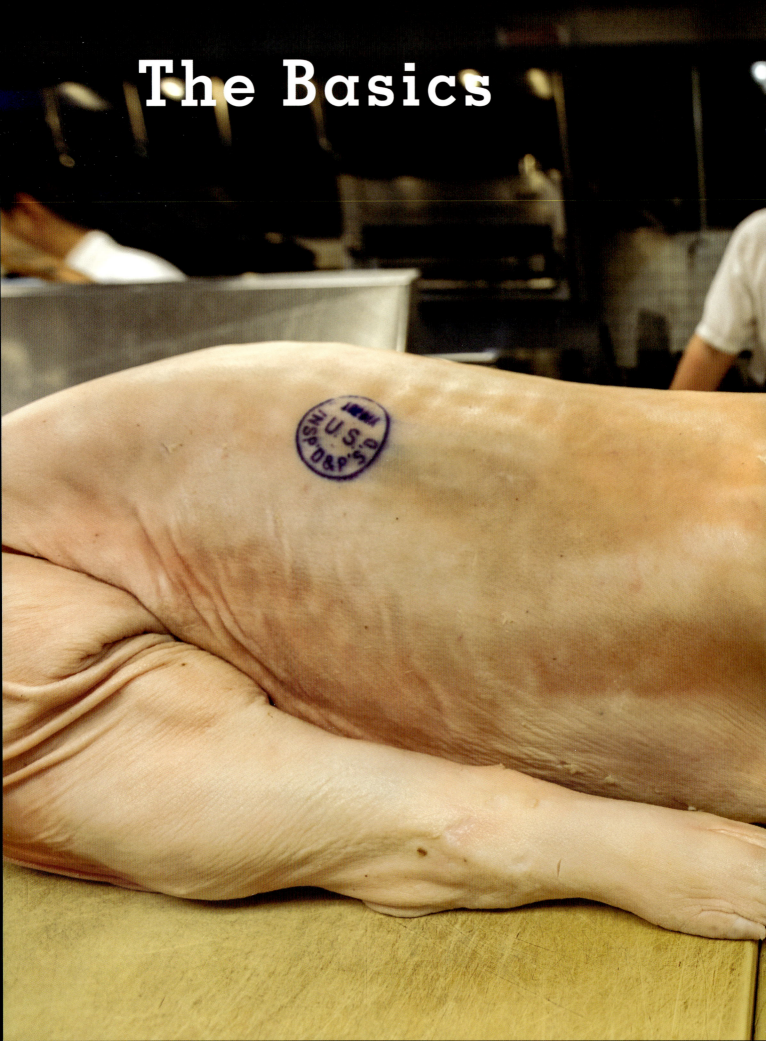

Butchering

BUTCHERING

Executive Sous Chef Taylor Melonuk butchering pig. Opposite: filleted red snapper.

I N THE KITCHEN EVERY MORNING, we are given the great responsibility to ensure that an animal that has given us its life is handled with respect and professionalism.

Without the proper training, a sharpened knife and the right space and temperature, many things can and will go wrong. Restaurants run on paper-thin margins, and not getting a full yield from any ingredient is wasteful and irresponsible. But if you don't work in restaurants, I get it. So what do you do if your buddy gives you some extra doves from his hunting trip? What happens when your cousin gives you a cooler full of fish and says, "Want these?" Will you study up or just wing it?

I honestly watched Chris Cosentino on YouTube for 3 hours straight before I touched my first pig head. I also had a teacher in San Francisco named Ming Lee who had a great sense of humor, but took butchering very seriously. I asked if I could butcher the branzino, the zino, one day.

He said, "Get the meat station set up early today and I'll save you a few." So there I was, clueless and eager as could be. "Do you have a slicer to butcher these fish? JP, do you have tweezers for the pinbones? We need to scale these fillets—do you know how to do that?" I was stumped and out of luck. He generously handed me everything I needed.

Carefully watching him, I imitated his every move. However, Chef Jason Berthold walked up to the table, and I felt my guts sink. Now this guy is a badass. I took every last thing he said to heart and always welcomed his advice. I don't think I ever saw him screw anything up. He butchered everything with more attention to detail than anyone I have ever seen. But that day I had blown it. "JP! You can never be clean enough when filleting fish! Clean up these scales! Look at all the meat you missed! Wipe your knife off! Don't make a mess!"

It was true. I had made a mess, and there was shit everywhere. I just wanted to jump right in because like

Executive Chef Jason Paluska carrying butchered pig. Opposite page: chicken ready to butcher.

most, you think, I'll learn as I go; it's all good. But it is not "all good."

If you end up mangling a fish because you leaned on it by accident or sliced it incorrectly or, even worse, you forgot to ice it down, then you are SOL. You instantly feel as if you failed. The flip side is you figure it out by paying attention and practicing. Go ahead and make fish fumet with fish frames (bones), grill the collars and beer batter those fillets. You will gain a sense of accomplishment that feels right for you and for that speckled trout you caught at Surfside Beach, Texas, or wherever you tear it up with your rod and reel.

HOW TO FILLET A FISH.

START WITH A SHARP KNIFE. Pat your fish dry to make it is easy to handle.

CUT DOWN TO THE SPINE right behind the pectoral fin.

BEGINNING ALONG THE BACK, CUT as deep as you can, parallel and flush to the spine, using the length of the blade, not the tip.

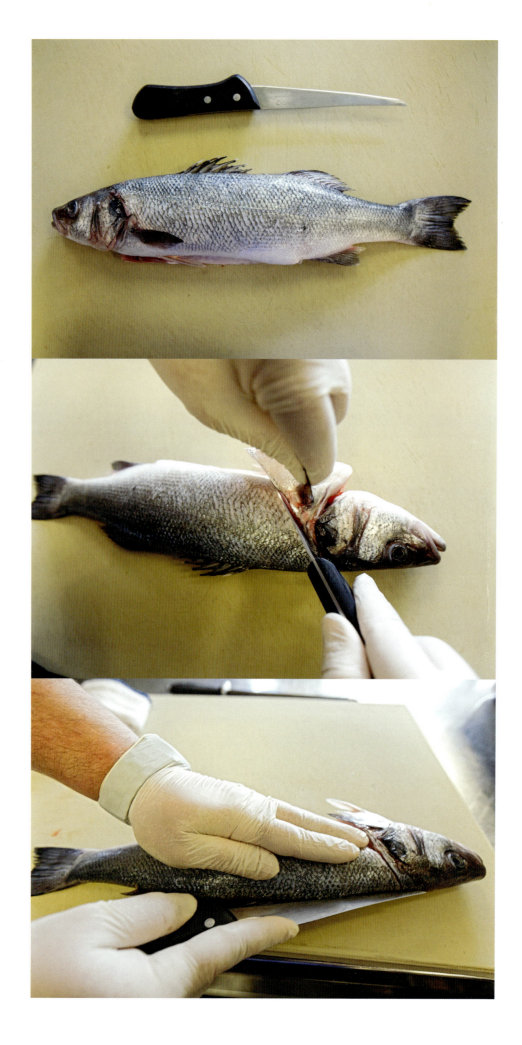

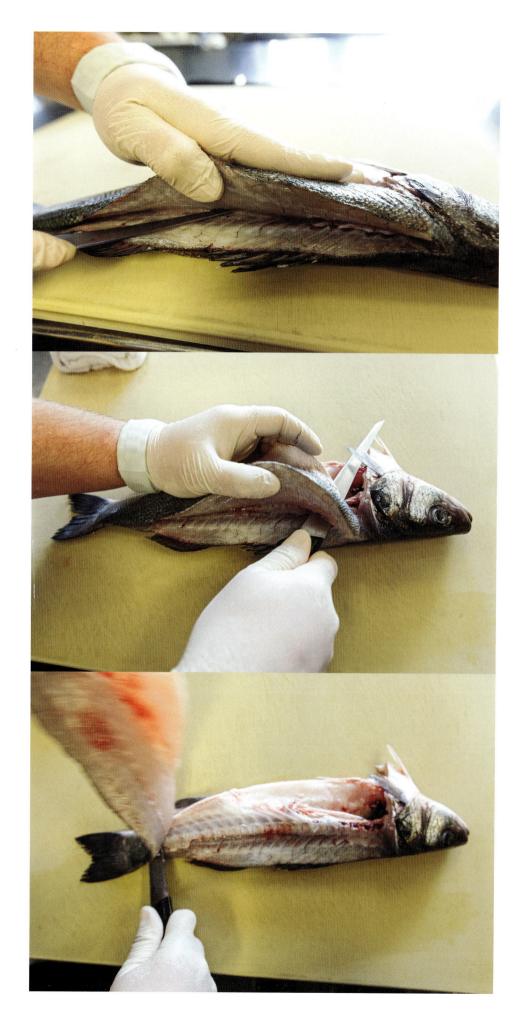

CAREFULLY CARVE THE FILLET AWAY from the spine, making sure to keep your knife against the bone.

PLACE YOUR KNIFE UNDER THE entire width of the fillet and angle your knife ever so slightly into the backbone.

SLIDE YOUR KNIFE CAREFULLY DOWN the backbone to release the fillet cleanly. Always keep the angle slightly down. A 10° angle works best so that you don't cut upward into the fillet.

THE FISH SHOULD LOOK AS IF it were butterflied with the tail still attached.

CUT OFF THE SKELETON AT the tail using scissors.

HOLDING YOUR KNIFE PARALLEL TO the cutting board, slice just underneath the rib cage, down and across, being careful not to cut into the flesh. You are carving the rib cage out of the fish. By butterflying it, you are saving all the meat below it.

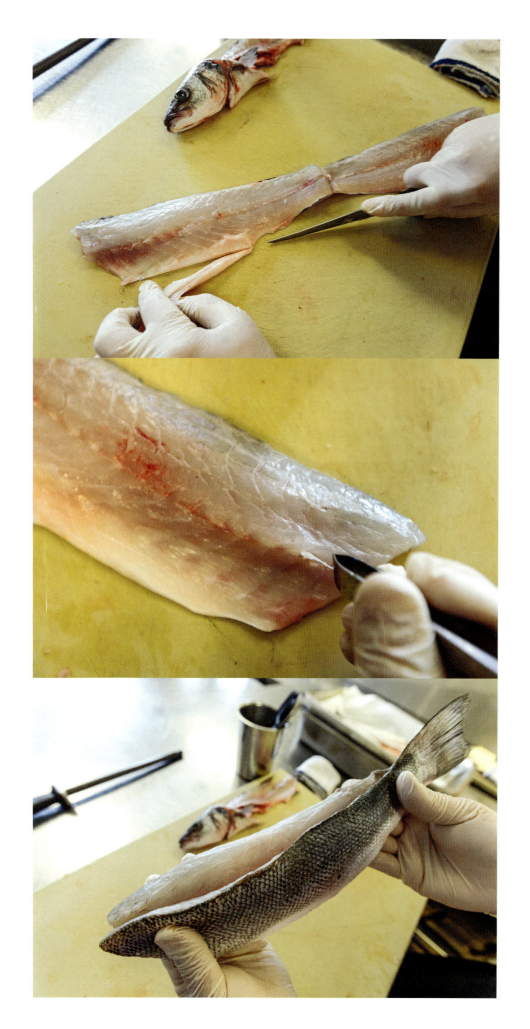

If you were to cut it off square, you would lose all that meat. It would be a very poor yield. For presentation purposes, I like to square up the belly.

Using fish tweezers, pull out each of the tiny pin bones in the same direction they protrude. If you pull the opposite direction, you will tear the fillet. If you run your finger across the center, you can feel the bones.

The fillets, still attached to the tail, are now ready to cook.

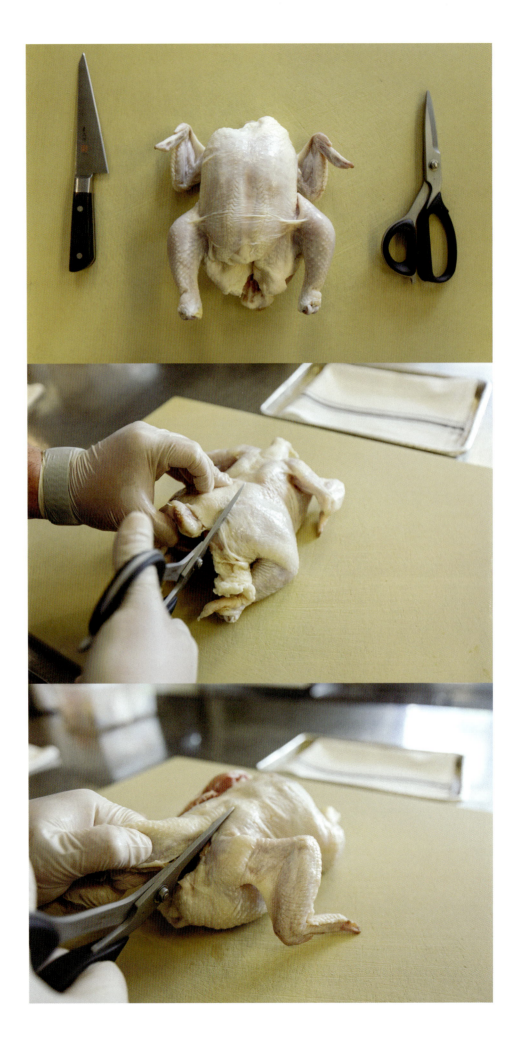

HOW TO BUTCHER
A CHICKEN.

START WITH A
SHARP BONING
knife and a pair
of good kitchen
shears.

TRIM THE BACK
OUT FIRST, using
shears, cutting
along the spine,
starting from the
tail.

ROTATE THE
CHICKEN AND
CUT along the
spine from the
opposite side,
starting at the
top of the neck.

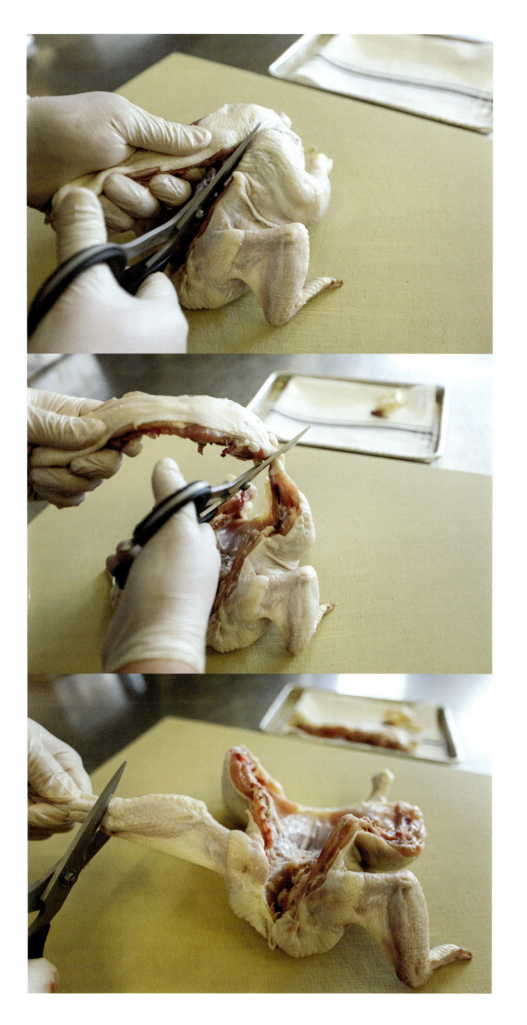

CONTINUE CUTTING PARALLEL TO THE spine, all the way through.

CLEANLY CLIP THE BACKBONE AWAY.

TRIM THE WING TIPS. THE reason is that when you roast the chicken the tips generally burn before the chicken has finished cooking.

269

THE FIRST
INCISION WITH
THE boning
knife should be
in between the
breast bone and
the breast.

GENTLY SLIDE
YOUR KNIFE
DOWN along the
sternum toward
the base of the
breast.

CAREFULLY
SLICE BELOW THE
BREAST meat,
holding the knife
firmly against
the sternum. You
must maintain
pressure against
the bone so that
you don't cut
into the meat.

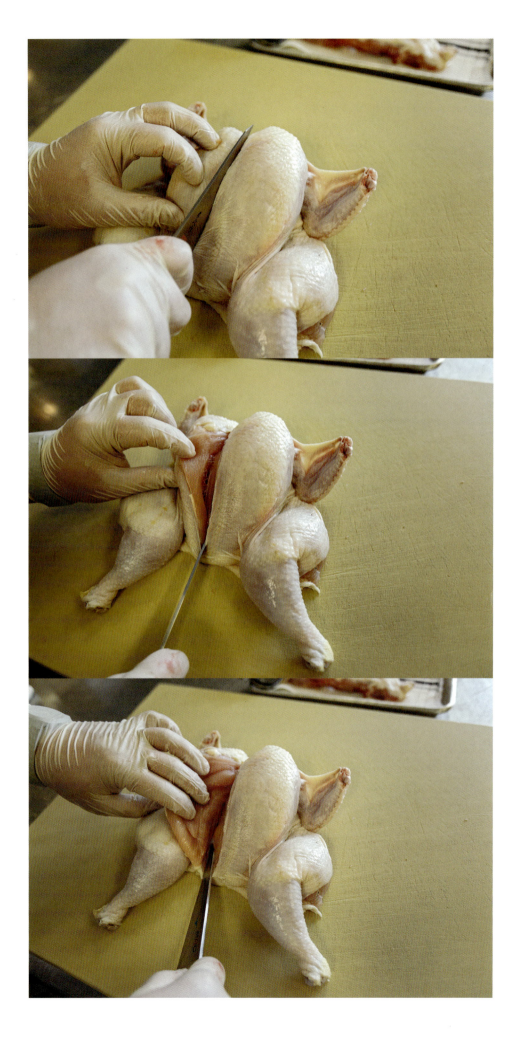

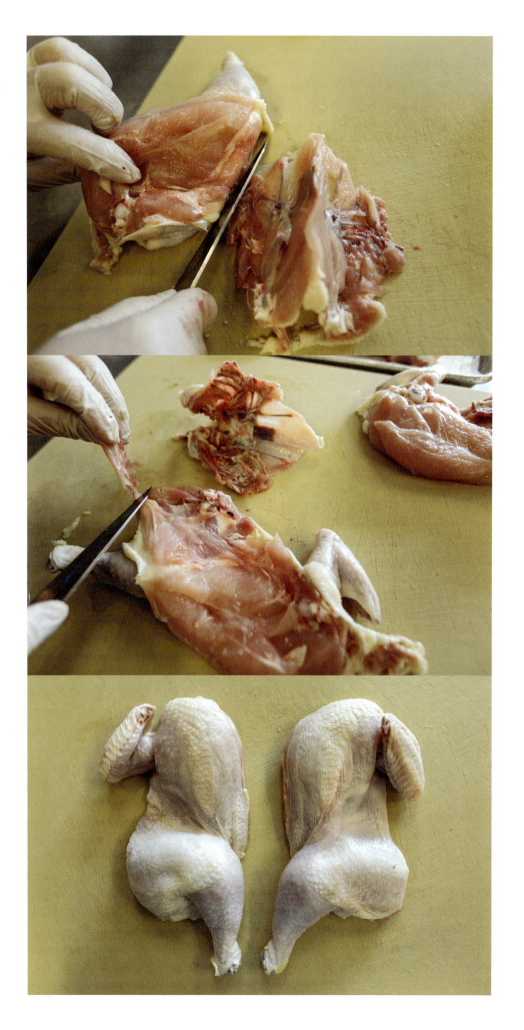

CONTINUE TO FOLLOW THE STERNUM all the way until the breast, leg and thigh are removed.

DOUBLE-CHECK FOR ANY REMAINING BONE fragments. Cleanly trim them away. When chicken is properly butchered, you can see that the sternum has little meat left on it.

TWO HALF CHICKENS READY TO be brined and then air-dried.

NOTES FROM THE EDITOR: TAMA TAKAHASHI

MISE EN PLACE

Mise in place is French for "everything in its place." Have your ingredients ready, assemble the pots and tools you need, be aware of the time each part of the final dish needs to be started. Think of how you will plate the dish for a beautiful presentation. Ingredients are listed in order of use and directions in order of the start time of each component—some need to start before the previous one is completed. For example, the Black Garlic Lamb Shank broth must be started while the shank is brining. Reading a recipe carefully is part of mise en place. So, though some of the recipes can be dashed off in half an hour or less, many recipes require preparation ahead of time.

QUALITY INGREDIENTS

The Lark cultivates relationships with local purveyors so their ingredients are incredibly fresh. They source responsibly and organically whenever possible.

WINE, VINEGAR AND OIL

Quality ingredients yield the best results.

SCRATCH KITCHEN

The Lark makes everything from scratch. They make their own pasta which they hand-cut; they create spice blends by toasting the ingredients whole, and then grind and blend them; they make their own jams and marmalades; they simmer their sauces for hours from stock made in-house that can include roasted bones, mirepoix and fresh herbs; they pickle their vegetables in peak season; and they butcher and then brine or cure their meats and poultry for up to 72 hours. The bread and pastries are all baked in-house.

MEASUREMENTS

Professional kitchens use weight measurements (grams, liters) instead of volume (cups, tablespoons). Weight is more precise, making it easier to scale a recipe up or down. Since most home cooks use volume measurements, we include both. An inexpensive digital scale is very helpful. The food at The Lark showcases robust flavors and Chef Jason has designed the various components of each recipe to create a harmonious whole. Rely on your palate as you cook for a final decision. Taste each step of the recipe.

EGGS

A medium egg weighs approximately 45 grams. Adjust for other sizes. A jumbo egg can be 50% larger. Eggs should be used at room temperature.

MIREPOIX

Mirepoix is another French culinary term. It is diced vegetables that The Lark uses as a flavor base. The traditional mirepoix is two parts onion, one part carrots, and one part celery. The Lark recipe calls for 500 g onion (1 large), 250 g carrot (1 large), 250 g celery (3 stalks), all roughly chopped unless otherwise noted.

BUTTER

All recipes call for unsalted butter.

SALT

Salt is an essential nutrient that is also critical to cooking. Applied in the right amount at the right time salt intensifies and enhances flavors. No other single ingredient has such a universal impact. Used in a brine it helps meat absorb richer and fuller flavors, and in curing it breaks down proteins and retain moisture.

All salts aren't created equal. The Lark recipes call for Diamond Crystal Kosher Salt—a tablespoon weighs 9.75 grams. You will need to make adjustments if you use any other type of salt. A tablespoon of table salt weighs a whopping 18.6 grams, whereas a tablespoon of Maldon Sea Salt weighs only 8.4 grams. Even kosher salts aren't the same. A tablespoon of Morton's Kosher salt weighs 14.75 grams.

SHAVED VEGETABLES

Several recipes call for shaved or thinly sliced vegetables. A mandoline is the best tool for uniformly thin slices. Do not become distracted when operating a mandoline.

HERBS, SPICES AND NUTS

Toast whole spices at 325°F for 8-10 minutes or until aromatic. Toast nuts at 300°F for 10-12 minutes. When blending spices, stop and stir occasionally to prevent spices packing the bottom of the blender. The Lark uses Italian parsley.

TASTE

Use your sense of smell and taste to guide you through the recipes. Pay attention to sensory cues. The aromas of cooking can be a cook's special pleasure or a warning. Pay attention to your food as you cook it. Taste every layer along the way. You are the final arbiter.

Many recipes yield extra servings of a particular component. I hope you will appreciate having jars of fragrant and tasty sauces, pickles, and dressings in your refrigerator as much as I did while testing these recipes!

Heirloom tomatoes from the Goleta Farmers Market.

In the Beginning

CLAY AURELL

CLAY AURELL OF AB DESIGN Studio Inc. is the architect who redesigned the historic property for adaptive reuse. "One of the biggest challenges was putting in a high-style, high-design, modern restaurant while utilizing as much of the original structure as I could. Any time we convert a historic building to a new use, we have to comply with new codes and generally update the structure and all of the system inside and out. For example, we needed to create a positive flow of water away from the doors (all 8 of them) to drain out to the parking lot and into planters, etc. I spent many nights with a red pencil and a glass of red wine, sitting at my kitchen table, working out the heights of the door thresholds and how the water would move away from the openings. This was a true challenge of intellect and 3-D thinking."

TED BRUCKNER

TED BRUCKNER IS THE SENIOR Project Manager for Young Construction who did all of the shell-core and tenant improvement work on the property. Ted's experience, steady leadership and creative problem-solving skills were invaluable throughout the two-year complicated construction process. Ted appreciated that The Lark warehouse spoke to Santa Barbara's history. "The building has been a fixture in Santa Barbara for close to a hundred years. Some of the original building structure was uncovered and left exposed as design elements, like brick walls, plank-sheathed roof structure, concrete columns, etc. New, rusting structural steel components were added, and some of the finishes were chosen as a nod to the industrial history of the building and the neighborhood."

DOUG WASHINGTON

DOUG WASHINGTON, OWNER OF THE acclaimed Town Hall, Salt House and Anchor & Hope restaurants in San Francisco and Irving Street Kitchen in Portland, designed the interior and exterior spaces using a fascinating array of repurposed elements by scouring flea markets and salvage yards throughout the state. Doug brings operations expertise to his dynamic design, setting the stage for efficiency while still creating a transformative experience for our guests. Doug's career in the restaurant business began at 15 as a busboy in a French restaurant in Vancouver, British Columbia, where he grew up. Doug has been a beloved Bay Area hospitality icon for more than 30 years and has received critical acclaim for his design, creative concept development and gracious style.

KATIE & DAVID HAY

KATIE AND DAVID HAY, OWNERS of Central Coast Real Estate, were Project Managers for the development of 131 Anacapa among numerous other properties in the neighborhood. Katie's tenacity and creative problem-solving were crucial in navigating a complicated development process with the City of Santa Barbara. David provided a strong and steady voice in managing the business details of the project. Their contributions were invaluable. They continue to manage the property today.

RICK MUSMECCI

RICK MUSMECCI, PROJECT SUPERINTENDENT, WAS on-site every day to ensure all the complex elements of construction flowed smoothly. "The vision Sherry and Doug had for the project was incredible, although at times I wondered how I was going to make the vision become reality. A 40-foot semitruck showed up one day, loaded with what looked like Sanford and Son's front yard. I was informed it would become part of the build. Amazingly enough, 90% of it was used inside and outside of the building. It worked, and the result was fricking amazing!"

DAN BUSH

DAN BUSH, AN ACCOMPLISHED BUILDER and finish carpenter, was Doug Washington's right-hand man. In addition to all the interior carpentry work, he made by hand all the tables for The Lark, including the one-ton, 18-foot-long, live-edge communal table at the heart of the restaurant. "I met Dan Burke (my buddy) up in the Oregon woods and saw this enormous tree with the top blown off during the Columbus Day storm back in October 1962. It was a huge, old-growth Douglas fir tree that had been slowly dying over the last 50+ years. It was near a private school that used this area for nature walks, and the tree was starting to become unsafe. So we cut the tree down at the bottom of this canyon and cut it up into 36-foot-long-by-3-inch–thick slabs right there in the woods as it lay on its side. We pulled those slabs up the canyon by hand to a staging area. Trust me when I say this: I will never do that again, but it was a great workout and experience to try only once."

The Lark under construction one month before opening.

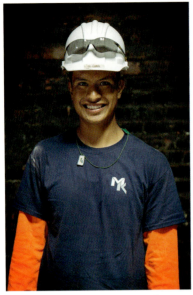
Guillermo Cervantes, construction.

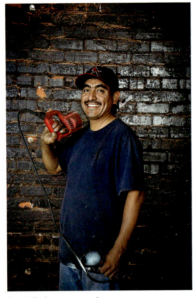
José Salazar, steel.

Nick Khreisat, steel.

Alexi Bayly, electric.

"Magic" Mike Lionello, electric.

Tommy Moreno, tile.

Durbiano, fire suppresion.

Art Grossman & Sons, HVAC.

Roy Rodriguez, electric.

Antonio Cervantes, concrete.

Miguel Cervantes, concrete.

Manuel Cervantes, concrete.

Homer Kelley, electric.

Damon Millar, doors and windows.

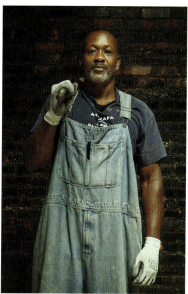

Willie Slone, plumbing.

"I MET INTERNATIONALLY RENOWNED PHOTOGRAPHER Macduff Everton at an exhibition of his work at African Women Rising, a local nonprofit I have been involved with over the last 10 years. Macduff's impressive body of work includes exploring culture and community around the world. Macduff and I started sharing the collective stories of the individuals who built The Lark and realized what an extraordinary example it was of the greater community of Santa Barbara. He began photographing the construction workers—the plumber, the concrete man, the tile setter—to document their work as part of the effort. Here in California, many of the craftsmen and laborers are Spanish-speaking. This was a great opportunity for me to practice my Spanish as we chatted regularly about their families and their lives. I hope when they see their images in our book telling their stories, they will feel empowered and recognized for their importance in building our business. Because not only do we serve a community, we employ a community, and that's been one of the best parts of this entire project."

SHERRY VILLANUEVA, CO-OWNER

Tim Benavente, Hugo Perez, Oscar Rodriguez and Raul Zamora, construction.

Juan Ortiz, Ignacio Ramos, Ceferino Ruiz, and Marco Antonio Ortega, construction

Crew from Mike Kelley Construction.

"WE DECIDED TO WRAP THE top of the three booths in The Lark with bison hide to give it an organic feel, while having the atmosphere of being inside an old railroad car. By this time, I'd been there for three months, working EVERY day, no days off, and my mind was needing some play time. I cut a piece of the hide, tied a Windsor knot in it and put it on around my neck. I started getting that look from some of the other subs like, 'What's that guy wearing?' so I started making more of them out of the scraps, and it became our uniform for Friday dress-up day. People started laughing and cracking jokes. This went on for weeks. Matter of fact, my original tie is hanging off of the sprinkler pipe in the ceiling in The Lark. How funny, all I tried was to get a good laugh, and it turned into more than that, memories that will always last.

"I spent four months here to get the job finished. It was my first time in Santa Barbara. Beautiful people were walking around everywhere. It was always sunny. I learned that Jason Paluska makes the best olives. I met new friends I still stay in touch with. I bought a Harley-Davidson and trailered it home. I went shark fishing and caught nothing. I golfed almost every day after work, wore hemp shirts for the first time, learned to played bocce ball and met Greg, the totem pole carver, who lived across the street from the project. I traded Greg some wood beams I brought down from Oregon for his boat. In return, he carved me a five-foot-tall custom totem pole. And not to forget, thanks to Dan Russo, the general manager, I experienced the worst hangover ever on record."
DAN BUSH, FINISH CARPENTER

"THERE IS A CERTAIN SOULFULNESS about The Lark that is hard to put your finger on. I think part of it comes from the intensity of purpose we all shared in building it. A great example is the fact that every table in the restaurant was built from the same tree that Dan Bush had milled in the forest. The tables, including the impressive communal table, are all connected in a visceral and powerful way.

"One of my most moving moments, as we completed the project, was receiving a gift that Rick Musmecci had made for me. Rick collected found objects from the early days of excavation and displayed them beautifully in a wooden box he made by hand from scrap wood and metal he also found on-site. I loved that it represented the history of the place, the heart he poured in to building the restaurant and that it was this sweet box with the beauty of a handcrafted object. We proudly hung it in the dining room for everyone to share."
SHERRY VILLANUEVA, CO-OWNER

"I AM VERY PROUD OF the end result. It couldn't have happened without everyone's contribution, from the people involved with the design to the craftsmen performing their trade."
TED BRUCKNER, GENERAL CONTRACTOR

Geoffrey Turner, Jerry Ignozzitto and Dustin Shepphird, equipment installation.

Jeff Dunch, Jr., Andrew Gerbac, Sergio Lopez, Pat Laughlin and Jeff Dunch, plumbing.

Miguel, Antonio, Guillermo and Manuel Cervantes, concrete and construction.

"THE LARK WAS SPECIAL, ONE of the most challenging (and involved) design projects I've ever done. It would be safe to say that this was the same for many of us who worked on it. From the construction chief to the many artisans and subcontractors to Sherry and Jason and Dan, everyone involved in creating it and getting it to opening day was in 110%. It was truly a collaborative effort with an amazingly talented group. When problems came up, there always was someone who knew someone somewhere that could fix it—by tomorrow! I can't remember a time when we allowed a great idea or detail to be thrown away because it 'couldn't be done.'

"One of the first things we agreed on was that we had no interest in transporting people out of Santa Barbara with the design and vision; we wanted the opposite. The Lark was to be a celebration of the history, the culture and the people of this great city with a mix of industrial (you can hear the train roar by every couple hours), warmth and natural beauty (it truly is the American Riviera) and organic elements (the country/the farm). When you enter the restaurant, we wanted you to feel a sense of all of these things without them being overt.

"Located in a historic warehouse originally built in the 1920s, The Lark connects the romance and nostalgia of the past with the excitement of a modern future through the blending of vintage, repurposed objects with original, urban industrial materials. We tried to utilize the outdoors as much as possible and to break down the walls between the two. In fact, the patios have more seating than the dining rooms. The intention was to have one flow into the other. The lighting throughout the entire place is original—I designed each fixture for each location.

"I incorporated a 100-year-old confessional from Provence, France, and three enclosed dining booths with stretched bison-leather ceilings into the design, along with French glass windows looking into an open kitchen, a solid steel bar top (in reference to the industrial style), vintage dining chairs and old steel-framed windows outside used to create the 8-foot-high perimeter patio wall. We built all the dining room tables and the 18-foot-long, live-edge communal table (mounted on three antique warehouse radiators) out of one tree. Dan Bush cut and dragged the 100-plus-year-old Douglas fir out of the forest where it had been struck by lightning 50 years ago. The heart of the restaurant is this communal table, center cut from the core of this enormous conifer.

"Sherry wanted people to walk in and be awed by the beauty and design, then immediately be disarmed by the graciousness and welcome from the staff. She envisioned The Lark as the 'train' that brings something new to town, something magical, something people would get excited about, plus feel proud of—like, 'This is one of our Santa Barbara places now and it's f'ing amazing!' I think Sherry's vision was for a place with sophistication and style that still retained 'funkiness,' earthiness and humor.

"I think we achieved all this…and more. I believe The Lark is one of those places where you dine and—even though you weren't there during the building of it, didn't experience the amazing people behind it or the all-night conversations—you feel these things. More importantly, you taste them on the plate, and you sense them the moment you interact with anyone working there…It's special."
DOUG WASHINGTON, DESIGNER

Doug Washington installing lighting in Les Marchands Wine Bar & Merchant, sister business to The Lark.

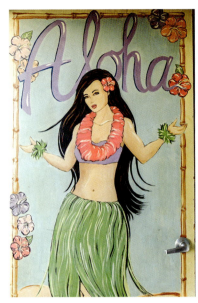

Surf-n-Wear.

Surf Museum.

Green House Studio artists Erika Carter (with Milly), Virginia McCracken, Donna Asycough and Liz Brady.

Train tracks bisect the Funk Zone.

Artist door.

Caroline and Steve Thompson, Cabana Home.

"Hurry Home" by Phoebe Brunner.

The Valley Project.

Mary Heebner with her books and drawings in the exhibition *Bridging Fine Art with Book Arts and Literature,* at The Arts Fund in the Funk Zone.

"In 2000, Carol Kenyon and I were on the Arts Advisory Committee. We approached Mayor Harriet Miller, concerned that a proposed development would seriously impact artists and makers in an area that they described as 'funky but filled with people who work, live and create, contributing a unique spirit to our community.' When Mayor Miller asked for some numbers, committee member Tom Moore took a survey and gathered more than 200 names. In 2004, Carey Berkus and Ginny Brush co-curated *Blur*, an exhibition and happening of emerging and established West Coast artists held in the vacant Bekins Building on Mason Street. *Blur* brought attention to the area and drew crowds of artists and art lovers.

"It has changed a lot. Now there are fewer studios and a lot more galleries, wineries, café/restaurants and new businesses. There is even a Funk Zone Public Art Program to find locations and create public art projects to carry on the creative signature of the area. An example is Phoebe Brunner's 2016 outdoor mural "Hurry Home," on Gray Avenue right off of Yanonali Street. It was facilitated by The Arts Fund and funded by Santa Barbara Beautiful. A goal is to attract a larger audience for the arts within the Funk Zone. Toward that objective, future plans include a permanent site for the Santa Barbara Museum of Contemporary Art."
Mary Heebner, artist

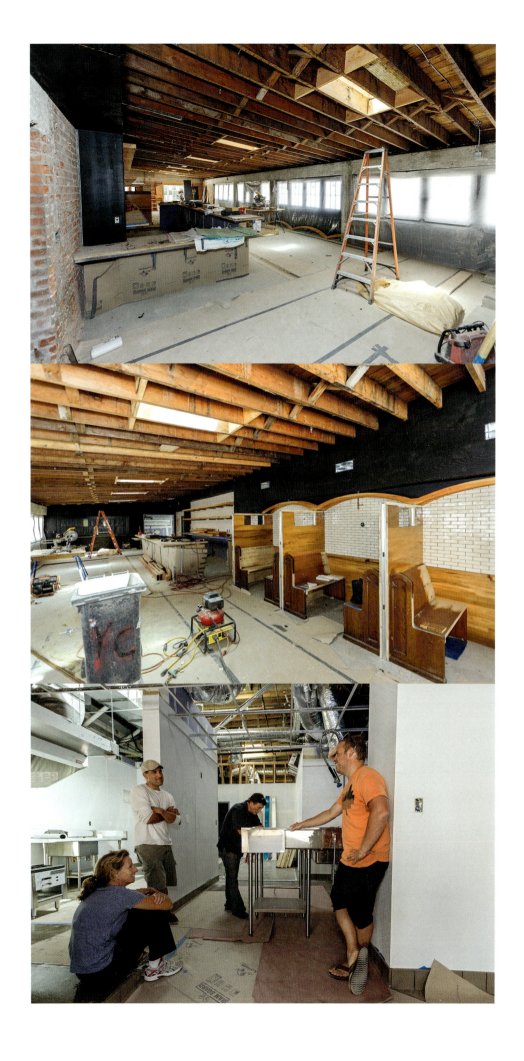

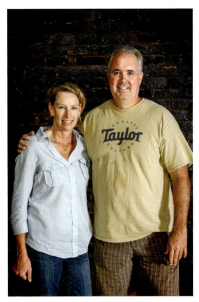

Sherry and Brian Kelly, co-owners.

Katy, Jim, Sherry, and Annie Villanueva.

The Lark had a thank-you dinner for the construction team, then a soft opening for friends and investors and then officially opened on August 5th, 2013.

"THERE WAS GREAT CAMARADERIE THAT showed up during the construction process—a lot of jovial times while all of us worked hard to get the project built."
CLAY AURELL, ARCHITECT

Jason, Sherry and Dan Russo giving project superintendent Rick Musmecci an award at pre-opening dinner.

Virginia Castagnola, whose father, George Castagnola, built the building with his brothers, Mario and Lino, as Castagnolas Fish Market, on opening night of The Lark.

The Lark staff celebrating after opening night. August 2013.

Family meal at the communal table.

Staff tasting new dishes before service.

"My favorite time in the restaurant is the hour leading up to the start of service. There is energy in the room. Everyone is focused. Everyone is busy with a specific job. There is anticipation. Every night is opening night for us. Every day."
Sherry Villanueva, co-owner

"The dining room is a universe of connections, enriched by the life and stories of our guests. Each night is special and different. People celebrate birthdays, anniversaries, holidays; they get engaged—it is a very emotional place. But it is also the place that people come that have just taken a walk on the beach or to the end of the pier. It is a comfortable and casual place. The relationship between the staff, kitchen and guests is complex. It feels like an elaborately orchestrated dance. We are creating all these memories and sharing in our guests' excitement. As a service team, we hold all of that in our hands. We transport our guests, seduce them with beautiful food and wine. Together we hope to spread that love and positive energy beyond the doors of our restaurant. I've never experienced this much energy and feeling at any other restaurant."
Skyler Gamble, General Manager

Dining outside, sharing plates and (below) tables inside The Lark.

NOTES FROM THE PROPRIETOR:

Elings Park, Santa Barbara.

"**Y**OU CAN DO HARD THINGS." This is the mantra that my husband, Jim, and I repeat regularly to our daughters, Annie and Katy, as they navigate the challenges of life. It wasn't until our youngest left home for college that I actually had to turn that sage advice back onto myself: developing and running The Lark is the hardest thing that I've ever done in my professional life.

Our family moved to Santa Barbara in 1999 when the kids were in grade school. We were immediately struck by the region's natural beauty, but even more so by the depth and complexity of the people who live here. As parents, we loved raising our girls surrounded by the mountains and the sea, and both were easy to explore every day. As a farmer at heart, I was thrilled to be so close to the people who grow our food, some of their crops mere miles from where we slept.

I was also blown away by Santa Barbara's strong and seemingly universal spirit of generosity. I learned from my mother at an early age that giving back, each day and in every way, was our collective and individual responsibility, so Jim and I made it a priority to weave this belief into our own family. After a few months in town, I realized that I had never lived in a place where everyone we met was filled with a deep sense of gratitude, simply for the privilege of being a resident.

Santa Barbara is a place where anything feels possible if you put your heart and soul into it, and that sense of entrepreneurship and unbridled creativity is infectious. The multifaceted nature of this community and the stories of the people who shared my dream in building The Lark are what drove me to create this book.

I first met Macduff Everton at my own home about six years ago, when we hosted an exhibition of his photographs to benefit African Women Rising (AWR), a Santa Barbara–based NGO that I'd supported for many years. An internationally known photographer, Macduff had recently traveled to Uganda with AWR's cofounder Linda Cole, and I was moved by the way

his photographs of that expedition told the stories of people living in war-torn northern Uganda. His images were both beautiful and provocative, capturing a sense of community values and personal sagas, and I wanted to know more about the people and places in each shot.

I wanted this book to convey a similar depth of field for all involved, and I hoped to somehow convince Macduff to use his talent to tell our stories. He's been an integral part of the Santa Barbara community all of his life, conveying many of our region's most important tales, and I was overjoyed when he accepted the challenge. I'm pretty sure he was quite excited himself to learn about the people and process that makes a restaurant possible.

Mesa Lane, Santa Barbara.

As the project unfolded, both Macduff and I were continually inspired by the craftsmen who built the restaurant and the farmers, fishermen and ranchers who provide the products we prepare. We came to appreciate that this book wasn't just about the development of a brick-and-mortar restaurant, but was a story about Santa Barbara itself, an exposé of the city's multifaceted values.

* * *

PRIOR TO MY PLUNGE INTO the life of a restaurateur, I was in marketing. Most recently, I was a partner in Twist Worldwide, a creative services agency that "went out into the world to bring back cool stuff" to the senior brass at Target. Twist was the brainchild of my friend, partner and mentor Mark Sottnick, who'd

worked for Target for years. But Twist's wild ride with Target came to an end in 2008, when the economic downturn roiled America from coast to coast.

That's when I met Brian Kelly, a visionary real estate developer who saw potential in Santa Barbara's Funk Zone. He was inspired by the seeds that had been planted over the years by the waterfront neighborhood's arts, design, wine and surf communities. I was soon entranced by the Funk Zone, especially the people who worked and lived there.

True originals at every address, from the pinot noir purveyors in tasting rooms down the block to the surfboard shapers around the corner, the Funk Zone was a quirky yet thriving community, unified in its values but diverse in their expression. An urban oasis just steps from the beach, it offers extraordinary opportunities for imaginative souls. It's a place where creative minds

can come together in pursuit of their dreams, allowing artistic expression to organically grow. I was in love.

Brian was buying properties in the neighborhood, and he hired me as a consultant to help him dream what we could make of them. We launched a full ideation effort around what would thrive in the Funk Zone while keeping the authentic flavor and vibe alive. It was a complex effort, to say the least. We met countless entrepreneurs, artists, neighbors, planning professionals and other visionaries. Then our expansive desires had to be honed to match the City of Santa Barbara's onerous planning guidelines, a process that required patience and the crucial guidance of Katie and David Hay.

We explored many great ideas, but my own was for a restaurant that had Santa Barbara baked into its core, one that focused on the highest quality Central Coast ingredients presented in a way for people to share with

each other. For me, building a restaurant was the best way I could imagine to honor the community I'd come to adore. It would be a place to bring our unique spirit together, where we could gather around a table to share our lives, toast triumphs, overcome challenges and enjoy each other's company.

So, we searched for an experienced restaurateur, but couldn't find anyone who could see our vision. Then, in one of those life-defining moments, Brian looked me in the eye and said, "You see it— you do it! I'll be your partner, and we'll hire a rock-star team."

Like many who often consider what could be with their lives, I had occasional dreams of owning a restaurant, but never really considered doing it. Aside from a cocktail serving gig in San Francisco in the early 1980s, I had zero restaurant experience. But I am a relentless researcher and have had strong female role

Overlooking Hendry's Beach, Douglas Family Preserve.

models, like my mother, so I decided to take a leap into the restaurant business.

It was daunting to say the least—just me, my computer and a big idea. I needed a road map, so I wrote my first-ever business plan, which is a monumental task for a woman with no previous spreadsheet skills. Jim suggested I reach out to "all my friends" in the restaurant industry for advice. Trouble was, I didn't have any.

Then I remembered my college boyfriend, Lance Cossey, had owned a bar in San Francisco, and I was pretty sure he still had a stake in it. We hadn't spoken in years, but I picked up the phone and nervously called. He was warm, supportive and immediately reconnected me with our mutual friend, Jeff Ames, who owns restaurants in Saratoga Springs, New York.

I became a voracious researcher, unabashed questioner and open-eyed learner. I was driven by a singular purpose: to understand as much as I could about every aspect of running a restaurant. Being a rookie helped because I had the freedom to ask questions without judgment. And ask questions I did—to anyone and everyone I encountered.

I read books, pored over magazines and scoured the internet for pro forma templates, sample business plans, restaurant ideas and anything else that might help. I studied demographic and competitive data while fine-tuning the restaurant's creative concepts. I developed detailed financial projections that I had vetted and re-vetted by industry pros.

My learning curve felt like a vertical line straight up, but every day I jumped back in to chip away at it a little more. I wrote and rewrote my business plan, pulling

more all-nighters than I had in all of my college years combined. Jeff was invaluable in validating whether my assumptions aligned with industry standards while Jim checked my formulas and advised on sound business principles for drafting the plans.

There were numerous moments of self-doubt, insecurity and fear, but Jim was my enthusiastic cheerleader, encouraging me to go on even when I was disheartened and overwhelmed. I put everything I had on the line for this dream, so I was determined to make it the best it could be. "You can do hard things," he often reminded me.

As the business plan continued to evolve, construction on the property was in full swing. As an adaptive reuse project, the initial phase involved substantial shell and core work as we upgraded every mechanical, electrical,

plumbing and structural system in the building. I am grateful for the patient tutelage of Ted Bruckner of Young Construction and Clay Aurell of AB Design, who both showed me the ropes of construction management.

Yet as construction moved forward quickly and my plan finally felt solid, I knew something was missing. I couldn't quite put my finger on it, but I needed someone who could translate the vision and passion for the restaurant into an interior space that not only functioned efficiently but also created a transformative experience for our guests. I started researching again, trying to rustle up any leads I could find.

My niece Laurén Ham was working for a group of innovative restaurants in San Francisco, and I had heard that their owner, Doug Washington, was a solid operator and a good man. I called her and asked her to

View of Los Padres National Forest behind Santa Barbara from crest of Santa Ynez Mountains.

introduce me. I can only imagine the look on his face and the roll of his eyes when she asked if he would take some time to help her aunt who has zero experience but wants to open a restaurant in Santa Barbara.

Nonetheless, he left me a message saying he could give me 30 minutes one day the following week, so I enthusiastically agreed on a time for our call. A couple of days later, I realized the call was on the afternoon of the same day I was scheduled for elbow surgery. But I didn't want to lose the opportunity, so I kept our appointment and hoped the pain meds wouldn't make me sound too crazy. With my arm held high in a plaster cast from wrist to shoulder, our conversation morphed from 30 minutes to nearly three hours.

Doug told me about his passion for restaurant design, shared his philosophies about creating spaces that make people feel good and emphasized that a restaurant must not only be beautiful but operate properly as well. Thankfully, Doug fell in love with the history of our building and the diversity of the Funk Zone much in the same way I had 18 months earlier and agreed to do the interior and exterior design. He has an extraordinary talent of taking an idea or emotion and manifesting it into a space that makes our guests feel they are being cared for, which, in the end, is our ultimate goal. Doug became my trusted friend, ally and advisor, and his contributions to The Lark are immeasurable

* * *

OUR DESIGN CONCEPT WAS TO marry vintage, industrial style with natural materials in a warm space. We scoured Craigslist, flea markets and secondhand stores all over the state, attending auctions and digging through dirty storage areas. At one point, I found myself carrying a large antique table on top of my head across the dusty grounds of the Rose Bowl in 100-plus-degree heat. No job was too difficult, which is obvious considering that we hand-glued 165,000 pennies to the exterior walls of Lucky Penny.

As the restaurant began to take shape physically, it was time to find the talent to make it come alive. I was introduced to Jason Paluska through a colleague who worked with him in San Francisco. JP, as he's known, was a young sous chef for Michael Mina's RN74 and ready for his next big challenge. I was immediately struck by his affable nature, sense of humor and sincere humility. He had all the qualities I was looking for in a chef, so I hoped to hell he could cook! And boy could he.

We were an unlikely pair: a first-time restaurateur and first-time executive chef taking on a very ambitious project. We took a giant leap of faith on each other, and JP continues to inspire me every day. He always pushes himself and his team to be better, and his uncompromising commitment to excellence is the core of our restaurant. He cares about every detail in both the front and back of the house, and he holds us all accountable to deliver on the promises we make to our guests every day. He is the epitome of our central values of community, hospitality, excellence, personality, integrity and profitability. His loyalty and dedication mean the world to me, and I am eternally grateful for him.

Sherry Villanueva, Dan Russo and Executive Chef Jason Paluska, pre-opening.

BUILDING THIS RESTAURANT HAS BEEN an intense labor of love. In my wildest dreams, I could never have imagined the actual amount of blood, sweat and tears that would go into building The Lark and the same amount that goes into running it every day. It is by tremendous leaps and bounds the most challenging and rewarding thing I have ever done in my career.

Yet, although I was a total rookie in the restaurant industry, this experience somehow feels like the perfect culmination of everything I've ever done before, even while it presents brand-new challenges. I'm often asked if I am a "foodie." My simple answer is no. I'm not up on the most exotic spice or the latest baking technique or the newest butchery trend. I am simply a person who loves the way that life and relationships are enriched around the table, and I wanted to create that opportunity for my community.

I hope this book honors the tremendous amount of time, energy and dedication that everyone involved with The Lark has poured into it. People wonder why the restaurant business is so hard. It's a business that changes daily, and you are only as good as you were last night for dinner. Every guest is important, and managing the hundreds of details it takes to ensure their excellent experience is complicated and intense.

The most difficult and most rewarding part is managing people. Some, frankly, have broken my heart. But most inspire me. They, like me, love being of service to others. We love to take care of people and to help them create lifelong memories. We collectively believe in authenticity, in connection and in family. Our guests have entrusted us with some of their most precious occasions and have given us the privilege of creating an experience that honors them. It's a huge responsibility that I take very seriously.

I'm grateful for this opportunity to "do a hard thing." It's been a wild ride, but I can't imagine it any other way. The communal table, the heart and soul of our restaurant, is the perfect example of everything that I hoped The Lark would be. It's where many stories unfold: new friends exchanging contact information, longtime locals meeting after years, grandparents chatting with other grandparents to set up playdates, couples getting engaged, people sharing tastes of their food with strangers. It is a true celebration of Santa Barbara and around the table that we've been proud to create.

Sherry Villanueva at an African Women Rising fundraiser.

View of Santa Barbara, Santa Barbara Channel and Santa Cruz and Anacapa islands from crest of Santa Ynez Mountains.

Elizabeth Poett and Austin Campbell, Rancho San Julian.

"**W**HEN YOU FIND A GOOD subject, shoot it six different ways," my first editor at *National Geographic* told me, "then shoot it six more ways." He wanted me to change my viewpoint, my angle and my lenses. His highest praise was when he told me my image was visual, informative and affective.

It is excellent advice. I was never again content with my first take. I am always looking to see if there is another vantage point, a fresh way to look at things. I think it is why I felt a bond with Executive Chef Jason Paluska as soon as we met. He too develops and pushes an idea until it works. It is why you will find some constants on the menu change with the seasons or when he discovers a new ingredient. It is fun to work with JP (Jason). When we are in the kitchen together, I might say, "What do you think of this idea?" about a photograph, and JP will offer me a spoon and say, "What do you think of the flavor? It needs a little more citrus, don't you think?"

"Try this," I'll say, showing him a handful of caviar limes I brought back after a visit with Jay Ruskey at his Goodland Organics farm. Neither of us had ever heard of them. We squeezed out little citrusy beads that burst and crunched like caviar in our mouths. As soon as Jay assured JP he could guarantee him a supply, caviar limes started appearing as an ingredient on the menu.

I hadn't planned on working on a cookbook until I met Sherry Villanueva. She was on the board of directors for African Women Rising, a particularly effective NGO. I'd visited Uganda, documenting the progress of their programs teaching literacy, microfinance and permaculture to refugees and victims of the Lords Resistance Army, the Christian cult led by Joseph Kony that devastated northern Uganda beginning in 1986.

Sherry told me she admired my work and knew my photographs hung in museums. She said she was opening a restaurant. Would I ever consider working on a cookbook?

"What kind of restaurant and what kind of cookbook?" I asked.

Sherry said she envisioned a place that would be fun, where the food would be healthy but not fussy, comfortable rather than a place you reserved for special occasions, where people might see their neighbors, where guests could come and relax after a walk on the beach or a hard day at work. The restaurant would be a place that reflected our community, where people would feel at home. She explained a sense of community meant everything to her because she'd grown up as an army brat and moved a lot. Long before she ever thought of opening a restaurant, she was involved in local charities and organizations in Santa Barbara. The thing about

Hendry's Beach.

community, she told me, is the more it gives to you, the more you need to give back.

I asked if she would source ingredients locally. "Yes," she replied. Would she want to profile the local providers? And would she want to include images of Santa Barbara to give context to her idea of community?

"That's exactly what I want to do," she said.

Sherry told me the restaurant was still under construction. Did I know where the old Castagnola fish market was on Anacapa Street? I knew exactly where it was. My family used to buy our fish there. Later there was a retired London bobby, a policeman, who opened a fish and chips stand there. And Ginnie Castagnola was a friend. She is an excellent photographer, intrepid traveler and philanthropist. It was a great location with a lot of history.

Restaurants always seem to be born fully formed, so the trade and craftspeople that make the dreams come true are rarely honored or acknowledged. I knew Sherry and I had connected when we talked about including portraits of the workers as a celebration of their contribution.

And then Sherry said something I found remarkable. She searched for a head chef based on personality and respect for other people as much as for their cooking success. "I was looking for a chef who is humble. I don't want a prima donna." That is how she came to hire JP. That afternoon we knew the story we wanted to tell.

Sherry had a vision and a passion for The Lark, and she would bring together a team to realize it. She kept her core values at the center. I was interested in working on a

cookbook that honored and celebrated the contributions of everyone who would be part of the story, from the architects and construction crew to the local fishermen, ranchers, farmers and winemakers to the cooks, kitchen crew and service staff. There wasn't any other restaurant in Santa Barbara with a cookbook. Sherry was already thinking in broad, creative terms. She wanted to be local and provincial without being unsophisticated.

* * *

IN 1986 I VISITED NEW YORK with my portfolio to try to get editorial assignments. I showed black-and-white images from my years of visual anthropological work documenting the lives of the contemporary Maya. As several magazine editors told me, it was not a typical California photographer's portfolio. Alice Rose George, who had been the photography editor at *Geo Magazine* for years, was then at *Fortune Magazine*. She liked my work and told me she wanted to give me an assignment but didn't want to ruin my eye shooting a studio executive in Hollywood. I explained that after years of living and working in the jungles of Yucatán, Hollywood was as foreign and exotic to me as the ruins of Chichén Itzá might be for her. Alice started giving me assignments.

Now with The Lark I had a chance to work on something else that would be new to me, focusing for an extended period on a restaurant. Of course I'd photographed food when it was part of a bigger story. I'd shot for *Gourmet*, *Saveur* and *Wine Spectator*. I'd shot features for *National Geographic Traveler* that included covering starred Michelin restaurants in Europe. I shot

Seagulls, sea anemones and eelgrass, low tide at Coal Oil Point Reserve.

in a photojournalistic style without elaborate lighting and setups. Sherry, JP and I agreed this approach, neither fussy nor precious, worked. I shot on location at The Lark with available light. For the panoramic images I used a Noblex film camera designed by Kornelius Schorle and manufactured in Germany. The lens rotates and covers an area that is comparable to what your eye sees with peripheral vision, nearly 150 degrees. It uses 120 film and I get six frames per roll of film.

Before construction was finished and the staff hired, before any meal was cooked in the kitchen, there were a lot of unknowns. JP, wearing his San Francisco Giants baseball cap, had just moved here from the Bay Area. I introduced him to some of the purveyors he would work with, a few I'd known since junior high school. We left the harbor before first light with Bernard Friedman

to harvest mussels from his pioneering open-ocean aquaculture farm off of Hope Ranch. We visited local farmers and ranchers. While Santa Barbara is known as a tourist destination famous as the American Riviera, few know the farming and ranching side. Agriculture in Santa Barbara County has topped over a billion dollars annually since 2006, and through the multiplier effect, it contributes nearly three billion to the local economy. One of its strengths is its diversity, with more than 40 different crops each worth more than a million dollars, including strawberries, broccoli, wine grapes, cut flowers, nursery products, head lettuce, cauliflower, raspberries, blackberries, avocados, lemons, celery, spinach, cabbage, bell peppers, dry beans and summer squash. They are sold locally and nationally and exported to 40 different countries. We have a group of exotic fruit farmers and a

huge cut-flower industry. We have biodynamic farmers, great farmers' markets and umpteenth-generation descendants raising grass-fed beef on land-grant ranches. Santa Barbara has a viable fishing fleet harvesting sustainable seafood, including our world-famous Santa Barbara uni (sea urchin). In Goleta Jay Ruskey, a coffee grower who scored a 90 with one of his varieties in a coffee tasting (his best coffee sells for $100 per pound on the gourmet coffee market), is confounding everyone as he's successfully growing commercial coffee 19 degrees latitude higher than anyone else. Santa Barbara County is important in the wine world because of a philosophy focused on farm-centered wineries—small family-owned producers with a small case count and lower alcohol. Our vintners are creating world-class wines. Santa Barbara County is on the cutting edge of agriculture. It

is from this wealth that The Lark gets a lot of its supplies. "There is no more intimate relationship we can have with our environment," writes Paul Greenberg in *American Catch*, "than to eat from it." It is this interrelatedness between a local grower and restaurant that builds a sense of community.

* * *

ONCE THE KITCHEN WAS READY, I watched JP put together his kitchen team to teach them what he expected. I listened as he told his cooks, "Be sure and taste everything as you cook and prepare. I don't want anyone sending back a plate you haven't tasted."

JP leads by example, putting in tireless days and nights of work. He created a scratch kitchen with real prep that features a seasonal menu to take advantage of local sourcing of fresh products. I would often arrive first thing in the morning and meet with Taylor Melonuk, the Executive Sous Chef in charge of the daily prep for the fish, meats, vegetables and fruits. JP and Taylor work closely together. He explained how brining meats infuses them with sublime flavors but it takes planning and time. Taylor is also in charge of making their own gnocchi, cutting up all their vegetables and herbs, preparing their own lemon zest, brining, pickling, butchering, deboning and receiving fresh-picked fruits and vegetables. JP has transformed even Brussels sprouts, never my favorite as a child, with spices and dates into something so savory and popular that it takes hours each morning to prepare enough. All of the ingredients, all the details are in place so when a diner places an order in the evening, the kitchen will soon have it ready to serve.

In the afternoon the staff prepares the front of the restaurant, setting the tables, filling water carafes, putting out bouquets of fresh flowers. One of the chefs cooks a staff meal, and the servers eat together. It is called the family meal because the crew is family. Afterward, the restaurant manager and the chef hold a group meeting to ensure everything runs smoothly and the chef describes the daily specials. He passes around plates so everyone can taste and describe it.

Then the restaurant opens, patrons arrive, and with their first orders, the kitchen kicks into gear. Guests are seated at booths and tables, or at the bar or the communal table. There is time for conversation and a few sips of their drinks before their plates start arriving. Most diners have no idea the time and care that went into preparing their meal, but they taste the intense flavors.

I have spent evenings in the kitchen photographing as JP choreographs the intricate dance of cooks and servers. The scene is made all the more exciting by scalding broths, flaming fires and delicate plates. He calls out the orders, and his cooks respond, acknowledging each one. Cooks create salads, others are at the stove, and servers sweep up their orders as soon as they are ready. JP oversees everything, with an experienced eye to detail. The kitchen is lined with windows on two sides so diners can watch this frenzied dance too. Everyone knows what he or she is doing. Working in the kitchen is both exhilarating and exhausting.

* * *

W E SHOT MOST OF THE plates starting around three in the afternoon before The Lark opens at five. During the winter that is close to sunset. During the summer we would still have hours of sunlight and hunted open shade as direct sunlight is usually too harsh. We developed a system. JP and I meet in the kitchen. I set a table outside in the open shade. JP brings the plate out. It is a plate off the line, as any guest would

order. I ask him how he sees it. What side do we shoot it from? What angle do we use? Or do we shoot it from overhead? Once we decide that, he will finish the plating if the dish includes a sauce, jus, or vinaigrette. Once we are ready, JP holds the reflector. We check the shot. Even though we've decided the best angle, I'll still shoot it from different angles with different lenses. It usually doesn't take us more than five minutes per plate. He has to get back to his kitchen.

I also photographed details in the kitchen during prep and cooking. Everything was progressing, but I wasn't happy with my images of the desserts. I consulted Nick Flores, the Executive Pastry Chef. I asked to see his cookbooks to find out who influenced him. That's when I discovered nearly half of his books were on architects. They were his inspiration. I needed to photograph his desserts as architecture. I brought in some black gabbro left over from our kitchen countertop, upon which Nick built his desserts. I liked the way they were reflected on its highly polished surface.

I also took images of details and patterns I found in the kitchen. One day JP told me he'd just received the most beautiful radishes from Ellwood Canyon Farm. He arranged a few on parchment on a kitchen tray. I thought his display had the beauty and grace of a botanical illustration. JP prepared other fruits and vegetables the same way. When I showed them to an artist friend, he commented he'd heard the difference between French and Italian cooking was in France it was all about the chef and in Italy it was all about the ingredients. He thought JP clearly revered the ingredients.

My wife, Mary, and I celebrated the 4th of July at Rancho San Julian. As is my wont, I got into a long conversation with Chris Thompson, a legendary local farmer. We both remembered his first meeting with JP at his farm. Chris pointed out he did all the work supplying a perfect product and all a chef had to do was add some balsamic vinegar and sprinkle of Maldon Sea Salt and get all the glory. When JP agreed that Chris should get the credit, it surprised the heck out of Chris. Ever since he has a grudging respect of Jason because he does sing the praises of the ingredients and the farmers, ranchers and fishermen who provide them.

* * *

T HE FOOD JOURNALIST AND AUTHOR Mark Bittman visited Santa Barbara and explained that most people don't eat food any more—or rather, many things in grocery stores and almost everything available at fast-food restaurants doesn't qualify when you use the definition of food as something that is healthy and good for you. His comments put into perspective what I find at The Lark. They serve healthy and good food made with fresh ingredients, and before it is plated it is put together with a lot of thought, work and care. This goes back to the dream Sherry shared with me the first time we met. The essence of The Lark is real food served in a restaurant where it is easy to feel comfortable, as if you belong. Serious food in a casual setting where eating is an immediate and unmitigated delight.

I also really enjoy the communal table, where it is easy to strike up a conversation with other diners. I had an assignment for *National Geographic Traveler* to photograph a story on Alsace, France. It included covering acclaimed vineyards and several three-star Michelin restaurants. The chefs insisted I eat at least one meal at their restaurants. It was really terrific food, yet I was disconsolate. I called Mary every night to tell her everything I ate. I understood clearly that part of my enjoyment of eating good food is sharing the experience. I was miserable eating alone. The communal table at The Lark is a great option. One can enjoy a fine meal that is both convivial and a divine pleasure.

Macduff Everton at work in rain forest, Corcovado National Park, Costa Rica.

Beverages

WINE PAIRINGS

Beyond its scenic beauty, Santa Barbara County is a geographically unique agricultural region. A 29-mile-long valley opening onto the Pacific Ocean is the longest transverse valley (east to west) found along the west coast from Alaska to South America. The uncommon orientation of the valley creates a wide-ranging collage of microclimates and terroirs in less than 30,000 acres of vines. The ocean winds sweep eastward through the valley, guided by the mountains and the hills on either side. As you get farther inland, to the foothills, the days are warm, and the nights are cool. On the west side, closer to the ocean, a maritime climate prevails, with moderate temperatures both day and night. There is a wide range of soil types as well, ranging from beach sand to limestone. These varied characteristics combine to make the area one of the most diverse wine-growing regions in the world.

The wine program at The Lark focuses on a handful of core criteria. First and foremost we believe wine is made in the vineyard. Grape growers or vignerons—that is, farmers—know that if you have a healthy, happy grape, you're more likely to end up with a clean, complex and balanced wine. Having respect for the grapes and allowing them to grow in a natural way without manipulation results in a wine with more depth and character. Also, the individual terroir of each vineyard greatly influences the wine. From the soil to the sun to the wind that blows between the vines, each vineyard puts its own stamp on the wine it produces. This philosophy is directly related to The Lark's philosophy in the kitchen. Our Chef is committed to local, sustainable and farm-to-table agriculture, and we choose to follow that path with our wines as well. We strive to support producers who are organic and/or biodynamic and believe that those who follow those practices produce wines that are naturally vibrant and full of life. You won't find wines with added chemicals, fillers or preservatives on our list.

On The Lark's wine list you will find local varietals side by side with European counterparts. The unique microclimates of Santa Barbara County offer a complex and vast array of wines from many different varieties (over 50 are grown here). Offering a contrasting European wine from the same grape variety provides an opportunity to explore not only the nuance of the grape itself but also the importance of geography, climate and terroir. Old World wines are different from local wines. A local pinot noir may have layers of ripe fruit while an Old World version may have more earthy undertones. This is a result of the varying soil, sun, wind and temperature factors that affect the grape as it's on the vine.

Our philosophy is based on two intentions. Our first route is to assess the components of the dish (its ingredients, weight, texture, vibe) and then choose wines that would either match or contrast those components. For example, a complementary pairing would be a rich, buttery pasta alongside a rich, buttery chardonnay, while a contrasting pairing would match the pasta's weight and heavy texture with an unoaked, crisp chenin blanc. We also look at each ingredient in the recipe, for example, bacon, or mint, or paprika. We consider what wine works well with these flavors. I think we've come up with some really wonderful pairings. We've focused on wine but for some recipes added alternative pairing of cocktails, spirits or beer. Similar to our philosophy in the kitchen, we like to keep our choices local to Santa Barbara County and the Central Coast. —Jeremey Bohrer, Les Marchands

HANDCRAFTED COCKTAILS AND BEVERAGES

OUR PHILOSOPHY AND APPROACH TO wine and spirits at The Lark starts with a sense of place, time and balance. We source the highest quality handcrafted products from small producers from around the world. It allows us to create a beverage program that pairs well with our food and offers something for every palate. Our goal is a streamlined and dynamic wine list so that we can introduce our guests to new and interesting varieties—wines of elegance and nuance.

Our wine list brings together the best of the old and new worlds, featuring wines from the unique terroir of Santa Barbara County alongside their counterparts from around the world. We support eco-conscious producers who farm responsibly. We look for wines made using traditional methods with minimal intervention in the winery to maintain their focus on the vineyard. Many of our producers have successfully made wine for centuries, but we also source from exciting new producers who carry on these traditions.

Whether a wine is 8% abv or 14%, the relationship among fruit, acid and tannin is what gives a wine harmony and versatility with food. This is a particularly exciting time for Santa Barbara County as more and more producers are returning to a balance in wines with less alcohol but full of nuance and sublime notes. In turn, we are doing our part to honor and embrace this cultural shift. At the end of the day, our wine list is what we like to drink, and we are excited to share our discoveries.

The spirits program at The Lark also embraces the same philosophical outlook. We feature small-batch craft spirits from domestic and international boutique distilleries. Our producers source the highest quality ingredients and handcraft their spirits using old-school production methods. Our beverage team pairs these spirits with the freshest locally sourced and seasonal fruits, vegetables and mixers. Add the right glass and ice, and you have the makings of a perfect cocktail.

The Lark Popcorn is popped in a large pot in canola oil and then flavored with a variety of seasonings. Here are four of our favorites.

Spicy Citrus Popcorn
1 cup popcorn kernels (225 g)
1 cup canola oil (225 g)
1 T salt (7 g)
1 tsp Calabrian chile oil (5 g)
2 tsp olive oil (10 g)
zest of 2 limes
zest of 2 lemons
2 T cilantro (10 g), chopped)
½ tsp citric acid (2 g)

Duck Fat Popcorn
1 cup popcorn kernels (225 g)
1 cup canola oil (225 g)
zest of 4 lemons
2 T thyme (10 g), finely chopped and de-stemmed
½ T Red Wine Salt (7 g) (recipe in index)
1½ T duck fat (20 g), melted
1 tsp garlic (3 g), finely minced

Pastrami Popcorn
1 cup popcorn kernels (225 g)
1 cup canola oil (225 g)
1 tsp each ground black pepper, ground allspice,
  ground caraway seeds, ground yellow mustard seeds,
  ground coriander seeds and ground fennel seeds (2 g)
1¼ tsp brown sugar (5 g)
zest of 4 oranges
zest of 1 lemon
¼ cup dill (10 g), finely chopped
1 T salt (7 g)

Black Pepper and Bacon Popcorn
1 cup popcorn kernels (225 g)
1 cup canola oil (225 g)
2 tsp black pepper (5 g)
2½ T crispy bacon (50 g), finely chopped
1 T scallion (10 g), finely chopped
1½ T bacon fat (20 g), melted
1 T salt (7 g)

DIRTY ONE-THIRTY-ONE

Ingredients:
2¹⁄₂ oz Lemon-and-Thyme-Infused Vodka
¹⁄₂ oz olive juice
3 blue-cheese-stuffed Castelvetrano olives

Directions:
Add vodka, olive juice and ice to a cocktail shaker and shake thoroughly. Strain into a chilled martini glass. Garnish with a skewer of stuffed olives.

Lemon-and-Thyme-Infused Vodka:
Pour a bottle of vodka into a quart container. Combine with peel of 6 lemons and 1 bunch of thyme. Refrigerate and infuse for 72 hours. Strain by pouring contents through chinois. Discard thyme and lemon peel. Pour vodka back into empty bottle.

THE HUMMINGBIRD

Ingredients:
2" sprig of rosemary
¹⁄₂ oz grapefruit juice
¹⁄₂ oz lime juice
1 oz agave nectar
³⁄₄ oz Campari
1 oz Junipero gin
1 egg white
1 grapefruit peel
1 trimmed thyme sprig

Directions:
Muddle the rosemary in a shaker. Add grapefruit and lime juice, agave nectar, Campari, gin and egg white and ice to a cocktail shaker and shake until frothy. Strain into a Collins glass filled with ice. Garnish with thyme sprig and grapefruit peel.

THE MULE

Ingredients:
1¹⁄₂ oz Cucumber-Infused Vodka
³⁄₄ oz lime juice
¹⁄₂ oz Yellow Chartreuse
¹⁄₄ oz simple syrup
ginger beer
lime wheel

Directions:
Combine vodka, lime juice, Chartreuse and simple syrup in a Mason jar with ice. Top with ginger beer. Garnish with a lime wheel.

Cucumber-Infused Vodka:
Pour a bottle of vodka into a mixing bowl. Combine with 3 thinly sliced English cucumbers. Cover with plastic wrap. Refrigerate and infuse for 72 hours. Strain by pouring contents through chinois. Discard cucumber. Pour vodka back into empty bottle.

LARK PISCO SOUR

Ingredients:
1¹⁄₂ oz Machu Pisco
³⁄₄ oz lemon juice
¹⁄₂ oz elderflower liqueur
¹⁄₂ oz simple syrup
1 egg white
Angostura bitters

Directions:
Combine Machu Pisco, lemon juice, elderflower liqueur, simple syrup, egg white and ice in a cocktail shaker. Shake thoroughly, then strain into a coupe. Garnish with dots of Angostura bitters.

OAXACAN NEGRONI

Ingredients:
½ oz Del Maguey Vida de San Luis del Rio Mezcal
½ oz Ancho Reyes Chile Liqueur
1 oz Punt e Mes
1 oz Campari
flamed orange peel

Directions:
Stir all ingredients over ice, then strain into double rocks glass over 1 large ice cube. Garnish with flamed orange peel.

CALIFORNIA RATTLESNAKE

Ingredients:
St. George Absinthe Verte (rinse)
1½ oz Lark Dickel 9 yr Tennessee Whiskey
¾ oz Meyer lemon juice
½ oz simple syrup
1 egg white
fennel frond

Directions:
Rinse double rocks glass with absinthe. Dry shake all other ingredients, then add ice and shake again. Double strain into rinsed glass over 1 large ice cube. Garnish with fennel frond.

JP'S PALOMA

Ingredients:
Kaffir Lime Salt
1½ oz Citrus-Infused Tequila
1½ oz lime juice
½ oz grapefruit juice
½ oz Aperol
¾ oz Jalapeño Simple Syrup
grapefruit soda
jalapeño slice

Directions:
Rim a Mason Jar with salt, then build in glass. Combine tequila, lime, grapefruit juice, Aperol, Jalapeño Simple Syrup and add ice. Top with grapefruit soda. Garnish with jalapeño slice.

Kaffir Lime Salt:
Combine 2 parts kosher salt to 1 part finely chopped Kaffir lime leaf.

Citrus-Infused Tequila:
Pour a bottle of tequila into a mixing bowl. Combine with the peels of a grapefruit, a lemon, a lime and an orange. Cover with plastic wrap. Refrigerate and infuse for 72 hours. Strain by pouring contents through chinois. Discard peels. Pour tequila back into empty bottle.

Jalapeño Simple Syrup:
Combine 1 cup water with 1 cup sugar in a saucepot. Bring to a boil. Add 2 jalapeños split in half. Pour into a quart container, refrigerate and infuse for 24 hours. Strain out jalapeños before using.

OLD AZTEC

Ingredients:
2 oz Old Overholt Straight Rye Whiskey
½ oz agave nectar
4 dashes chocolate bitters
4 dashes orange bitters
lemon and orange peel

Directions:
Stir all ingredients over ice, then strain into double rocks glass over 1 large ice cube. Garnish with orange and lemon twists.

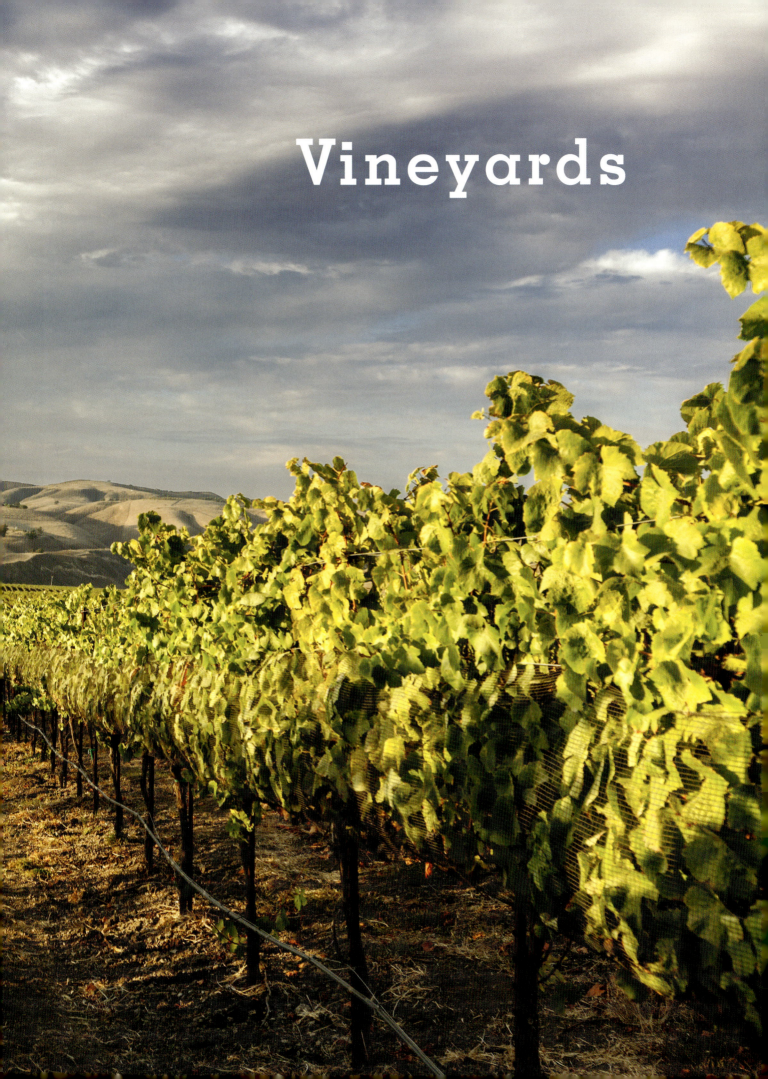

Vineyards

SANTA BARBARA COUNTY WINEMAKING HISTORY

IF GIVEN A BLANK CANVAS to paint the perfect place to grow a wide range of wine grapes, you'd be hard-pressed to craft anything better than Santa Barbara County, where the terminus of our Tranverse Mountain Ranges creates one of the most unique geographic settings on the planet.

Compared to almost every other mountain range in the cordillera that runs the length of western North and South America, our east-to-west peaks smash right into the cold, blue sea, opening up the mouths of both the Santa Ynez and Santa Maria valleys to the crashing waves of the great Pacific Ocean. This brings cool weather and fog to the western end of these valleys, creating prime vineyard locations for the Burgundian varietals of pinot noir and chardonnay, outstandingly in the Sta. Rita Hills AVA.

Average temperatures gradually increase as you travel the 25 or so miles east toward the arid reaches of Happy Canyon and, on the backside of the mountains, the high desert of the Cuyama Valley. One pioneer in the early 1970s tracked the change as one degree per mile. Bordeaux grapes such as cabernet sauvignon and sauvignon blanc can reach peak ripeness in these climes. In between, everything from Rhône rock stars like grenache and mourvèdre to Italian stunners like sangiovese and nebbiolo are settling into happy homes. Throughout, vintners experiment with different expressions of all these grapes, which means you can first taste a peppery, cool-climate syrah, then a jammy, tarry version of the same grape from just a dozen or so miles away.

In the grand scheme of history, the thriving Santa Barbara County wine scene is a recent development. For a few millennia, the Chumash natives and their thriving shamanistic culture preferred native tobacco paste and hallucinogenic flowers to fermented fruits. The Spanish missionaries arrived in the late 1700s. One of the friars' first moves was to plant grapes for altar wine, so small vineyards were soon established at Mission Santa Barbara, Mission Santa Inés and Mission La Purísima near Lompoc. Their grape of choice is referred to today simply as "Mission" and a few stringy vines have been discovered in recent years, with at least one producer turning it into the fortified wine called Angelica that these padres preferred. (Red table wine made from Mission grapes can be quite rustic, to put it kindly.)

Fast-forward to the late 1800s, when a commercial wine industry was starting to take off, with hundreds of vineyard acres off the coast on Santa Cruz Island. Prohibition killed this nascent industry. It wasn't until the late 1960s that table grape farmers from the Central Valley, including Dale Hampton, Uriel Nielsen and his former Little League star Louis Lucas, heeded UC Davis research and began planting wine grapes in the Santa Maria Valley. Most grapes were shipped north to Napa producers, a trend that continues today.

Pioneers like Firestone Vineyard, Richard Sanford, Pierre Lafond of Santa Barbara Winery and the now-defunct Santa Ynez Winery experimented with planting to mixed results. The riesling, for instance, was a hit, but the cabernet was way too green, initially putting Santa Barbara County in an unpromising light. Critical success did not come until the later 1970s, when pinot noir in a chilly stretch of Santa Rosa Road near Lompoc planted by Richard Sanford and Michael Benedict won widespread accolades. The acclaim established the Sta. Rita Hills as a prime place for growing wine grapes, rivaling Burgundy in France.

Waves of plantings in the 1980s and 1990s were followed by waves of federally recognized appellations starting with Santa Maria Valley in 1981 and Santa Ynez Valley in 1983. The Sta. Rita Hills AVA debuted in 2001, followed by Happy Canyon of Santa Barbara in 2009, an expansion west for Santa Maria Valley that same year, Ballard Canyon in 2013 and the Los Olivos District in 2016. There's talk of more to come, including an Alisos Canyon District and perhaps even a Santa Maria Bench AVA. Altogether, the six distinct areas exemplify the diversity that is to be found in the region, so restaurant wine lists can truly offer a local option for every dish on their menu. Local farm-to-table restaurants like The Lark can be vineyard-to-table as well.

Pinot noir from the Sta. Rita Hills and the Santa Maria Valley remains Santa Barbara County's current crowning achievement. Aside from the globally

Harvest, syrah grapes.

respected quality, this popularity is inextricably tied to the 2004 Oscar-winning hit Hollywood film *Sideways*, which added jet fuel to both the ethereal Burgundian grape and to Santa Barbara wine country tourism. It's been a rocket ride ever since for pinot noir production, with seemingly dozens of new producers popping up each vintage year and critical acclaim increasing.

As such, wine today drives Santa Barbara culture in ways that were unimaginable just a decade ago. One of the top crops in the county, it really impresses when one factors in how much it plays into the restaurant and tourism business. Over 100 wineries are based here, and I estimate there are more than 1,000 brands nationwide using Santa Barbara grapes. The city of Santa Barbara alone boasts more than 20 tasting rooms, quite a feat when it had just one in 2002. Wine is driving the reinvigoration of the Funk Zone, formerly a rag-tag

neighborhood of artists now gentrifying into a bustling food and wine destination for tourists and locals alike.

Yet despite this rise to fame and awards, Santa Barbara wine country retains soul. Many winemakers can be found in the vineyards, happy to chat with anyone about their projects. Modesty is reflected in the region's lower bottle prices for comparable quality, and our great sense of pride for the region's past can be savored in the traditional tri-tip and pinquito bean meals still served at many winery dinners. As winemaking continues to be refined over the years, the focus is continually on how to best express this land, the terroir, rather than by the winemaker's hand. In a place shaped so exquisitely by a rare and perfect geography, what could be a better strategy?

—Matt Kettmann, Editor, *Wine Enthusiast* and *Santa Barbara Independent*

"We were the first winery in Santa Barbara County post–Prohibition. That was 1962. It would be 10 or so years before another winery opened its doors. Today there are more than 200." Pierre Lafond, Lafond Winery & Vineyards, Buellton

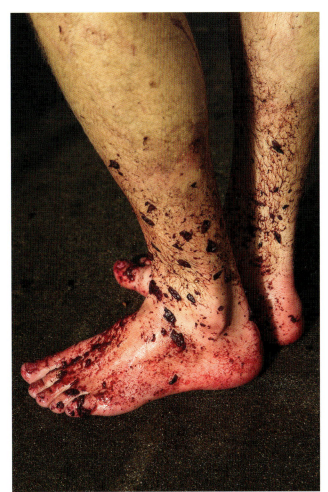

Ken Brown, of Ken Brown Winery, was the first to introduce syrah to Santa Barbara County. He was the founding winemaker of Zaca Mesa Winery in 1977.

Fully clothed, participants at the First Annual Grape Stomp at Andrew Murray Vineyard in 2014. For the Mountain Drive grape stomp, Paramount paid the community $5,000, and brought up a huge wooden vat and tons of grapes. The money was held in trust and loaned to those in the community who needeed it.

WHEN IT COMES TO HOLLYWOOD portrayals, some longtime Santa Barbarans see wine country as less about *Sideways* than *Seconds*, John Frankenheimer's 1966 sci-fi flick in which Rock Hudson (as an urban sophisticate exploring bucolic California byways in search of the meaning of existence) crashes a bacchanalian grape stomp hosted by the hot-tub-loving residents of Mountain Drive. What these films have in common besides the plot: Men have mid-life crises, only hippies like merlot and out-of-towners come to Santa Barbara for wine-fueled epiphanies. While some things don't change, regionally produced libations have evolved dramatically over the decades—from 1960s rotgut to silky chardonnays, lushly aromatic pinot noirs, heavenly syrahs, heady Rhône-style red blends and promising grenache blancs. Both films were nominated for Academy Awards, with *Sideways* winning Best Adapted Screenplay.

Mountain Drivers started making wine in 1952 under the direction of Bill Neely, Frank Robinson and Jack Boegle. Everyone would drive to a Central Coast vineyard in the fall, camp out, dance and drink through the night, then pick grapes in the sunlight and haul them back on flatbed trucks. The men would choose a Wine Queen, who would start the wine stomp wearing only an elegant garland of gold painted grape leaves on her head. Soon everyone else was naked in the wooden vat. The wine was bottled under the Pagan Brothers label for consumption within the community.

Frank Robinson bought their wine crusher and basket press for $50 from Santa Cruz Island. Recently Rob Robinson, a current Pagan Brothers winemaker and Frank's son, traded these historic implements to the Santa Cruz Foundation in exchange for newer equipment. They currently make approximately 75 cases a year.

—Trish Reynales & Macduff Everton

"We were just blown away by how good the wines were turning out, but I don't think any of us visualized how big the wine industry would get." Ken Brown, Ken Brown Winery, Buelton, speaking of the early days of Santa Barbara winemaking.

RICHARD SANFORD

IN 1971, RICHARD SANFORD AND Michael Benedict initiated the cultivation of wine grapes in the western end of the Santa Ynez Valley, marking the beginning of profitable modern wine production in the area. Their seminal pinot noir vineyard, planted in 1972, laid the groundwork for the worldwide recognition the grape would bring to Santa Barbara County. In 2001, Sanford, along with other pioneering winemakers including Wes Hagen, Bryan Babcock and Rick Longoria, successfully petitioned to establish the Sta. Rita Hills AVA. Through the years, Sanford has been instrumental in promoting the distinctive wine being produced in the appellation. He is the first and only Santa Barbara County winemaker to be inducted into the Vintners Hall of Fame. A tall, quiet, unassuming man, Sanford downplays his historic leadership role, saying, "I always poo-pooed the idea of me being a pioneer, but I'm able to accept now that it's true and I'm proud of it. I don't talk a lot about it, but I am proud and it is a part of my history."

Journalist Steve Heimoff lauds Sanford both for helping create pinot noir's popularity in the U.S.A. as well as for his role in establishing Sta. Rita Hills AVA, saying Sanford is beyond important in the field—he is "over-the-top historical."

Sanford didn't grow up tasting fine wine. His first sample of it was as a young man in the U.S. Navy when a shipmate took him to dinner at a restaurant in La Jolla. "He introduced me to this beautiful Volnay [from Burgundy, France]. It had the texture of velvet. I'd never had a wine like that before. I thought, 'I want to be involved in agriculture and create something with that texture, character and finesse.'"

After studying geology at UCSB and graduating with a degree in geography from Berkeley, he paired with botanist Michael Benedict to find a place to grow pinot noir. He recalls, "I went back 100 years in the climate record from the known stations around California and Oregon, comparing them with Burgundy. I compared the heat summation units for the different areas, and something quite dramatic jumped out at me—that was the Transverse Ranges. The Transverse Ranges cause westerly winds to moderate the climate. The flora and fauna of Northern and Southern California meet—and there are upwelling waters from the Japanese current creating the Channel Islands environment. It was obvious to me that this is a really remarkable part of the world. I ended up driving up and down the valley with a thermometer hanging out my car and people thinking, 'This guy is nuts.'"

Not only did Sanford find the perfect climate, but he also found the dirt to match the vines. "This particular location, the Sanford-Benedict Vineyard, is an old landslide that collapsed. It's a Monterey formation—a Miocene deposit—from about 30 million years ago. There's a lot of diatomaceous earth and all these little chert pieces that are mixed up in the soil that give excellent drainage. It's what I was looking for—so between climate and drainage, it's a very, very special place."

Sanford and Benedict's first release was in 1978, and the 1976 Pinot Noir met with immediate acclaim. Dan Berger of the *Los Angeles Times* said the pinot was "a wine of cult proportions" and critic Robert Balzer compared it to a Grand Cru wine from France—the area with the best pinot noir at the time.

Today, Sta. Rita Hills boasts over 35,000 acres of vineyards. The wine business has grown exponentially since Sanford's first release. Income from the wines and visits to the wineries contribute to over $200 million spent each year in Santa Barbara County on wine-industry-related tourism expenditures. But Sanford has never been focused on money; his expertise and passion have always gone into crafting elegant wines that express the full potential of the exceptional terroir. He pours us glasses of his 2013 Alma Rosa El Jabalí Vineyard Brut Rosé—a gorgeous, vibrant, sparkling wine made from pinot noir in the traditional French *méthode champenoise*. Fresh and aromatic, with a lovely flavor of wild strawberry, it has a nice minerality to it that harks back to that unique Miocene soil.

Sanford and his wife, Thekla, have always been protective of the earth. She came from an agricultural background and grew the couple's vegetables in a large, organic kitchen garden. She encouraged him to follow suit in the vineyard, so Sanford again became a pioneer, creating the first certified organic vineyard in the county. Their advocacy and activism in environmental concerns led to a sustainability award named in their honor. In 2015, Edible Communities in Santa Barbara created the Richard and Thekla Sanford Sustainability Award for Business that will be awarded annually. In summation, Sanford reflects, "I am grateful for having found something in my life that so resonates with me and is so fulfilling. I would say to anyone interested in making wine to just follow their passion. There is soul in fine wine, and if you are going to be in fine winemaking, you have to capture that soul."

—Tama Takahashi

"Natural diversity makes Santa Barbara County very special. It's where the Northern and Southern California flora meet with a multitude of climate possibilities." Richard Sanford

BRYAN BABCOCK

WINEMAKER BRYAN BABCOCK BEGAN WORKING during the "second wave" of illustrious Santa Barbara winemakers who founded their wineries in the late 1970s and 1980s. The notable list is long and includes Dan Gainey of Gainey Vineyard, Bill Wathen and Dick Doré of Foxen Vineyard & Winery, Fred Brander at Brander Vineyard and Jim Clendenen at Au Bon Climat. It was a time that saw great advances in modern "New World" winemaking techniques as producers discovered better ways to adapt "Old World" traditions to their local land and climate. Babcock was a young man at this time, a graduate student at UC Davis. He and a classmate went above and beyond in their winemaking. They gleaned dropped fruit from the university's test vineyard and fermented it in Babcock's bath tub. He couldn't use the shower for two weeks and the wine was not great, but his fearless quest to be at the leading edge of innovation had begun.

In 1981, just one semester shy of receiving his degree, Babcock worked harvest in his parent's winery. His 1984 Estate Grown Sauvignon Blanc won gold medals at both the Los Angeles and Orange County Fairs, so he didn't return, instead continuing to work on crafting elegant wines. He was honored by being selected for both the "Ten Best Winemakers of the Year" list and by being lauded as "Most Courageous Winemaker of the Year" by the *Los Angeles Times*.

Rather than resting on his laurels, Babcock has continued to be inspired by progress. Since 2008, he has been working on a radical reshaping of his vineyards, which could spark a fundamental change in the 600,000+ acres of wine grapes planted in California if his cost-effective viticulture is emulated by other wine grape growers. Traditionally, local grapes are grown in the vertical shoot positioning (VSP) system where the long, leafy canes are trained with wires upward, against gravity, so they are essentially pinned into a two dimensional "wall." In Babcock's system, the grapes grow at shoulder height, and the supported canes are allowed to trail down toward the ground in three dimensions—a more natural configuration.

Benefits are many, including easier and more ergonomic pruning, less damage to next year's canes, harvest time cut in half and best of all, approximately 30% savings on vineyard labor costs. The revelation of a better way to farm grapes came to Babcock in 2008 when the recession sparked a desire to find a more cost-effective method of farming. As he explains, "When I started the new farming, there was a day when I went down with my vineyard manager into one of my lower vineyards. I must have stood there for two hours just looking at one vine, projecting how it would naturally grow." What he saw was that the VSP system was essentially 180 degrees from the way the vines grow in nature. He realized, "I've come to the conclusion that VSP is fundamentally rigid. You are working against gravity, and you are working against the nature of the vine."

Babcock produces a coveted portfolio of pinot noir, chardonnay, pinot gris, sauvignon blanc, syrah, grenache and sauvignon blanc, many with 90+ point ratings. His "micro-lot" Sta. Rita Hills pinot noir has gained cult status, often selling out quickly. Babcock is the only American winemaker selected by the prestigious James Beard Foundation to be included in their list of "Top Ten Small Production Winemakers in the World." Of his choice of Babcock for this recognition, David Moore wrote, "Bryan Babcock best exemplifies the traits I look for in a great winemaker. The quality of Bryan's wines speaks for themselves, yet it is his personal commitment to excellence that stands out so much. His relentless experimentation, his willingness to explore the possibilities with so many grape varieties and his aesthetic are a world apart from the usual American approach to winemaking."

Along with Richard Sanford, Rick Longoria, Pierre Lafond and other early Santa Barbara winemakers, Babcock was instrumental in developing the Sta. Rita Hills appellation. For his Terroir Extraordinaire Pinot Noirs, he favors the western edge of the AVA where the cooling maritime influence is the most pronounced. Babcock explains, "With the Bentrock Vineyard being slightly farther east than the Radian Vineyard, this now gives me a straight line of terroirs along Santa Rosa Road in the cool western end of the Sta. Rita Hills. To the east is the Je Ne Sais Quoi section; then as you go west, we have Radical in the middle and Appellation's Edge at the boundary of the appellation. Put another way, this gives me a line of tour de force terroirs that are producing amazingly concentrated pinots. All three are layered and seductive, but at the same time are dramatically different in their personalities: the result of three different soils."

—Tama Takahashi

"The ocean has such a profound influence on the region because of the orientation of our coastal mountain ranges. This, along with a complementary diversity of soil types, offers an existential cornucopia of winegrowing and winemaking opportunities." Bryan Babcock

ERNST STORM

ORIGINALLY FROM SOUTH AFRICA, ERNST Storm is a young Santa Barbara winemaker garnering praise and attention from wine critics and sommeliers. His name is often included when talking of other young local winemakers like Sashi Moorman of Sandhi Wines, Graham Tatomer of Tatomer, Angela Osborne of Grace Wine Company, Justin Willett of Tyler Winery and Dave Potter of Municipal Winemakers who, like Storm, are using New World techniques minimally and selectively while looking stylistically to Old World wines. As Storm comments, "There are a group of winemakers making wine where you can say, 'Okay, this is the vineyard'—as you can in Burgundy where you know Romanée [Conti] tastes different than Chambertin because they don't manipulate the wine." Winemakers like Storm seek to express the specific flavors derived from the terroir rather than introducing flavors during the winemaking process. For example, other producers may use high percentages of new French oak barrels for aging that can impart flavors of smoke, vanilla, clove and other spices that can enhance (or detract) from the flavors of the wine. Storm uses mostly neutral oak barrels to convey the flavors of the grape and create wines that are "more transparent to vintage and site."

His vineyard-specific portfolio includes pinot noir, sauvignon blanc, syrah and a Rhône-style blend of mourvèdre, grenache, cinsault and syrah. Sourcing his fruit from select vineyards is only part of the equation for creating great wine. As he says of Presqu'ile Vineyard, "I've been friends with the owners since the beginning. I have long-term contracts with them. It's important to not just look at the site, but at the people who farm it, to have similar philosophies." Storm has input on leaf pulling, watering, cluster development and when to pick. "Picking the fruit is the most important decision—making sure you have your potential alcohol, your flavors, your acids, your wine style—everything gets locked in to the picking decision."

Storm can use whole-cluster fermentation "to tone down the fresh, bright California fruit so there is a fruit component but also other components," a technique that adds complexity—like earthy tones, forest floor and mouth feel. For his Duvarita Pinot Noir, Storm has blocks of clones 115, 667 and 113 that individually can see a different percentage of whole-cluster use, length of maceration and type of oak barrel. They are fine-tuned into a site-specific blend. He remarks, "The goal is to figure out which sites have certain characteristics and how to bring that out best."

Storm received his degree from the Elsenburg Agricultural School in the Cape Winelands region of South Africa and his older brother attended Hannes University of Stellenbosch to study viticulture and enology. Storm worked for Amani Vineyards for a year before moving to Renwood in the Sierra Foothills, then Firestone in Santa Barbara, then Curtis Winery. He launched his own label in 2006. When asked why he chose to move to Santa Barbara to make wine, he answers, "It's very diverse. There's all these little pockets, different little microclimates, different soils. It's a Mediterranean climate very similar to the Western Cape, where I'm from, and there's the potential to make really good, world-class wines here."

Bold, high-alcohol, fruit-forward California wines still sell well to consumers, but Storm's balanced wines are a refreshing change. He is not concerned about competition, saying, "It's good there are different styles; otherwise, it would be really boring and even more competitive. We don't all show up at a party with the same car. It's the same with wines. Everyone has a different taste; it's very subjective."

Currently, Storm produces 2,000 cases under his label and 1,000 cases under the Notary Public label owned by The Lark. He does most of the work himself with seasonal help from his brother Hannes, who also makes wine in South African under the Storm name. Unlike a large, more than 10,000-case production winery, Storm has no marketing team or publicist. He says, "I let the wine do the talking." The story Storm wines tell is obviously compelling. For a small-lot winemaker, Storm wines have gained great popularity simply through word of mouth. Prominent wine critic Antonio Galloni calls Storm "one of the most promising young winemakers in California" and Matt Kettmann of *Wine Enthusiast* called Storm's 2013 Presqu'ile Vineyard Sauvignon Blanc "one of the most memorable white wines I've ever tasted."

Storm isn't looking for acclaim; he says he is simply making wine that he likes to drink. "I have a lot of friends that make this style of wine, and it's the style of wine we like to drink. I'm looking to make unpretentious, site-specific wines with authenticity." —Tama Takahashi

"When I think of Santa Barbara wine country, I picture a group of winemakers pushing the boundaries to make wines with a sense of place. That started before any wines were made—it started when Richard Sanford realized that pinot could grow in the Santa Rita Hills in the early 1970s." Ernst Storm

Opposite: Pioneer winemaker Bruce McGuire, Lafond and Santa Barbara Winery.

"Quickly, bring me a beaker of wine, so that I may wet my mind and say something clever." Aristophanes

Desserts

Recipes by
Executive Pastry Chef Nick Flores

Citrus Pavlova
basil puree, white chocolate ganache, passion fruit curd, winter citrus

Wine Pairing:

Santa Barbara Winery Late Harvest Riesling, Sta. Rita Hills
Kunin Late Harvest Viognier, Santa Ynez Valley

Chef's Notes:

Santa Barbara has a beautiful array of citrus that grows here, and surprisingly, passion fruit does too. We re-created this classic dessert for our dining room manager Ryan Stowers, a native of New Zealand, where the dessert originated.

Prep Time:

45 minutes active preparation plus 2 hours baking and refrigeration

Special Equipment Needed:

piping bag with large and small tips, double boiler or bain-marie, ice bath, offset spatula

Servings:

6-10

Editor's Note:

For best results, purchase Valrhona Opalys from www.valrhona-chocolate.com or on Amazon. Make sure your mixing bowl and beater are spotlessly clean for making meringue. Use only 100% passion fruit juice.

INGREDIENTS

Vanilla Meringue:
5 egg whites (100 g)
¼ cup each granulated and 10x sugar
  (50 g each) (option: use superfine sugar
  in place of 10x)
2 vanilla beans, seeds scraped
½ tsp citric acid (2 g)

Passion Fruit Curd:
⅔ cup 100% pure passion fruit juice
  (160 ml) (option: mango)
6 T + 1 tsp sugar (82 g)
3 egg yolks (60 g)
2 eggs (90 g)
5 T butter (70 g), melted
½ tsp gelatin

Whipped White Chocolate Ganache:
1 cup heavy cream (240 ml)
2 vanilla beans, seeds scraped
5 oz Valrhona Opalys (150 g) 33%
  cocoa white chocolate
5 tsp glucose (30 g) (option: corn syrup)
6 T crème fraîche (90 g)

Basil Puree:
1 bunch fresh basil, de-stemmed
4 tsp sugar (17 g)
salt to taste
2 tsp agar (4 g) or gelatin
water

Garnish:
ruby red grapefruit segments
tangerine segments
fresh basil

DIRECTIONS

Vanilla Meringue:
Preheat oven to 200°F and sift the two sugars separately. Whip egg whites to soft peaks, then slowly add granulated sugar and whip to STIFF peaks. Add sifted 10x sugar and vanilla bean seeds and whip on medium until well combined. Spoon into piping bag fitted with large tip and pipe out to desired shapes on a parchment-lined sheet pan. Bake in oven for 1½ hours or until dry. Turn off heat, leave the door ajar and let meringue cool in the oven.

Passion Fruit Curd:
Blend together passion fruit, sugar, yolks and eggs in a pot and bring to a boil, stirring constantly. Stir butter and gelatin together in a mixing bowl, then strain fruit mixture into it. Whisk until emulsified.

Whipped White Chocolate Ganache:
Bring half of the cream to a boil with vanilla bean seeds. Remove from heat and let infuse for 10 minutes. Meanwhile, melt white chocolate in a double boiler or bain-marie. Return cream to a boil, then strain into the chocolate along with glucose. Whisk until emulsified. Whisk in crème fraîche and the remaining heavy cream until emulsified. Let rest for 24 hours in the refrigerator before use.

Basil Puree:
Fill a 5-quart pot three-quarters full with water and bring to a boil. Season the water with salt until it tastes like the ocean. Blanch the basil until tender. Transfer to an ice bath when cooked, stirring to speed up the cooling process. Drain excess water. Blend with sugar, salt, agar and enough water in a Vitamix or high-powered blender to form a thick puree. Place puree in a shallow bowl. Refrigerate. The puree will set up like a rubber ball. Blend again in a Vitamix or high-powered blender to form a thick gel-like consistency, and pass through a chinois. Transfer to a squeeze bottle.

Plating:
Spread Basil Puree on serving plate with an offset spatula, then place Vanilla Meringue. Pipe dots of Passion Fruit Curd and Whipped White Chocolate Ganache on the plate. Garnish with fresh citrus and basil leaves.

Grand Macaron Tart
almond macaron, coconut cremeux, basil puree, fresh berries, chocolate mousse, finger lime

Wine Pairing:

Paul Lato Late Harvest Grenache Kiss Me Again, Santa Barbara County
Jonata NV La Miel de Jonata, Santa Ynez Valley

Alternative Pairing:

The Bruery Or Xata Blonde Rice Ale
Ascendant Spirits American Star Caviar Lime Vodka with tonic

Chef's Notes:

I love everything about the macaron. Fad or no fad. They're a little tedious and a great challenge for new cooks piping each one out to the exact same size. I still like to watch them "jump" and develop their little foot. Texturally they're crispy and chewy. They lend themselves to being a great medium for sweet and savory treats. Fillings such as duck liver mousse with pickled rhubarb and candied Niçoise olives or in this case coconut ganache with blackberry curd and fresh Santa Barbara berries.

Prep Time:

2½ hours (plus 24 hour chilling)

Special Equipment Needed:

bain-marie or double boiler, 2 ice baths, pastry brush, piping bag with 1" tip

Servings:

30-35

Editor's Note:

Purchase Valrhona Opalys and Caraïbe from www.valrhona-chocolate.com. Coconut puree is available from www.perfectpuree.com. Pay attention to the temperature of ingredients and the exact steps in this recipe—for instance, when adding warm milk to the caramelized sugar—otherwise the results may be disappointing.

INGREDIENTS

Coconut Cremeux:
7 oz Valrhona Opalys 33% cocoa
  white chocolate (190 g)
²⁄₃ cup coconut puree (160 g)
¼ cup each coconut cream and
  coconut milk (60 ml each)
2 T glucose (25 g) (option: corn syrup)
1½ cups heavy cream (360 ml)
4 tsp Malibu rum (18 ml)

Almond Macaron:
2 T blackberry juice (26 ml)
¾ cup superfine sugar (150 g)
1¾ cup almond flour (150 g)
3 egg whites (60 g)
½ vanilla bean, seeds scraped
¾ cup granulated sugar (150 g)

Basil Puree:
1 bunch fresh basil, de-stemmed
4 tsp sugar (17 g)
salt to taste
2 tsp agar (4 g) or gelatin
water

Blackberry Curd:
5½ T butter (75 g)
1 tsp granulated gelatin (5 g)
2 cups blackberries (150 g)
6 T sugar (78 g)
3 egg yolks (60 g)
2 eggs (90 g)

DIRECTIONS

Coconut Cremeux:
Melt white chocolate in a double boiler or bain-marie. In a separate pot, bring coconut puree, half the coconut milk and glucose to a boil. Remove from heat, then whisk in the melted white chocolate until emulsified. Fold in heavy cream, the rest of the coconut milk and Malibu rum. Place in the refrigerator for 24 hours, then whip until fluffy right before assembling dessert.

Almond Macaron:
Preheat oven to 275°F. In a small pot, bring blackberry juice to a boil to reduce by half. Let cool. The result should be a thick but pourable reduction that will add color to the macarons.

Blend 10x sugar and almond flour in food processor until finely textured. Whip the egg whites in a stand mixer just until foamy. Mix in scraped vanilla bean seeds. With the mixer on low, slowly add the granulated sugar in a thin stream. Turn mixer to high and whip until stiff peaks form and meringue is glossy. Fold almond mixture into meringue.

Separate half of the batter into another bowl. Add 1 tsp of the reduced blackberry juice to the stand mixer and mix it into the batter on low. Add more for color as long as it doesn't thin the batter. Place some of the colored batter in a piping bag along with some of the plain batter. Pipe onto parchment-lined sheet tray. (Tip: use a ring mold to draw circles with a pencil on the parchment for piping guides. Turn parchment over and tack it to the baking sheet with a dab of batter at each of the four corners to keep the edges from curling up.) You can bake the macarons in batches with only one baking sheet or use multiple baking sheets—trading rack positions when you rotate them.

Let macarons sit for 20 minutes before baking. Bake with fan on high for 10 minutes, then turn fan to low, rotate the baking sheets, then continue baking for approximately 10 minutes. (Note: if your home oven has only one fan speed, leave fan on for entire baking time.) Macarons are ready when they are slightly firm and the bottoms are dry. Do not let them brown. Let cool before using.

Basil Puree:
Fill a 5-quart pot three-quarters full with water and bring to a boil. Season the water with salt until it tastes like the ocean. Blanch the basil until tender. Transfer to an ice bath when cooked, stirring to speed up the cooling process. Drain excess water. Blend with sugar, salt, agar and enough water in a Vitamix or high-powered blender to form a thick puree. Place puree in a shallow bowl. Refrigerate. The puree will set up like a rubber ball. Blend again in a Vitamix or high-powered blender to form a thick gel-like consistency, and pass through a chinois. Transfer to a squeeze bottle.

Blackberry Curd:
Stir butter and gelatin together in a mixing bowl. In a small pot, heat blackberries just until softened, then strain through a wide-meshed sieve to make a puree. In a medium-sized pot, blend together blackberry puree, sugar, egg yolks and whole eggs. Bring to a boil, stirring constantly. Strain into the bowl with butter/gelatin and whisk until emulsified, then place the bowl inside an ice bath to cool.

INGREDIENTS

Chocolate Mousse:
8 oz Valrhona Caraibe 66% chocolate
 baking bar (225 g)
1½ cup heavy cream (360 ml), in two parts
6 T sugar (78 g)
4 egg yolks (80 g)

Garnish:
1 pint fresh berries, mixed
1 finger lime, halved, pulp squeezed out

DIRECTIONS

Chocolate Mousse:
Melt chocolate in a bain-marie or double boiler. Warm ½ cup of cream in a small pot. In another pot, caramelize the sugar over low heat, then whisk in the warmed cream until sugar is completely dissolved. Bring to a boil, then turn off heat.

Whisk egg yolks in a small bowl; set aside. Temper the yolks by whisking in a small amount of the sugar/cream mixture, then vigorously whisk the rest of the mixture. Whisk in the melted chocolate until completely emulsified, then place the bowl inside an ice bath. Whip the rest of the cream to soft peaks and fold it into the mousse.

Plating:
Dot the serving plate with Basil Puree. Pipe Blackberry Curd on the macarons, then pipe Coconut Cremeaux on top. Add fresh berries and a quenelle of Chocolate Mousse. (Tip: heat 2 small spoons by running them under hot water, dry, then immediately use to make a smooth quenelle that releases easily from the spoons.) Garnish with finger lime.

Meyer Lemon Almond Gateau
vanilla buttermilk glacé, hibiscus-poached figs, oatmeal streusel, mint

Wine Pairing:

Fess Parker Winery Marcellas White Wine, Santa Barbara County
Carr Vineyards & Winery Late Harvest Viognier, Santa Ynez Valley

Alternative Pairing:

Cutler's Artisan Spirits Vodka Lemon Drop

Chef's Notes:

Cake and ice cream, plain and simple. Moist cake, lemon cream filling, jammy figs and frozen buttermilk to cut through all the richness....

Prep Time:

3 hours, plus 2 overnight periods of chilling

Special Equipment Needed:

candy thermometer, ice cream molds, ice bath, two 9" x 13" baking pans, pastry brush, immersion blender, two Silpats, round cookie cutter, food processor

Servings:

12-16

Editor's Note:

Remove cake from the freezer 3 hours before plating and serving. Trimoline is difficult to find in small quantities, I've added a recipe for the home cook.

INGREDIENTS

Vanilla Buttermilk Parfait Glacé:
7/8 cup heavy cream (210 ml)
1$\frac{1}{2}$ vanilla beans, seeds only
6 T sugar (78 g)
$\frac{2}{3}$ cup buttermilk (160 ml)
3 egg yolks (60 g), lightly beaten
1 tsp salt (3 g)

Poached Figs:
1$\frac{1}{4}$ cups red wine (287 ml)
7 T red verjus (98 ml)
10 T sugar (130 g)
2 T dried hibiscus flower (6 g)
1 vanilla bean, seeds scraped
1 tsp black pepper (3 g)
1 pint black figs, halved

Almond Cake:
$\frac{1}{2}$ cup almond paste (126 g)
$\frac{1}{2}$ cup granulated sugar (100 g)
1 tsp salt (3 g)
13$\frac{1}{2}$ T butter (189 g), at room
   temperature
6 eggs (270 g)
6 T trimoline (see recipe below) or
   invert syrup (130 g)
2 cups flour (250 g)
1 T baking powder (11 g)
3 T milk (50 ml)

Option: Homemade Trimoline:
1 cup water (230 ml)
2 cups superfine sugar (200 g)
splash citric acid or cream of tartar

Oatmeal Streusel:
$\frac{1}{4}$ cup sugar (50 g)
$\frac{1}{2}$ cup oatmeal (50 g)
2 T butter (28 g), melted
1 tsp ground cinnamon (4 g)

Meyer Lemon Curd:
1 tsp granulated gelatin (5 g)
13 T butter (182 g)
1 cup lemon juice, in two parts (225 ml)
5 eggs (225 g)
1 cup + 2 tsp sugar (225 g)
4 tsp lemon zest (9 g)

DIRECTIONS

Vanilla Buttermilk Parfait Glacé:
Heat cream over low heat; do not boil. Split the vanilla beans and scrape the seeds into the cream. Stir, cool, then let infuse in the refrigerator overnight. In a small pot over medium heat, boil sugar and buttermilk to 117°C (242°F), then immediately remove from heat. Put yolks into stand mixing bowl and add sugar mixture, then whip until cool. In a separate bowl, whip the vanilla/cream mixture with salt to soft peaks, then fold into yolk mixture. (Tip: pour mixture into a spouted container to make filling molds easier.) Freeze into desired ice cream molds.

Poached Figs:
Bring wine, verjus, sugar, hibiscus, vanilla bean seeds and black pepper to a boil for 2 minutes, then turn off heat. Add figs and let infuse for 20 minutes before removing with a slotted spoon. Reduce syrup to a glaze consistency—so it will coat the back of a spoon but still run off. Strain glaze into a bowl inside an ice bath. Pour over figs and let rest overnight in the refrigerator before use.

Almond Cake:
In food processor, mix almond paste, sugar, salt and butter in food processor, then add eggs one at a time. When mixture is smooth, mix trimoline in completely, then mix in flour and baking powder, then mix in milk. Cover and let rest overnight in the refrigerator.

Preheat oven to 325°F. Grease two 9" x 13" baking pans with pan spray and add a Silpat to each (option: parchment cut to fit the bottom, then sprayed). Divide the batter between the two pans; the layers will be thin. Spread Oatmeal Streusel Topping on only one of the pans with batter. Bake both for 30 minutes or until a toothpick inserted in the center comes out clean. Let cool.

Option: Homemade Trimoline:
In a small pot, bring sugar, water and citric acid or cream of tartar to a boil in small pot. Do not stir. Wet a pastry brush in water and brush down any sugar crystals stuck to the side of the pan, to prevent trimoline from crystallizing. Boil until the mixture reaches 236°F (114°C) on the candy thermometer. Remove from heat and cover pan. Cool.

Oatmeal Streusel:
Mix sugar, oatmeal, butter and cinnamon together. Place on sheet tray lined with parchment. Bake at 325°F for 15 minutes or until golden brown.

Meyer Lemon Curd:
Place gelatin, butter and half the lemon juice in a large bowl. In a pot, combine half the lemon juice, eggs, sugar and zest. Whisk until smooth. Stirring constantly, bring to a boil, then immediately remove pot from heat. Strain over the gelatin/butter along with remaining lemon juice. Using the immersion blender, mix until emulsified. Cool to room temperature over an ice bath, then pour onto the bottom layer of the cooled almond cake, top with the second layer of cake and freeze for 24 hours. Cut into portions with a bread knife.

INGREDIENTS

Almond Croquante:
1 cup ground almonds (185 g)
½ cup sugar (105 g)
¼ cup water (58 ml)
6½ T simple syrup (120 ml)

Fig Jam:
1 pint black figs, de-stemmed,
  chopped
9 T sugar (117 g)
2 T glucose (31 g) (option: corn syrup)
¼ cup red verjus (65 ml)
½ vanilla bean, seeds scraped
2 pods star anise (2 g)
1 tsp black pepper (3 g)
1 tsp cardamom (3 g)
1 T dried hibiscus flower (3 g)

Garnish:
mint leaves, de-stemmed

DIRECTIONS

Almond Croquante:
Preheat oven to 400°F. Grind almonds to a powder in food processor then add to a small pot. Do not use almond flour. Fold in sugar, water and syrup, then boil to 238°F (114°C). Spread mixture on a Silpat, lay the second Silpat on top, then press with a baking sheet to level the mixture. Cut into rounds with a cookie cutter. Bake on a parchment-lined baking pan for 10 minutes or until golden brown, rotating pan halfway through. Let cool.

Fig Jam:
Place all ingredients in saucepot and cook over low heat until figs are soft. Pass mixture through food mill (option: fine-meshed sieve) into a bowl, then place the bowl in an ice bath.

Plating:
Spread the Fig Jam on the serving dish. Add the almond cake, Poached Figs, Vanilla Buttermilk Parfait Glacé and Almond Croquante and mint leaves.

Meyer lemons.

Butternut Squash Roulade
butternut squash cake, dulcey cremeux, honey-poached pear, shortbread

Wine Pairing:

Tatomer Vandenberg Riesling, Santa Maria Valley
Wylde Honey Wine, Wildblossom Chaparral Bouchet, Santa Barbara County

Alternative Pairing:

Third Window ABDIJ VI

Chef's Notes:

At one of my first jobs in a bakery, we used to make roulade cakes or jelly rolls. We used them for lining the molds of different mousse or cream filled cakes, Bûche de Noël cakes, or just simply dusted with powdered sugar. The idea for this dessert came just from that in a plated version.

This is a really delicious way to enjoy autumn. The butternut squash keeps the cake incredibly moist and the creameux puts it over the top. — Jason Paluska

Prep Time:

4 hours (plus overnight chilling)

Special Equipment Needed:

double boiler or bain-marie, ring molds, cast iron pan, ice bath, cookie cutter, offset spatula

Servings:

12-16

Editor's Note:

Purchase Valrhona Dulcey, crunchy pearls and feuilletine flakes from www.valrhona-chocolate.com or on www.chefshop.com. Use thin-skinned pears such as Barletts for the compote; thick-skinned ones such as Bosc pears should be peeled.

INGREDIENTS

Dulcey Presse:
3 oz Valrhona Dulcey 32% cocoa
baking chocolate (80 g)
¾ cup cookie crumbs (80 g)
½ cup feuilletine (50 g)
½ cup crunchy pearls (80 g)

Pear Compote:
2 tsp granulated gelatin (8 g)
¼ cup cold water (58 ml)
canola oil
4 pears (800 g), cored, diced
¾ cup sugar (150 g)
5½ T heavy cream (82 ml)
4 T butter (56 g)
2 tsp bourbon (9 ml)

Dulcey Cremeux:
9 oz Valrhona Dulcey 32% cocoa
  baking chocolate (250 g)
1⅓ cups warm vanilla custard (420 g)
1 tsp granulated gelatin (4 g)

Shortbread:
13½ T butter (189 g)
1 tsp salt (3 g)
½ cup powdered sugar (62 g)
1 egg yolk (20 g)
1 cup + 6 T all-purpose flour (172 g)
¼ cup cornstarch (30 g)

Honey-Poached Pears:
¾ cup honey (250 g)
½ cup verjus (345 ml)
1 star anise pod
1 tsp ground coriander (3 g)
½ tsp black pepper
1 vanilla bean
2 pears, halved, cored

Butternut Squash Cake:
pan spray
½ medium butternut squash
1 egg (45 g)
½ cup milk (122 ml)
6 T butter (84 g)
3 T ras al hanout spice (24 g)
2 tsp salt (6 g)
2½ tsp baking soda (12 g)
1 cup sifted all-purpose flour (150 g)
1 cup sugar (200 g)

DIRECTIONS

Dulcey Presse:
Melt chocolate in a double boiler or bain-marie. Gently fold in cookie crumbs, fuilletine flakes and crunchy pearls. Press into ring molds on a parchment-lined sheet tray and chill overnight. (Tip: using a bit of plastic wrap on the top of the sticky mixture will help press it into the molds. Remove before chilling.)

Pear Compote:
Bloom gelatin in water and let sit 10 minutes. Have all your ingredients measured and ready. Heat cast iron pan until hot, coat evenly with a thin layer of oil, then caramelize the pears on all sides and set aside.

Caramelize sugar in a clean pan, then deglaze with cream. Whisk in butter, followed by gelatin and bourbon, then fold into pears and chill in a bowl inside an ice bath.

Dulcey Cremeux:
Melt chocolate in a double boiler or bain-marie. Whisk in custard and gelatin until emulsified.

Shortbread:
Preheat oven to 300°F. In a stand mixer with the paddle attachment, slowly cream all ingredients together until homogenous. Press into baking pan, then bake for 25 minutes or until golden brown. Cut with cookie cutter into desired shapes.

Honey-Poached Pears:
Preheat the oven to 300°F. Spread star anise, coriander and black pepper on a baking sheet. Toast until aromatic, about 2 minutes, then set aside. Place honey in a small pot over low heat. Stir constantly until it starts to simmer, then stop stirring. Let cook 1-2 minutes or until the honey darkens and emits a nutty aroma. Deglaze with verjus. Add spices and bring to simmer, then add pears and gently simmer until knife tender, stirring occasionally.

Butternut Squash Cake:
(Note: time your preparation of the components so they will be ready when the cake is still warm—this will help roll up the roulade.) Preheat oven to 325°F. Prepare a 9" x 13" baking pan for the cake by spraying with span spray. Cut a sheet of parchment to fit, with an extra 2" on the shorter sides of the pan, lay on the pan and spray with pan spray.

To bake the butternut squash: line a baking sheet with parchment with pan spray. Scrape out seeds from butternut squash half, place face down and bake 1 hour or until tender. Cool completely, remove skin and puree in a food processor with egg and milk.

INGREDIENTS

Garnish:
2 T each pomegranate seeds and
  pistachios
fresh mint, de-stemmed

DIRECTIONS

Heat butter in a small saucepan until it bubbles. Whisk until it becomes light amber and smells caramelized, then remove from heat. (Note: it will transition quickly from brown to burned, so watch carefully!) In a large mixing bowl, whisk together raz al hanout spice, salt, baking soda, flour and sugar. Stir in the puree, then fold in brown butter. Pour batter into pan. The layer will be thin. Bake 20 minutes or until a toothpick inserted into the center comes out clean.

Let cool just until warm. Spread a thin layer of Pear Compote on one end of the cake, using an offset spatula to smooth the surface. Spread Dulcey Cremeux on the rest of the cake, then roll up from one of the short ends of the cake, using the parchment paper to help roll it evenly. Chill in the refrigerator for ½ hour before slicing with a bread knife.

Plating:
Build a tower of sliced Butternut Squash Cake on a shortbread and Dulcey Presse base. Garnish with Honey-Poached Pears, pomegranate seeds, pistachios and fresh mint.

A pastry cake cutter.

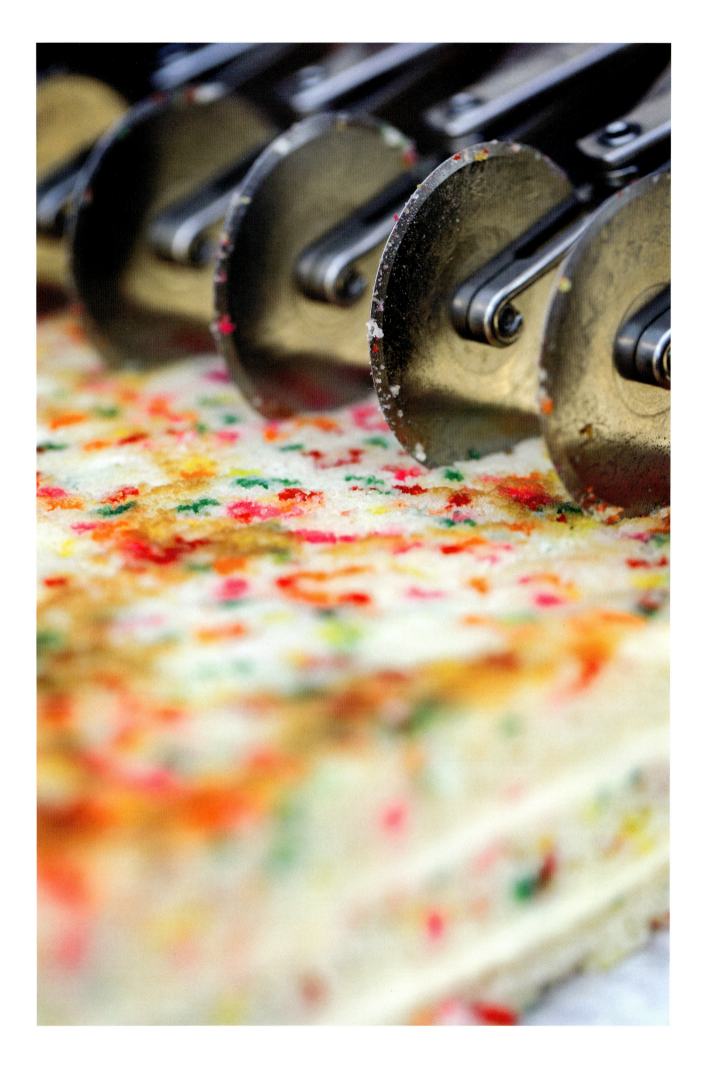

Bourbon Vanilla Ice Cream Sandwich
cocoa nib 'blondie,' vanilla ice cream, miso butterscotch apples, mint

Wine Pairing:

Beckman Vineyards Late Harvest Sauvignon Blanc, Santa Ynez Valley

Alternative Pairing:

Brothers Spirits Bourbon Old Fashioned
Third Window Oko Bomb!
Anchor Brewing Company Bock Beer
Jester King Brewery Black Metal Farmhouse Imperial Stout

Chef's Notes:

Fresh-spun vanilla ice has been a huge perk as pastry chef. Even better is being able to make ice cream sandwiches out of any cake or cookie you have left laying around for your staff. Riff this idea with an apple pie, cocoa nib for added texture and to balance out the sweetness. The miso brings more of the needed salt to highlight all the butterscotch notes and deepen the complexity with umami.

Prep Time:

1½ hours, plus two overnight chilling periods

Special Equipment Needed:

candy thermometer, ice bath, three quarter-sheet pans or three 9" x 13" glass baking dishes

Servings:

6-12

Editor's Note:

The fluffy ice cream is made without an ice cream maker.

INGREDIENTS

Bourbon Vanilla Ice Cream:
2⅓ cups heavy cream (540 ml)
1 tsp salt (3 g)
1½ vanilla beans, seeds scraped
6 egg yolks (120 g)
½ cup water (115 ml)
¾ cup sugar (150 g)
⅓ cup cocoa nib (75 g)
2 T bourbon (30 ml)

Cocoa Nib 'Blondie':
pan spray
1⅔ cups all-purpose flour (200 g), sifted
1 tsp baking powder (4 g)
1½ tsp salt (4 g)
1 cup butter (224 g)
2 cups brown sugar (440 g), firmly packed
2 eggs (90 g)
½ vanilla bean, seeds scraped
¼ cup cocoa nib (30 g)

Miso Butterscotch Apples:
1¾ cups brown sugar (385 g),
  firmly packed
¼ cup butter (56 g)
2 T miso (50 g)
½ cup heavy cream (120 ml)
½ tsp salt
canola oil
4 apples, peeled, cored, chopped

Garnish:
several mint leaves, de-stemmed

DIRECTIONS

Bourbon Vanilla Ice Cream:
Bring cream to a boil with salt and vanilla bean seeds, then remove from heat and cool. Chill in the refrigerator overnight before whipping to soft peaks. Whisk the yolks until creamy in a stand mixer. Bring water and sugar to a boil with a candy thermometer in the pot. When the sugar syrup reaches 120°C (248°F), remove from the heat at once. Drizzle the syrup onto the yolks in the stand mixer while beating on full speed for 3-5 minutes until you have a firm, yellow foam. Cool in a bowl inside an ice bath. Fold in whipped cream/vanilla mixture, cocoa nibs and bourbon. Chill in a quarter sheet pan or 9" x 13" glass casserole dish in the freezer overnight.

Cocoa Nib 'Blondie':
Preheat the oven to 350°F. Spray two quarter sheet pans or 9" x 13" glass baking dishes with pan spray, then line each with parchment paper cut to fit the bottom. Pan spray the parchment. In a small bowl, sift together flour, baking powder and salt and set aside. Melt butter and brown sugar over low heat. Whisk eggs into mixture. Whisk in the flour mixture and vanilla bean seeds, then fold in cocoa nibs. Divide the batter between the pans (the layers will be thin). Bake approximately 25 minutes or until light brown and a toothpick inserted into the center comes out clean. Remove from oven and let cool slightly, then invert on a rack to cool completely.

Miso Butterscotch Apples:
Bring brown sugar to a boil with butter, then whisk in miso and cook for 1 minute. Deglaze with cream, stir in salt and set aside. Evenly coat a hot skillet with canola oil and caramelize the apples until tender, then fold into the Miso Butterscotch.

Plating:
Place one of the cooled Blondies on work surface. Pass the bottom of the baking dish containing the ice cream quickly over a flame to make it easier to lift out the ice cream. Place the frozen block on the Blondie, then press the other Blondie on top. If you want precise edges, trim with a bread knife. Cut into triangular portions, then serve immediately with Miso Butterscotch Apples and fresh mint garnish. Extra ice cream sandwiches can be stored in the freezer.

Milk Chocolate Pot de Crème
chocolate pot de crème, smoked marshmallow, graham cracker, almond, lemon zest, mint leaves

Wine Pairing:

Fess Parker Winery Traditions Port Style Wine, Santa Barbara County
Longoria Syrah Vino Dulce, Santa Barbara County
Buttonwood Winery & Vineyard P.O.S.H. 100% Syrah Dessert Wine, Santa Ynez Valley

Chef's Notes:

This is like the ultimate pudding cup you had in your lunch sack as kid. This has taken on a few different faces in my dessert menus over time, and I'm always reaching back to the s'mores-themed version evoking memories as a kid of being able to light your dessert on fire.

Prep Time:

1½ hours, plus 3 hours chilling

Special Equipment Needed:

bain-marie or double boiler, 9" x 13" glass baking dish, 6 4-ounce ramekins, ice bath, candy thermometer, piping bag, blowtorch (option: middle rack of the oven)

Servings:

6

Editor's Note:

Purchase Valrhona Jivara and Caraïbe from www.valrhona-chocolate.com

INGREDIENTS

Chocolate Pot de Crème:
1 cup milk (240 ml)
1 cup heavy cream (240 ml)
4$\frac{1}{2}$ oz Valrhona Jivara 40% cocoa milk chocolate (125 g)
3$\frac{1}{2}$ oz Valrhona Caraïbe 66% cocoa dark chocolate (125 g)
4 egg yolks (80 g)

Smoked Marshmallow:
6 egg whites (126 g)
1$\frac{1}{4}$ cup smoked sugar (225 g)
1 cup glucose or corn syrup (320 g)
$\frac{1}{2}$ cup water (115 ml)
$\frac{1}{2}$ tsp salt
1$\frac{1}{2}$ tsp granulated gelatin (6 g) or 1 gelatin sheet

Graham Cracker Almond Streusel:
5 T butter (70 g), melted
$\frac{1}{4}$ cup sugar (50 g)
1 T honey (21 g)
zest of $\frac{1}{2}$ lemon
1 T salt (9 g)
$\frac{1}{2}$ cup almonds (75 g), chopped
$\frac{1}{2}$ tsp cinnamon
2 T whole wheat flour (20 g)

Garnish:
mint leaves

DIRECTIONS

Chocolate Pot de Crème:
Preheat oven to 325°F. Bring milk and cream just to a simmer in a heavy-bottomed medium-sized pot, then remove from heat. Melt the milk chocolate and dark chocolate in a bain-marie or double boiler, then whisk into the warm milk/cream mixture. In a large, heavy bowl, whisk the yolks, then add the chocolate/milk mixture slowly, in a thin stream, while whisking continuously. Cool 10 minutes and skim off any foam.

Divide chocolate mixture among the ramekins and cover each with foil. Place ramekins in the baking pan. Bring 3 cups of water to a boil, then carefully pour it into the baking pan so the level is halfway up the sides of the ramekins. Bake for 55 minutes or until the pot de crème is set but still jiggles slightly when gently shaken. Place ramekins in a shallow ice bath to bring them to room temperature, then remove and chill in the refrigerator for at least 3 hours.

Smoked Marshmallow:
In a small pot, combine smoked sugar, glucose, water and salt, then clip in a candy thermometer and bring the mixture up to 117°C. Immediately remove from heat. In a very clean stand mixing bowl, whip egg whites to medium peaks.

Pour about a $\frac{1}{4}$ of the sugar syrup into a small bowl, then whisk in the gelatin to bloom it. Pour back into the pot of sugar syrup and whisk to combine. With the mixer on low, slowly pour the sugar syrup into the whipped egg whites in a thin, even stream. When all the syrup is added, turn mixer to high and whip until the mixture is thick and lukewarm. Place into a piping bag and pipe onto the top of each Chocolate Pot de Crème. (Note: if there is more marshmallow mixture than needed, grease a small tin, dust it with a mixture of equal parts cornstarch and powdered sugar, spread the marshmallow mixture inside and let sit overnight before cutting into squares with a knife dusted with the cornstarch/powdered sugar mixture.)

Graham Cracker Almond Streusel:
Preheat the oven to 275°F. Stir the melted butter, sugar and honey together thoroughly. Stir in the zest, salt, almonds, cinnamon and flour. Spread over a parchment-lined baking sheet. Bake for 20 minutes or until golden brown and crisp. Let cool completely before crumbling.

Plating:
Brown the top of the marshmallow topping with a blowtorch or put the ramekins on the middle rack of the oven and broil. (Note: watch the ramekins carefully. The marshmallow topping can transition from golden to burnt in one second.) Garnish with Graham Cracker Almond Streusel and fresh mint leaves.

ACKNOWLEDGEMENTS

MACDUFF EVERTON

This all began when Linda Cole of African Women Rising introduced me to Sherry. When she asked if I would work on a cookbook, I had no idea I would learn such detail about the restaurant business. JP (Jason) allowed me unreserved access to his kitchen. He is an artist in both the culinary arts and in life. Our collaboration and friendship is made better by our love of habanero chiles and cheladas. His team, especially Nick Flores, Taylor Melonuk and Sergei Simonov, have been especially welcoming, helpful and exceptionally patient and kind to explain processes in detail. I appreciate the time and help everyone extended me to photograph the profiles of purveyors and friends in the Funk Zone including Elizabeth and Austin, Marianne and Jim, Chris, Stephanie, Jay, Bernard, Jack, Tom, B.D., Andrew, Richard, Bruce, Brian, Ernst and Green House Studio. Tama has done yeoman's work testing recipes, and writing and interpreting the instructions. Andy Johnson and Kate and Hilary Dole were very kind to share with me their family stories about Nikita Khrushchev's visit. Jeff Cable expertly scans my film. It is a delight to work with Betty Fussell. May we all be as wise, charming and delightful at any stage in our lives. And most of all to my wife, Mary, I so appreciate she has supported me yet again on a project that has taken a long time to reach fruition. Her patience and love mean everything to me. She and John Balkwill of Lumino Press have been incredibly helpful with their suggestions for improving the design and layout. No successful project is going to be easy. I love collaborations. I've especially enjoyed working with Sherry and JP over the years, even before the restaurant had a name or a kitchen and was just Sherry's dream.

JASON PALUSKA

I wouldn't be anywhere today without the ultimate support, love and freedom that my parents instilled in me to chase this impossible dream. And my Nana who introduced me to Southern cooking in her ranch house kitchen in the middle of nowhere in Brazoria, Texas. To the chefs I have worked for, who had no patience for me and to the chefs who took a risk in giving me a chance to succeed, thanks for always showing me the right way. To all the real friends I've made in kitchens along the way, you know who you are, thank you for pushing me and helping me understand again why we actually do this crazy, unstable, ridiculous and wildly rewarding job. To Sherry, thank you for letting me be a part of your dream and believing in me to make it a reality. To Macduff, thank you for sacrificing your time to make this book with me, which I will be forever proud of. To my family, Helen and our twin daughters, Marlowe and Penelope, thank you for letting so many days and nights pass without me, as I continue to learn and grow as a chef. To my brother, who has been begging me to move back to Texas ever since I left, I want to thank you for always being rad.

TAMA TAKAHASHI

I thank Macduff for the extraordinary opportunity to watch him so beautifully express the sculptural quality of Chef Jason's platings and to witness his artistry in creating this visually stunning book. Many thanks to Sherry for allowing me to be a part of this project. I am in awe of Sherry; she is a fireball of energy and creativity. I am a Santa Barbara resident and witnessed how The Lark brought a galaxy of vitality to the Funk Zone. Working with Sherry has only increased my respect for her as one of the most influential and creative "go-getters" in this town. With his experience and skill, Chef Jason doesn't need recipes to create his complex dishes, but he had created component recipes for The Lark kitchen. My task was to scale these down to a size appropriate for a home kitchen, work with him to obtain each recipe's ingredients and techniques, then test each recipe for both volume and weight measurements. Between Chef Jason's dedication to the restaurant and having twin babies, he did not have much free time. I thank him for devoting some of this precious free time to meet with me. I (and my family and friends) also thank him for the techniques and flavor combinations I learned from him that have elevated my daily meals. Thanks to my chef friends Rose Pizzorno and Claudia Romero for assisting in my kitchen for several of the dishes. I would also like to thank Lana McIntyre, Tamara Riley, Yvette Giller, Liz Dewell and Rebecca Ingram, who home-tested some of my recipe versions and my husband, Paul Arganbright, #1 taste tester! I have done my best to translate Chef Jason's vision for you to use in your home, adding options for specialized equipment when possible, but none of the recipes have been dumbed down. A culinary adventure awaits you as you cook through these recipes. I'm sure you will enjoy it as much as I did.

SHERRY VILLANUEVA

As hard as I've tried, it's impossible for me to acknowledge all of the people who have contributed to the success of The Lark. For those I've inadvertently missed here—you know who you are and I am eternally grateful. I appreciate our loyal guests who regularly patronize our restaurant and trust us with their most precious occasions. We do what we do every day for you. I'd like to publicly congratulate our team at The Lark and its sister businesses for their commitment to excellence, hospitality and our restaurant family. Without the support and trust of our investors, this restaurant would not exist. Rebecca Ingram, Weston Richards and the other "OGs" have been loyal team members throughout the years. Thank you to Macduff Everton and Tama Takahashi, who shared their unique talents with this project and whose perseverance in extracting this book from some very busy people made it real. Macduff and his lovely wife, Mary Heebner, showed great dedication and patience throughout the four years it took to make this book. I appreciate the contributions from Jeremy Bohrer, Vern Kettler, Marc Nespoli and Lunden Desmond to our wine program and the beverage pairings listed here. This extraordinary journey would not have been possible without the love, wisdom and mentorship of many along the way, including Jeff Ames, Chris Robles, Doug Washington and my sister, Kathleen Cochran. I'd like to thank Brian Kelly, Dan Russo, Skyler Gamble, Nick Flores and particularly JP for believing in me and trusting in the dream and Treg Finney and Lunden for their dedication in carrying it forward. To my dad, Lew, and my angel mom, Anne, thank you for giving me the confidence to spread my wings. To my daughters, Annie and Katy, who are my reason for being, thank you for loving and unconditionally supporting me through the long weeks, months and years it took to make this dream come true. And none of this would have been possible without the loving support of my sweet husband, Jim, who loyally served as coach, financial advisor, tireless cheerleader and picker-upper-of-the-pieces-when-everything-seemed-like-it-was-falling-apart. I love you with all my heart.

Ingredients for braised octopus.

INDEX

A

Aioli
  Buttermilk Thyme Aioli 60
  Chimichurri Aioli 178
  Saffron Aioli 68
  Shiner Bock Aioli 42
  Spanish Chorizo Aioli 34
Apples
  Miso Butterscotch Apples 381
Artichokes 158

B

Babcock, Bryan 348
Beef
  Beef Cheek Jus 229
  Beef Cheeks 227
  Bone Marrow Crust 228
  Grilled Ribeye 219
  Hanger Steak 201
  Herb-Crusted Bone Marrow 185
  Steak Tartare 177
Beets, Roasted 101
Beurre Blanc
  Beurre Blanc 163, 210
  Grapefruit Beurre Blanc with Clams 171
  Smoked Tomato Beurre Blanc 220
Biscuits, Aleppo Pepper Buttermilk 186
Blondie 381
Bouillabaisse, Lark 133
Breadcrumbs
  Bacon Breadcrumbs 116
  Brown Butter Breadcrumbs 214
Brining and Curing 248–251
Broccoli, Charred in Calabrian Chile Vinaigrette 202
Brussels Sprouts 29
Butchering 260–271
Butter
  Brown Butter 45
  Carrot-Miso Butter 96
  Quince Butter 199
  Whip Tempered Butter 45

C

Cabbage, Bacon-Braised Red 198
Cake
  Almond Cake 369
Candied
  Candied Grapefruit Peel 186
  Candied Orange Peel 126, 186
Candied Grapefruit Peel 186
Caramel
  Calvados Caramel 82
  Medjool Date Caramel 194
Caramelized

Caramelized Cauliflower 116
Caramelized Mushrooms 210
Carrots
  Rainbow Carrots 95
  Roasted Carrots 229
Cassoulet
  Black-eyed Pea and Pork Sausage Cassoulet 214
Cauliflower, Caramelized Gratin 115–117
Cheese
  Fromage Blanc 82, 93
  Parmesan Crisps 108
  Southern Pimento Cheese 41
Chicken
  How to Butcher a Chicken 268–271
  Roasted 233
Chips
  Red Garnet Yam Chips 178
  Spicy Root Vegetable Chips 47
Chutney
  Almond and Pomegranate Chutney 224
Cocktails and Beverages 331–335
Coffee
  Caramelized Coffee Bean Powder 88
  local coffee grower 84
Compote
  Pear Compote 375
Corn Bread
  Brown Butter and Rosemary Corn Bread 45
  Grilled Scallion and Okra Corn Bread 45
  Jalapeño & Foie Gras Corn Bread 45
Corn, Grilled Sweet 235
Crab, Dungeness 161
Cracker
  Black Sesame Cracker 146
Crème Fraîche
  Black Pepper Crème Fraîche 142
  Crème Fraîche 38
Cremeux
  Coconut Cremeux 364
  Dulcey Cremeux 375
Crisps, Parmesan 108
Croutons 78
Crumble
  Niçoise Olive Crumble 112
Curd
  Blackberry Curd 364
  Meyer Lemon Curd 369
  Passion Fruit Curd 360
Curing
  Citrus-Cured Salmon 142

D

Dautch, D.B. 105
Desserts
  Almond Cake 369
  Almond Macaron 364
  Bourbon Vanilla Ice Cream Sandwich 380
  Butternut Squash Roulade 374
  Citrus Pavlova 359

Cocoa Nib 'Blondie' 381
Dulcey Presse 375
Graham Cracker Almond Streusel 384
Grand Macaron Tart 363
Honey-Poached Pears 375
Marshmallow, Smoked 384
Meyer Lemon Almond Gateau 368
Meyer Lemon Curd 369
Milk Chocolate Pot de Crème 383
Miso Butterscotch Apples 381
Poached Figs 369
Trimoline, Homemade 369
Vanilla Meringue 360
Douglas fir needles, fried 54
Duck
Duck Cure 207
Duck Leg Confit 206
Duck Liver 181

E

Earthtrine Farm 105
Eggs, Deviled 37
Ellwood Canyon Farms 70, 73
Emulsion
Oyster Emulsion 54

F

Farro 112
Fennel, Grilled 158
Fish
Citrus Cured King Salmon 141
Grilled Branzino 157
Grilled Red Snapper 153
How to Fillet a Fish 264–267
Roasted Arctic Char 149
Yellowtail Hamachi Crudo 125
Flatbread, Grilled 225
Friedman, Bernard 129
Frito Misto 158
Fruit, Compressed
Compressed Pineapple 166
Funk Zone 10–14, 342

G

Ganache
Whipped White Chocolate Ganache 360
Gastrique
Pineapple/Habanero Gastrique 166
Roasted Blackberry Gastrique 190
Vanilla Sage Gastrique 207
Glaze
Pomegranate Glaze 214
Gnocchi 163
Goat
Goat Cheese Dip 48
Goat Confit 210
Goodland Organics 84
Granita

Early Girl Tomato and Strawberry Granita 136
Persian Cucumber Granita 146
Gremolata
Carrot Top Gremolata 96
Grits, Black Pepper 235

H

Habanero Fireball Hot Sauce 257
Honey
Eureka Lemon Honey 93

I

Ice Cream
Bourbon Vanilla Ice Cream 381
Vanilla Buttermilk Parfait Glace 369

J

Jam
Fig Jam 370
Jus
Beef Cheek Jus 229
Chicken Jus 234
Lamb Jus 224
Pork Jus 198

L

Lafond, Pierre 339, 342, 345, 348
Lafond Winery 342, 353
Lamb
Black Garlic Lamb Jus 224
Lamb Ribs 193
Lamb Shank 223
Lamb Stock 224
Leeks, Grilled 229

M

Marmalade
Grapefruit-Campari Marmalade 186
Spicy Kumquat Marmalade 182
McGuire, Bruce 353
Motter, Jack 70
Mousse
Avocado Mousse 126
Duck Liver Mousse 182
Mushrooms, Caramelized 210
Mussels, Hope Ranch 129–133
Mutz, Stephanie 51

N

Nuts
Almond Romesco 158
Candied Black Walnuts 82
Duck Fat Roasted Pecans 182
Graham Cracker Almond Struesal 384
Pine Nuts 150
Roasted Sliced Almonds 158
Spicy Pecans 78

Toasted Hazelnuts 88
Toasted Pistachios 102

O

Octopus, Grilled Spanish 165
Olives
    Fried Castelvetrano Olives 33
    Niçoise Olive Crumble 112
Oysters 135

P

Parsnip
    Crispy Parsnip 154
    Steamed Parsnip 154
Pasta
    Handmade Pappardelle 209
Paste
    Harissa Paste 225
Pear
    Caramelized Pear 88
    Honey-Poached Pears 375
    Pear Compote 375
Pea, Spring and Farro Risotto 111
Peppers, Jimmy Nardello and Shishito 133
Pesto
    Cilantro Pesto 48
Pickled Vegetables
    Ginger Pickled Carrots 96
    Pickled Butternut Squash 82
    Pickled Carrot 166
    Pickled Cippolini Onions 254
    Pickled Corno di Toro Peppers 190
    Pickled Curry Cauliflower 150
    Pickled Fresno Peppers 126, 171
    Pickled Nameko Mushrooms 182
    Pickled Okra 234
    Pickled Ramps 108
    Pickled Serrano Chile and Bell Pepper 42
    Pickled Shallot 142
    Pickled Watermelon Radish 198
    Pickled Watermelon Rind 74
    Red Wine Pickled Shallots 228
    Whiskey Pickled Jalapeño 198
Pickling and Fermenting 254–257
Pistou
    Mint Pistou 150
Poached
    Honey-Poached Pear 375
    Poached Figs 369
    Soft Poached Eggs 108
Poett, Elizabeth 216–217
Popcorn 331
Pork
    Chicharron 190
    Chorizo Crumb 163
    Crispy Pancetta 38
    Crispy Pig Ears 199
    Crispy Suckling Pig Confit 197

Cure Pork Belly 250–251
    Glazed Bacon 78
    Ham Hock 234
    Porchetta di Testa 239
    Pork Chop 213
    Pork Jus 198
    Pork Sausage 214
    Smoked Pork Belly 189
    Suckling Pig 198
Potatoes, Boiled Fingerling 171
Preserve
    Preserved Lemon 68, 116
    Preserved Lime Puree 150
Puree
    Basil Puree 360
    Cauliflower Puree 150
    Rutabaga and Carrot Puree 229
    Thai Basil Puree 171
    Yukon Potato Puree 220

R

Rainbow Chard, Sautéed 214
Rancho San Julian 216–217
Ruskey, Jay 84
Rutabaga
    Rutabaga and Carrot Puree 229
    Rutabaga, Pan-Roasted 229

S

Sage, Crispy 207
Salads
    Central Coast Spring Vegetables 107
    Ellwood Canyon Farms Melon and Cucumber 73
    Frisée Salad 42, 142
    Granny Smith Apple Frisée Salad 154
    Little Gems 'Wedge' 77
    Mâche Salad 102
    Red Kale and Pears 87
Salt
    Red Wine Sea Salt 178, 228, 241
Sanford, Richard 339, 347
Santa Barbara Mariculture Company 129
Sauces
    Beurre Blanc 163
    Grapefruit Beurre Blanc with Clams 171
    Mornay Sauce 116
    Salsa Verde 194
    Smoked Tomato Beurre Blanc 220
Scallops
    Herb-Roasted Diver Scallops 170
    Hokkaido Scallop Crudo 145
Sea Stephanie Fish 51
Shallots, Crispy 202
Shortbread 375
Soups, Stews, Broths
    Coconut and Kaffir Lime Broth 154
    Lark Bouillabaisse 133
Spice

Chai Spice 207
Clement Street Spice 150
Goat Spice Blend 210
Ras El Hanout Spice 68
Ribeye Pepper Blend 220
Root Vegetable Chip Spice Blend 48
Spiced Chickpeas 158
Squash
Butternut Squash 81
Butternut Squash Cake 375
Butternut Squash Roulade 374
Squash Blossoms 68
Steak Tartare 177
Stock
Pork Stock 241
Veal Stock 228
Stone Fruit, Marinated 93
Storm, Ernst 351

T

Thompson, Chris 118
Tomatoes
Fried Green Heirloom Tomatoes 59
Smoked Tomato Base 220

U

Uni, Urchin 51–55

V

Vegetables
Roasted Vegetables 166, 207
Root Vegetables with Swiss Chard 225
Spring Vegetables 108
Vinaigrette
Calabrian Chile Vinaigrette 202
Fines Herbes Vinaigrette 78
Fish Sauce Vinaigrette 30
Hibiscus Vinaigrette 102
Parmesan Vinaigrette 108
Poppy Seed Vinaigrette 93
Tangerine Vinaigrette 126
Yuzu Vinaigrette 142

W

Waffles, Belgian 182
Washington, Doug 279, 287
Winemaking, Santa Barbara County 339–352

Y

Yogurt
Charred Orange and Kalamata Yogurt 224
Coriander-Lime Yogurt 166

Z

Zucchini
Ras El Hanout Spiced Zucchini 67

Fall foliage, Sta. Rita Hills vineyard.

RECIPE FROM VIRGINIA CASTAGNOLA-HUNTER
DAUGHTER OF GEORGE CASTAGNOLA, WHO BUILT THE CASTAGNOLA
FISH MARKET IN THE HISTORIC WAREHOUSE THAT IS NOW HOME TO
THE LARK

My father's swordfish marinade
(overnight or 18 hours with fish in large container in refrigerator)

1 pint virgin olive oil
2 pints catsup
2 T Worcestershire sauce
2 dashes hot sauce
6 bay leaves
fresh rosemary
salt, pepper and fresh pressed garlic

Shrimp marinade for barbecue
(several hours or more in refrigerator)

¼ cup olive oil or truffle oil
1 cup catsup
⅔ cup fresh lemon juice
chopped parsley, fresh pressed garlic
2 T Worcestershire sauce
salt, pepper, rosemary, bay leaf

Enjoy!